D1250891

Organizing Audiovisual and Electronic Resources for Access

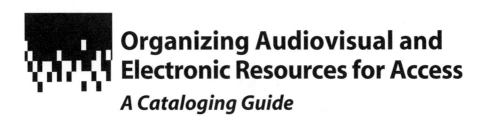

Organizing Audiovisual and Electronic Resources for Access
A Cataloging Guide

Ingrid Hsieh-Yee

2000
LIBRARIES UNLIMITED, INC.
Englewood, Colorado

Dedicated to the memory of my father, Hsi-chuan Hsieh, whose life exemplifies love, responsibility, and kindness and to my husband, Cordell, for his love and faith in me.

Libraries Unlimited, Inc.
P.O. Box 6633
Englewood, CO 80155-6633
1-800-237-6124
www.lu.com

Library of Congress Cataloging-in-Publication Data

Hsieh-Yee, Ingrid.
    Organizing audiovisual and electronic resources for access: a cataloging guide / Ingrid Hsieh-Yee.
        p. cm.
    Includes bibliographical references (p.) and index.
    ISBN 1-56308-629-8
        1. Cataloging of computer files--United States. 2. Anglo-American cataloguing rules.
    3. Cataloging of interactive multimedia--United States. I. Title.

Z695.615 .H78 2000
025.3'44--dc21   99-052467

CONTENTS

EIGHT—CATALOGING AND THE CHANGING INFORMATION ENVIRONMENT

LIST OF FIGURES

 **PREFACE**

Sound recordings and videorecordings have become important components of many library collections. Increasingly, libraries have collected computer files and multimedia. Many libraries have also started collecting Internet resources. The cataloging of these materials, however, is not covered in depth by all library and information science programs. Those interested in this subject rely on special workshops to gain some knowledge in this area. This book was developed to meet the increasing need for assistance in cataloging these materials.

Cataloging rules for sound recordings and videorecordings remain stable, and new guidelines have been published to supplement Chapter 9 (Computer files) of *Anglo-American Cataloguing Rules, 2nd edition (AACR2R)* for the description of interactive multimedia and Internet resources. This book illustrates these standards with examples and uses fully cataloged records to explain cataloging issues specific to each type of material. The objective is to help students, librarians, educators, and anyone new to these media to gain competency in cataloging them. The book is designed either for self-study or for classroom use. Readers can study the subjects at their own pace, and educators may find the text useful for courses on media cataloging, advanced cataloging, and the cataloging of Internet resources.

Chapter One explains the relationship between information organization and cataloging and discusses how librarians have been organizing the types of material covered in this book. Chapter Two provides an overview of the cataloging process to prepare readers for the other chapters. Chapters Three through Seven cover the cataloging of sound recordings, videorecordings, computer files, interactive multimedia, and Internet resources. Each of these chapters begins with an introduction—followed by a discussion, with examples, of current standards for descriptive cataloging, choice of access points, and subject analysis—and concludes with analyses of 10 bibliographic records. Options for arranging audiovisual and electronic resources are included in the appropriate chapters. Chapter Eight discusses the changing information environment and places cataloging in this context. The book contains a list of cataloging resources on the Web. A supplementary Web site to facilitate access to important cataloging tools and recent updates on the treatment of audiovisual and electronic resources is available on the "Textbook Supplements" page of the Libraries Unlimited Web site (http://www.lu.com.textsupp.html).

Items cataloged for this book came from public, academic, and special libraries. The author created records according to the current standards and presented the records in the MARC format. All access points were checked against the name and subject authority files on OCLC PRISM. New names were established according to *AACR2R*. Some records were found in PRISM and revised to meet the current standards.

The author and her colleagues reviewed literature of cataloging to gain an understanding of how rules have evolved for the selected audiovisual and electronic resources. To keep current with issues related to electronic resources, the author monitored several listservs, including Autocat, Diglib, InterCat, Lita-L, Metamarda-l, USMARC, and Web4Lib. In addition, the author monitored electronic journals such as *D-Lib Magazine* and *Current Cites* and electronic newsletters such as *LC Cataloging Newsline* and *ALCTS Network News*. The archives of Autocat were reviewed for discussion on relevant issues. To understand how libraries arrange the selected media for access, the author visited libraries in the Washington Metropolitan areas. To gain a broader perspective, the author conducted a survey of the 100 largest public and academic libraries.

As a teacher of cataloging for nearly a decade, my goal is and has always been to give students enough practical details to perform original cataloging and to provide them with the principles of cataloging to adapt to a changing information environment. In addition to the immediate goal of helping readers gain some competency in cataloging selected types of material, I hope that readers will also recognize that the future of cataloging lies in the application of cataloging principles. The future of our profession depends on lifelong learning and collaboration with other information professionals. Librarians have successfully integrated sound recordings and videorecordings into their services. If history is our guide, catalogers will turn the challenges posed by electronic resources into opportunities and help make libraries an essential player in the future information environment.

Ingrid Hsieh-Yee

ACKNOWLEDGMENTS

The preparation of this book involved many people. I would like to thank the librarians who allowed me to use their collections and helped me understand how audiovisual and electronic resources are organized for library services. Their dedication and expertise are impressive. They include Beth Picknally Camden, Adele R. Chwalek, Genevieve Clemens, Lawrence E. Clemens, Brooke W. Harding, Ruth Hennessy, Patricia J. Herron, Meredith Horan, Carleton L. Jackson, Patti Patterson, Rick Provine, Chiyono Sata, Jackie Shieh, Allison Mook Sleeman, Judith Thomas, Patricia E. Wallace, and Lauren S. Windisch. My gratitude also goes to Edward Gaynor, Rebecca Guenther, Sherry Kelley, Daniel Pitti, and David Seaman who shared their knowledge of metadata development and applications with me.

A research grant from The Catholic University of America supported this research. Dr. Elizabeth Aversa, then dean of the School of Library and Information Science, was very encouraging and helpful. My colleagues at the School provided much-needed moral support—their friendship and encouragement are greatly appreciated.

Many students were generous with their help and time. Scott Davidson, Honora Nerz, and Craig McGrath helped me gather data, monitor listservs, and prepare bibliographies. Michael Smith and Connie Lee helped me to update the URLs. Liselle Drake and Connie Lee provided much help in proofreading the text and correcting the indexes. Michael Smith helped me to create the Web site for this book.

I would like to acknowledge the staff at Libraries Unlimited for their work in producing this book. Edward Kurdyla, managing editor; Mary Cullen, project editor; and Pamela J. Getchell, typesetter; were flexible and very helpful. I also wish to thank Ron Maas, who was instrumental in the development of this project.

Last but not least, my appreciation goes to my husband, who has provided tremendous support for me. His love and encouragement have given me the determination to press on. I could not have completed this project without him.

Ingrid Hsieh-Yee

ONE ← ORGANIZATION OF INFORMATION AND CATALOGING

Cataloging is the cornerstone of librarianship. Some people perceive it narrowly as a subject that involves rigid rules and forced logic. But it is cataloging that enables patrons to search, browse, and access information. Cataloging provides the bibliographic structures that support reference services and ensure effective and efficient collection management. An understanding of how cataloging relates to information organization will prove helpful as librarians integrate information of all formats into collections.

■ THE INFORMATION TRANSFER CYCLE

Cataloging is a form of information organization, as well as a critical part of the information transfer cycle. As Figure 1.1 shows, information transfer is cyclical. A potential author can begin at the **Access** stage by researching for materials for a project. The author will consult information tools, computerized and human, to locate known items, to search for works on selected subjects, to find out what experts have said about the topics, to determine the relevancy of retrieved items, and to request access to relevant items. At the **Synthesis** stage, the author takes time to review those items, discards irrelevant ones, synthesizes relevant literature, develops theses and antitheses, adds personal insight, and moves on to the **Creation** stage. When a work is complete, it is sent forward to peer reviewers or editors. When the work passes review, it becomes available to the public. The **Information Organization** stage begins next. The work could be included in a directory such as *Books in Print*. It could be indexed by an abstracting and indexing service or listed in a bibliography. In a library, the work is most likely to be cataloged. Descriptive information, access points, subject indicators (descriptors, subject headings, classification or similar devices) would be provided, and the item would be placed on the shelf for access. After such treatment the item is ready for the **Access** stage, and the cycle continues.

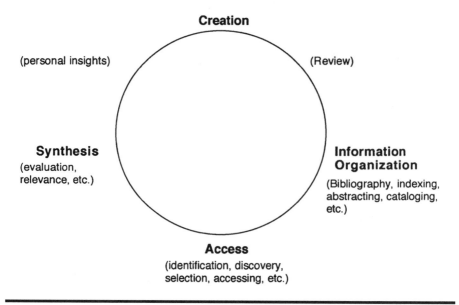

Figure 1.1   The information transfer cycle.

Different methods of information organization result in different outputs—a directory, an index, a bibliography, or a catalog. But the objectives are similar—to identify, to discover, to select, and to obtain a work. If **Information Organization** is removed from this cycle, the gap between creators and users of information becomes very costly to bridge. Patrons will have to spend much time and energy determining what is available, searching for the desired items, and evaluating the relevancy of everything they happen to find. This is, in fact, the current predicament of Internet users. In spite of the large number of search engines and directories, users still have to sift through a lot of materials to find something satisfactory—many have found nothing useful after extended exploration.

■ THE PRINCIPLES OF INFORMATION ORGANIZATION

Organizing information for access is a major concern of library and information science professionals. Various methods have been developed to organize different types of information for access, resulting in tools such as catalogs, indexes (print and online), abstracts, finding aids, bibliographies, and pathfinders. The large number of such tools gives the impression that these methods are very different and cover separate parts of the information universe. But these tools all serve the important functions advocated by Charles A. Cutter in his

Rules for a Dictionary Catalog in 1904: identifying, collocating, evaluating, and locating functions.[1] The importance of such functions were underscored by an IFLA report that describes finding, identifying, selecting, and obtaining access as the functional requirements of bibliographic records.[2] While their procedures may be different, these bibliographic tools, in fact, apply the same principles. The principles have been shared but rarely articulated. Taylor[3] and Hagler[4] are probably the first writers to successfully describe the important principles of information organization. Drawing on their ideas, a full set of the principles of information organization can be set forth as follows.

Principle One: Definition of Scope and Selection Criteria

The first principle for organizing information, regardless of the method an organizer chooses, is the definition of the tool's scope. While it is desirable to have one tool that organizes the entire information universe, that tool does not exist, nor would it be feasible to do so. The part of the information universe a tool covers could be the holdings of one archive, materials in a selected subject area, or resources relevant to a particular user community. Many factors should be considered when one defines the coverage of an information organization tool. Knowledge of users' information needs is the most critical factor.

With information on user needs, the organizer then can develop selection criteria and begin searching the information universe for appropriate resources. In a library, activities entailed by the first principle are usually in the domain of the collection development department. The recent dramatic growth of electronic resources, however, has resulted in the increased participation of reference staff and cataloging staff in this process.

Principle Two: Creation of Representation

Once resources have been identified for coverage, the next concern is the creation of a representation, or surrogate. The step is necessary because it is generally believed that a representation is better than the source material itself for access purposes. For example, instead of having an entire research report available for searching, a record of the work with author, source, and subject information can be created to make searching more efficient.

The procedure for creating a representation varies by tools, but two objectives are common to all. First, the representation should contain enough detail to identify a resource. Second, it should include sufficient information to distinguish one resource from another.

To ensure consistency in representation creation, various standards have been created. Indexing agencies have guidelines on how to describe resources, and citation style manuals offer similar advice. For cataloging purposes, the key standards are the *Anglo-American Cataloguing Rules, 2nd ed., 1998 revision* (*AACR2R*) and the MARC format standards.

Principle Three: Analysis for Access

Related to representation creation is the analysis of a resource for access. The goal of this principle is to ensure that a tool serves the evaluation and collocation functions. The organizer typically identifies people or organizations who are responsible for, or have contributed substantially to, the intellectual content of a work. Depending on the tools, authors, co-authors, and editors are likely candidates to be selected as access points. Series titles, journal titles, and related works have also been included as access points.

In addition, the organizer analyzes the subject matter, or the "aboutness," of a work to inform users of its content. Indexers assign descriptors, abstractors create abstracts, bibliography compilers prepare annotations, and catalogers assign subject headings. Some tools also make use of classification codes or product codes. The objective is to enable users to conduct subject searches and select from similar items.

Besides non-subject and subject access points, authority control also is needed to facilitate access and ensure collocation. Most tools strive to control synonyms, homographs, and variant spellings, and to represent the relationships of concepts in their subject authority lists. But not all tools make an effort to control non-subject access points. The lack of consistency in non-subject access points, as experienced in some online databases, becomes a burden on the searcher and negatively affects access.

Principle Four: Organization of Resources and Their Representations

The final principle is to decide how resources and their representations will be organized for access. If resources are owned locally, some kind of location notation such as a call number is provided. The objective is to facilitate retrieval of the needed item and to provide collocation on the shelf so that users, especially shelf browsers, can select from similar items.

If resources are located remotely, some mechanism such as a hypertext link can be provided for online access. Many online services have well-established document delivery services and some have made full-text available online on request, too.

This principle also applies to the organization of representations. This step is critical because it affects access to resources, especially in an online environment. Unlike the manual environment where a user can thumb through pages or drawers of cards, online tools provide few physical cues to users. The screen display of representations informs the user of what is available. It then becomes critical that the order of the elements in a representation and the screen display of multiple items be carefully designed. A successful design presents collocation on the screen and enable users to make good use of the resources covered by the tool.

■ THE PRINCIPLES AND CATALOGING

As one of many methods for information organization, cataloging closely follows the principles described above. A brief discussion of how these principles are applied in cataloging and a summary of the standard procedure of cataloging follow. The purpose is to prepare users new to cataloging for the work in the next few chapters. Users familiar with cataloging procedures may find this a good way to refresh their memory of the subject.

In a library, the collection development staff usually performs the selection of resources, thus carrying out Principle One. Cataloging typically begins after items arrive. In many libraries newly arrived items are searched in bibliographic utilities such as Online Computer Library Center (OCLC) to determine if records exist. If such records are found, copy cataloging procedures are followed. If not, catalogers perform original cataloging on the items. Cataloging consists of several major steps: description, assignment of access points, subject analysis, authority control, MARC record creation, and contributing records to a bibliographic utility. The purpose of descriptive cataloging is to create a representation for an item. The representation must contain enough details for an item to be identified and to be distinguished from others. This step puts Principle Two into practice.

The assignment of access points and the process of subject analysis result in access points, subject and non-subject, for the bibliographic record. Authority work is performed on all access points to ensure consistency and to enhance retrieval. Thus, Principle Three is applied.

The actual items and their representations are then processed for access. They are assigned call numbers and placed on shelves, while their representations are put into machine-readable format and parsed for further manipulation. Catalogers and system designers have decided how elements of the representations are displayed, and how multiple items are organized and displayed on screen.[5] This step puts Principle Four into practice.

■ ORGANIZING AUDIOVISUAL AND ELECTRONIC MATERIALS

Libraries have always organized, provided access to, and preserved information that is believed to be meeting the needs of their users. The format in which information is presented has expanded from physical to virtual, but the focus of librarians continues to be on organizing information for access. Recent studies have reported the proliferation of nonprint collections in libraries. In a survey of Canadian libraries, Weihs and Howarth found that 93.7 percent of responding libraries have collected one or more types of nonprint media. Videorecordings were the most frequently collected medium, followed by microforms, sound recordings, cartographic material, computer software, and film, all owned by more than 50 percent of the libraries surveyed.[6] A survey of the largest 100 American academic and public libraries also found videorecordings to be the most popular medium (collected by 99.3 percent of responding libraries) and sound recordings are close behind (98.6 percent). Computer files are popular as well (96.6 percent) and Internet resources are making an inroad (77.2 percent).[7] Regarding the method for organization, the Canadian study reported 75.1 percent of libraries with nonbook collections used *AACR2R* to catalog all or part of their collections. The U.S. study found a higher percentage of full cataloging activities among the large libraries owning media—97.9 percent of the responding libraries fully cataloged their sound recording collections, 95.1 percent fully cataloged videos, 88.6 percent fully cataloged computer files, and 61.6 percent fully cataloged Internet resources. Data suggest that *AACR2R* rules for sound recordings, videorecordings, and computer files are accepted as the standards for cataloging such materials.

The latest additions to library collections are Internet resources. Their organization remains a work in progress. Many librarians believe libraries should integrate Internet resources into their collection because users demand access[8] and some valuable materials are available only on the Internet. Internet resources are of varying quality, but librarians can add value to such resources through careful selection and organization.[9] From bookmarking to full cataloging, librarians have attempted to impose order over parts of the Internet. Some rely on simple grouping of resources, while others provide rating information (e.g., *Argus Clearinghouse*[10]) or employ control vocabularies for better access—for example, *INFOMINE* organizes resources with modified LC subject headings,[11] *The Scout Report Signpost* uses LC classification and subject headings,[12] and *Beyond Bookmarks* includes many projects that use classification schemes.[13] Some projects focus on a particular audience or a subject area (e.g., *Kids Click!*[14] and *SunSite's Digital Library* page[15]), while others have broader scope (e.g., *Sailor*[16]). An effort that has the potential for organizing Internet resources on a larger scale is cataloging. The dynamic nature, volatility, and large number of Internet resources have caused many to question the validity of cataloging Internet resources.[17] Some catalogers have worried that the Internet resources would be difficult to catalog because they are hard to examine.[18] But if evaluation criteria are applied, the number of resources to be cataloged will become manageable,[19] and new technology and technique such as PURL (persistent URL) will address the problem of link maintenance.[20] The InterCat project has created an experimental catalog to show that cataloging is a sensible solution to the management of Internet resources if the resources are carefully selected and if libraries cooperate in this venture.[21]

Although Internet resources are different from print resources, the principles of bibliographic access can be applied to them. Mandel and Wolven have discussed how these principles can be applied with the help of the latest technology and techniques such as Z39.50, field 856, encoding standards and metadata.[22] Projects such as InterCat and CATRIONA[23] have demonstrated that cataloging Internet resources is feasible. More libraries are actively including such materials in their catalog. Chances are that libraries will be able to find reasonable solutions to the organization of Internet resources because they have done so with other formats of information successfully. In the 1960s and 1970s the concern was about new nonprint resources such as sound recordings and videorecordings. In the 1980s microcomputer files dominated catalogers' attention. In the 1990s Internet resources have presented catalogers with challenges and opportunities.

■ PURPOSE OF THIS BOOK

This book was developed to meet an increasing interest in cataloging sound recordings, videorecordings, computer files, interactive multimedia, and Internet resources. While the *AACR2R* rules for sound recordings and videorecordings remain stable, new guidelines have been published to supplement Chapter 9 (Computer files) of *AACR2R*. This book uses examples to illustrate the current standards and analyzes fully cataloged records to explain cataloging considerations specific to each type of material. The objective is to help students, catalogers, educators, and anyone new to these media gain competency in cataloging them. The book is designed both for self-study and for classroom use. Readers can study the subjects at their own pace, and educators may find the text useful for courses on media cataloging, advanced cataloging, and the cataloging of Internet resources. Chapter Two provides an overview of the cataloging process, which students new to cataloging will need to be prepared for the next few chapters. Students and catalogers with some knowledge of monograph cataloging can use this material to refresh their memory of the subject. Those familiar with monograph cataloging can skip ahead to the chapters covering the specific media. Chapters Three to Seven are devoted to the cataloging of sound recordings, videorecordings, computer files, interactive multimedia, and Internet resources, respectively. Each chapter begins with an introduction, followed by a discussion of current standards and examples for descriptive cataloging, choice of access points, and subject analysis. Each chapter concludes with analyses of 10 fully cataloged records. The records were created according to the current standards for descriptive cataloging and subject analysis. All the access points were checked against the name and subject authority files on OCLC PRISM. New names were established according to *AACR2R*.

■ CONCLUSION

Libraries have successfully integrated new types of material into their collections by developing sensible solutions to organize such materials. The best way to organize sound recordings, videorecordings, computer files, interactive multimedia, and Internet resources is to become familiar with the standards. Then improvements can be made. Changes in technology will be continuous, which will make the task of information organization both challenging and exciting. To operate well in a changing information environment, librarians can take comfort in knowing they have the proven principles of information organization. Those principles, if applied intelligently and coupled with new technology and techniques, will help them manage and organize information in all formats.

■ NOTES

1. Charles A. Cutter, *Rules for a Dictionary Catalog*, 4th ed. (Washington, D.C.: Government Printing Office, 1904; reprint, London: The Library Association, 1962).

2. International Federation of Library Associations, *Functional Requirements for Bibliographic Records: Final Report*, available: http://www.ifla.org/VII/s13/frbr/frbr.pdf, accessed June 2000. (Adobe Acrobat Reader required to view this document)

3. Arlene G. Taylor, "The Information Universe: Will We Have Chaos or Control?" *American Libraries* 25 (July/August 1994): 629–32.

4. Ronald Hagler, *The Bibliographic Record and Information Technology*, 3rd ed. (Chicago: American Library Association, 1997).

5. Martha M. Yee and Sara Shatford Layne, *Improving Online Public Access Catalogs* (Chicago: American Library Association, 1998).

6. Jean Weihs and Lynne C. Howarth, "Nonbook Materials: Their Occurrence and Bibliographic Description in Canadian Libraries," *Library Resources & Technical Services* 39 (April 1995): 184–97.

7. Ingrid Hsieh-Yee, "Organization of Nonprint Resources in Public and Academic Libraries," unpublished report, May 30, 1999.

8. Janet Swan Hill, "The Elephant in the Catalog: Cataloging Animals You Can't See or Touch," *Serials Librarian* 23 (1996): 6–7.

9. See, for example, Ron Chepesiuk, "Organizing the Internet," *American Libraries* 30 (January 1999): 60–63; Eric Lease Morgan, "Possible Solutions for Incorporating Digital Information Mediums into Traditional Library Cataloging Services," *Cataloging & Classification Quarterly* 22, nos. 3/4 (1996): 143–70.

10.   *Argus Clearinghouse*, available: http://www.clearinghouse.net/, accessed June 2000.

11.   *INFOMINE*, available: http://infomine.ucr.edu/, accessed June 2000.

12.   *The Scout Report Signpost*, available: http://www.signpost.org/signpost/, accessed June 2000.

13.   *Beyond Bookmarks: Schemes for Organizing the Web*, available: http://www.public. iastate.edu/~CYBERSTACKS/CTW.htm, accessed June 2000.

14.   *Kids Click!*, available: http://sunsite.berkeley.edu/KidsClick!/, accessed June 2000.

15.   *Berkeley Digital Library SunSite*, available: http://sunsite.berkeley.edu/, accessed June 2000.

16.   *Sailor*, available: http://www.sailor.lib.md.us, accessed June 2000.

17.   See, for example, Roy Tennant, "The Art and Science of Digital Bibliography," *Library Journal* 123 (Oct. 15, 1998): 28, 30.

18.   See, for example, Kyle Banerjee, "Describing Remote Electronic Documents in the Online Catalog: Current Issues," *Cataloging & Classification Quarterly* 25, no. 1 (1997): 5–20; Jean Weihs, "Solving the Internet Cataloging Nightmare," *Technicalities* 16 (April 1996): 4–8.

19.   Diane I. Hillman, " 'Parallel Universes' or Meaningful Relationships: Envisioning a Future for the OPAC and the Net," *Cataloging & Classification Quarterly* 22, nos. 3/4 (1996): 97–103.

20.   *Persistent URL*, available: http://purl.oclc.org/, accessed June 2000.

21.   Martin Dillon and Erik Jul, "Cataloging Internet Resources: The Convergence of Libraries and Internet Resources," *Cataloging & Classification Quarterly* 22, nos. 3/4 (1996): 197–238.

22.   Carol A. Mandel and Robert Wolven, "Intellectual Access to Digital Documents: Joining Proven Principles with New Technologies," *Cataloging & Classification Quarterly* 22, nos. 3/4 (1996): 25–42.

23.   Dennis Nicholson and Mary Steele, "CATRIONA: A Distributed, Locally Oriented, Z39.50 OPAC-Based Approach to Cataloguing the Internet," *Cataloging & Classification Quarterly* 22, nos. 3/4 (1996): 127–41.

■ SUGGESTED READINGS

Hagler, Ronald. "Principles of Bibliographic Control." In *The Bibliographic Record and Information Technology*, 3rd ed. (Chicago: American Library Association, 1997).

Hillman, Diane I. " 'Parallel Universes' or Meaningful Relationships: Envisioning a Future for the OPAC and the Net." *Cataloging & Classification Quarterly* 22, nos. 3/4 (1996): 97–103.

International Federation of Library Associations and Institutions. 1998. *Functional Requirements for Bibliographic Records: Final Report.* Available: http://www.ifla.org/VII/S13/frbr/frbr.pdf (Accessed June 2000).

Mandel, Carol A., and Robert Wolven. "Intellectual Access to Digital Documents: Joining Proven Principles with New Technologies." *Cataloging & Classification Quarterly* 22, nos. 3/4 (1996): 25–42.

Taylor, Arlene G. "The Information Universe: Will We Have Chaos or Control?" *American Libraries* 25, no. 7 (July/August 1994): 629–32.

TWO ← CATALOGING: AN OVERVIEW

■ TREATMENT OF NONPRINT RESOURCES

The cataloging of nonprint resources has evolved over time. Weihs presented a historical perspective on bibliographic control of nonbook materials,[1] Intner[2] and Frost[3] detailed the development of cataloging rules for nonprints, and Maillet described efforts to provide subject access to film and video.[4] Among the issues debated, uniformity in bibliographic access and equality in physical access were the most critical. Uniformity in bibliographic access refers to the application of the same cataloging rules to all types of material. This practice results in an integrated catalog where users can retrieve items of interest regardless of their format. Advocates of this omnimedia approach believe it would make retrieval easier for users and encourage the use of nonprint resources.[5] But opponents have cited unique qualities of nonprints and recommended special treatment.[6] The cost of full cataloging has also caused concern and led libraries' to adopt the departmentalized approach, which separates nonprints from the book collection and from the catalog. After several major changes, acceptable cataloging rules have emerged and most libraries have adopted the omnimedia approach. A 1989 survey, for instance, reported that 73 percent of American libraries serving population over 25,000 fully cataloged their nonprints.[7] A 1995 report of the cataloging practice of Canadian libraries of various types found 89.7 percent of libraries owning sound recordings cataloged them, with 72.6 percent of them following *Anglo-American Cataloguing Rules, 2nd edition* (*AACR2*); 89.3 percent of libraries owning videorecordings cataloged them, with 72.1 percent of them follow *AACR2*; and 70.9 percent of libraries owning computer files cataloged them, with 63.4 percent using *AACR2*.[8] A 1998 study of the largest 100 public and academic libraries found more than 95 percent of responding libraries fully cataloged sound recordings and videorecordings.[9] The integrated approach seems to have been prevalent among large libraries, especially when sound recordings and videorecordings are concerned. The omnimedia approach has been endorsed by many practitioners and researchers.[10]

11

Equality in physical access is a less settled issue. The goal is to provide the same access to print and nonprint resources, and one major approach is intershelving all types of material. Patrons benefit from this approach because all materials are organized under one system, and all works on the same subject are collocated on the shelf. This approach may also attract new patrons and increase use of the library.[11] Concerns for security, maintenance, and space, however, have led some libraries to adopt other methods for arranging nonprint resources. For instance, Scholtz indicated that genre classification, not classification by *Dewey Decimal Classification* or *Library of Congress Classification*, was popular among public libraries.[12] A 1998 study of top 100 public and academic libraries found public librarians expressing a commitment to browsing and 99 percent shelved sound recordings by format, while 94 percent shelved videorecordings by format.[13]

▪ DESCRIPTION

Current cataloging rules reflect a strong interest among librarians to integrate various types of resources into the catalog. This chapter presents descriptive cataloging rules and subject analysis approaches applicable to sound recordings, videorecordings, computer files, interactive multimedia, and Internet resources. Special issues related to these types of material are discussed in the chapters devoted to the specific media.

To ensure consistency in record creation and to support international sharing of bibliographic records, catalogers follow the *Anglo-American Cataloguing Rules* (*AACR*), which are based on the International Standard Bibliographic Description (ISBD) and the Paris Principles. The current standard is the revised edition of the second edition of *AACR*, commonly known as *AACR2R*. *AACR2R* incorporates many changes to the second edition and the Library of Congress's interpretations to the rules. Because of the emergence of new types of resources, new guidelines have been developed to describe interactive multimedia[14] and Internet resources.[15] *Library of Congress Rule Interpretations*[16] continues to be an important tool for clarifying the application of *AACR2R*.

The USMARC format continues to be the main guideline for catalogers. Bibliographic utilities have developed their own MARC guidelines, too. Since OCLC (Online Computer Library Center) is one of the most popular bibliographic utilities, the OCLC guidelines for MARC records are followed in this book.

The goal of descriptive cataloging is to create a bibliographic record with sufficient details for an item to be identified and distinguished from others. Part I of *AACR2R* is devoted to this effort. Chapter 1 presents general rules that can be applied to materials of all formats, and is followed by chapters on specific media. The structure of Chapter 1 is used in all other chapters in Part I. For example, Chapter 1 stipulates eight areas for description:

Area 1. Title and Statement of Responsibility (MARC field 245)

Area 2. Edition (MARC field 250)

Area 3. Material Specific Details

Area 4. Publication, Distribution, Etc. (MARC field 260)

Area 5. Physical Description (MARC field 300)

Area 6. Series (MARC field 4xx)

Area 7. Notes (MARC field 5xx)

Area 8. International standard numbers (MARC fields 020 or 022)

And the same rule structure is repeated in chapters on specific media in Part I. For instance, Rule 1.4 instructs catalogers to transcribe information related to the publisher, Rule 2.4 explains how to transcribe the place, name, and date of a book publisher, and Rule 6.4 provides instructions on how to record the place, name, and date of a sound recording publisher. Catalogers consult Chapter 1 and also the chapter dealing with the medium being cataloged. The parallel structure in the rules simplifies the use of *AACR2R*.

The next section summarizes Chapter 1 and Chapter 2 of *AACR2R* to give readers an overview of the basics of cataloging.

Rules for Descriptive Cataloging

Levels of Description

Following Charles A. Cutter's model, *AACR2R* allows three levels of description. The first level is brief and contains few basic elements to identify an item (see 1.0D1 for example). Libraries with limited resources sometimes adopt this level of description to make their holdings known to users. The second level of description has been considered the standard level of cataloging. It includes the eight areas stipulated by 1.0B1 and contains elements listed under 1.0D2. Most libraries catalog their materials by this level of specification. The third level of description offers far more details than the second level and is often used for materials of local significance or rare book materials.

Chief Source and Prescribed Sources of Information

In describing any type of publication, the cataloger looks for the chief source of information first. The chief source is specified at the beginning of each chapter in Part I of *AACR2R* to ensure consistency in cataloging. Information in the chief source of information is preferred to information from other areas of the item. For each area of the description *AACR2R* prescribes one or more sources. The cataloger should use square brackets for information taken from outside the prescribed sources.

Area 1. Title and Statement of Responsibility (MARC field 245)

245 __ Title proper $h [GMD] : $b other title information / $c statement of responsibility ; subsequent statement of responsibility.

Area 1 includes several elements, and the order of the elements and the punctuation pattern are shown above. In this area the main task is to record the title proper verbatim, following exactly its wording, order, and spelling, but not necessarily its punctuation or capitalization. The objective is to show users how the title is presented in the chief source.

If a general material designation (GMD) is used, it follows the title proper in square brackets. A GMD is useful for indicating the medium of any nonprint materials. Libraries in Australia, Canada, and the United States use terms on List 2 provided in *AACR2R*, and the Library of Congress makes use of only a small number of these terms, including computer file, filmstrip, kit, microform, motion picture, slide, sound recording, transparency, and videorecording (CSB 44: 10).

Other title information is transcribed according to the same rules for the title proper. Statements of responsibility appearing prominently are transcribed, and people performing different functions for the item, such as authors and editors, are separated by semicolons.

Area 2. Edition (MARC field 250)

250 Edition statement / $b statement of responsibility relating to the edition.

If an edition statement is found on the item, it is transcribed using abbreviations in Appendix B and numerals in Appendix C of *AACR2R*. If a statement of responsibility is related to one particular edition, it is transcribed after the edition statement.

250 Definitive ed. / $b edited, with an introduction, by Susan Sontag.

One caveat about the edition statement is that it should be a formal statement found on the item. The cataloger should not infer an edition from an item. For example, "first published in America in 1988" should not be interpreted as the first American edition.

Area 3. Material Specific Details Area

Only four types of materials—cartographic materials, music, computer files, and serials—make use of this area. Some microforms also have this detail. This area will be discussed in detail in chapters devoted to some of these materials.

Area 4. Publication, Distribution, Etc. (MARC field 260)

260   Place of publication : $b Name of publisher, $c Date of publication.

The place of publication is transcribed as it appears. The first place of publication is always transcribed, using abbreviations from Appendix B. The name of country, state, province, etc. is added in square brackets if it is necessary to distinguish between places or identify a place.

In the prescribed source: DeKalb, Illinois   Transcribed as: DeKalb, Ill.
In the prescribed source: Madison   Transcribed as: Madison, [S.D.]

If the name of a larger jurisdiction appears with a place name in the prescribed source, the Library of Congress adds it to Area 4 even though it may not be necessary for identification purpose. If the name of a larger jurisdiction does not appear with a place name in the prescribed source, the Library of Congress adds it in square brackets when there is a need to distinguish between places or identify a place.

In the prescribed source: Indianapolis, Indiana
Transcribed by LC as: Indianapolis, Ind.
In the prescribed source: San Francisco
Transcribed by LC as: San Francisco

If the first place of publication is not in the home country of the cataloging agency or if the layout or typography suggests another place to be more important, then a second place of publication should be added.

In the prescribed source: Toronto   London   Chicago
A US library will transcribe: Toronto ; Chicago

The name of the publisher should be recorded in the shortest possible form that is recognizable internationally. Reference tools such as *Books in Print* are good sources to determine to what extent the name of a publisher can be shortened. Initial articles and terms such as "limited" and "incorporated" are dropped. If in doubt, the cataloger should not shorten a publisher's name.

If a publisher responsible for an item is a subordinate unit of a parent organization, the name of the division, not that of the parent organization, should be recorded.

In the prescribed source: Beginners Books, a division of MacMillan
Transcribed as: Beginners Books

Phrases indicating the function or responsibility of the publisher other than publishing should be recorded. This is typical of association publications that are contracted out to commercial publishers.

In the prescribed source: Published for the American Society for Information Science by John Wiley.
Transcribed as: Published for the American Society for Information Science by J. Wiley.

The publication date of the edition in hand is the third element for Area 4. Publication date is preferred to copyright date or printing date. If a publication date is not available, the cataloger records the copyright date. If a copyright date is not available, a printing date is used. *AACR2R* offers an option to include both the publication date and the copyright date if they are different. The Library of Congress decided in 1989 that it would not apply this option to monographs or print serials.

260   Toronto ; $a Chicago : $b Beginners Books, $c 1990.

Area 5. Physical Description (MARC field 300)

300   Extent : $b Other details ; $c Dimensions + $e Accompanying material.

The extent of an item is recorded as the number of physical units in Arabic numerals and the specific material designation. For books the cataloger records the number of pages, such as "320 p." For nonprint materials, the cataloger should consult the .5B subrules in the relevant chapter. For example, for sound recordings (covered in Chapter 6 of *AACR2R*), consult 6.5B.

If playing time is available, it follows the physical units description in parentheses.

300   2 sound cassettes (60 min.)

If other physical details of an item are available, they are included as the second element in the field 300. Examples include color, tracks, recording methods, and playing speed. For dimension of the item, the cataloger will need to consult rules in the relevant chapters.

300   1 sound disc (62 min.) : $b digital, stereo. ; $c 4 3/4 in.

Accompanying material can be included in the record in several ways. A common approach is to provide the number of physical units in Arabic numerals and a descriptive term of the material at the end of Area 5.

300   1 sound disc (62 min.) : $b digital, stereo ; $c 4 3/4 in.
                       + $e 1 booklet.

Area 6. Series (field 4xx)

440   _   Series title, $x ISSN ; $v

490   _   Series title.

490   _   Series title as it appears in the item [not to be used for added entry]

830   _   Series title as added entry.

Series titles are usually found in the chief source or other prescribed sources. A series title should be transcribed according to the same rules for transcribing title proper. If the International Standard Serial Number (ISSN) appears on the item, it is transcribed in Area 6. The number of an item within a series is in Arabic form. Abbreviations in Appendix B are used and the numbering appears as the last element in Area 6.

Other title information is rarely included in the transcription of Area 6. The statement of responsibility is usually not included in Area 6, however, *AACR2R* instructs that if a statement of responsibility is needed to identify a series, it can be included. The Library of Congress interprets this to mean adding statements to titles which are meaningless by themselves (CSB 22: 16), for example, Occasional papers / National Geological Society.

Series information can be entered in the 440 field if it is to serve as an added entry; otherwise 490 is used. When a series title is to be used as an added entry but in a form different from that on the item, both 490 and 830 are used. In this case, the series title on the item is recorded in 490, and the series title to be used as an access point is recorded in 830.

440   0   Contribution to information science studies ; $v 25

Area 7. Notes (field 5xx)

Notes supplement information formally presented in the first six areas of a record. Some notes provide identifying information, some indicate the nature of an item, while others offer background information such as the intended audience. Rules under 1.7 cover various types of notes the cataloger may want to provide. The notes for specific types of materials can be found in chapters on specific media.

Notes serve at least two major purposes:

1. They offer additional information about an item that cannot be recorded in one of the first six areas.

2. They justify the provision of additional access points.

The content of a note can be taken from any suitable source. Quotations can be used in notes. For quotations not taken from the chief source of information the cataloger will need to indicate the source:

"Proceedings of a Symposium on Hypertension"--T.p. verso.

Notes providing general information about an item as a whole are presented first. The rest of the notes are presented in the same order as the eight areas specified by *AACR2R*. Some of the more popular notes are:

1.7B1. Nature, scope, or artistic form (field 500)

1.7B2. Language of the item and/or translation or adaptation (field 546)

1.7B3. Source of title proper (field 500)

1.7B4. Variations in title (field 500)

1.7B6. Statements of responsibility (field 500)

1.7B7. Edition and history (fields 500, 518, etc.)

1.7B13. Dissertation (field 502)

1.7B14. Audience (field 521)

1.7B16. Other formats (field 530)

1.7B17. Summary (field 520)

1.7B18. Contents (fields 504, 500, and 505)

1.7B19. Numbers borne by the item (fields 023-030, 036, 037)

Area 8. International Standard Numbers (field 020 or 022)

020   Ten digits without hyphens (qualifier) $a availability

The International Standard Book Number (ISBN) or International Standard Serial Number (ISSN) should be recorded in Area 8. If more than one standard number is available, the one describing the item in hand should be recorded first. Both *AACR2R* and the Library of Congress allow the option of including additional standard numbers with qualification added.

020   2378456333 (alk. paper) $c $42.50

The ISSN for a monograph is usually entered with the series title in Area 6. But for a serial record, the ISSN will be recorded in Area 8.

222   ISSN 1047-949X = ALCTS newsletter

Assignment of Access Points

Part II of *AACR2R* is based on the Paris principles. Chapter 21 stipulates how access points should be selected, and Chapters 22 to 25 offer details for developing headings. The chief source of information of the item being cataloged is the main source for potential access points. Other statements that appear prominently (i.e., in the prescribed sources for the first two areas of the type of materials cataloged) should be considered as well.

Personal authorship: *AACR2R* defines a personal author as "the person chiefly responsible for the creation of the intellectual or artistic content of a work" (21.1A1, p. 312). The choice of access points follows the tradition of honoring individuals responsible for a work, and catalogers' rule of three applies. That is, if there are no more than three authors involved in the creation of a work, all three authors will be assigned access points, with the first one as the main access point if no indication of principal authorship is available. But if more than three authors are involved, then the main access point is the title and only the first named author is used as an access point. The rule of three applies to editors as well.

Corporate bodies: *AACR2R* defines a corporate body as "an organization or a group of persons that is identified by a particular name and that acts, or may act, as an entity" (21.1B1, p. 312). The rules for using corporate bodies as the main access point have evolved and become more stringent. A work must emanate from one or more corporate bodies and must belong to one of the six categories of materials for it to be entered under a corporate body (see 21.1B2 for details). In case of doubt, *AACR2R* encourages catalogers not to use a corporate body as the main access point.

Title as the main access point: There are only four occasions when title becomes the main access point:

1. When there are more than three authors (see 21.6C2) or when the authorship is unknown (see 21.5).

2. When the item being cataloged is a collection of works by many people or corporate bodies (see 21.7).

3. When the item emanates from a corporate body but does not belong to any of the six categories stipulated by Rule 21.1B2.

4. When the item is a sacred scripture of a religious group (see 21.37).

AACR2R also stipulates how adapters, illustrators, revisers, commentators, translators, and persons being honored by a work should be used as access points (see 21.9-21.15). In addition, it offers guidelines for determining access points for artworks, musical works, and sound recordings (see 21.23). Rules under 21.29 provide general rules for added entries and Rules under 21.30 include specific rules on when to assign individuals, corporate bodies, titles, and series as added entries. Rule 21.29C gives catalogers the authority to make an added entry "if some catalogue users might suppose that the description of an item would be found" under the added entry (p. 354). Rule 21.29F also states that if the description does not clearly indicate why an added entry is made, a note should be provided. *AACR2R* DOES NOT specify the order of added entries in a description, but an LC interpretation (21.29:CSB 12) gives the order of added entries:

1. Personal name;

2. Personal name/title;

3. Corporate name;

4. Corporate name/title;

5. Uniform title (all instances of works entered under title);

6. Title traced as Title-period;

7. Title traced as Title-colon, followed by a title;

8. Series.

Within each group the added entries should follow the order in which the data appear in the bibliographic description. Nonprint materials are often the results of many individuals' efforts, and it is not unusual for a work to have many added entries. Rules relevant to the selected resources in this book and the Library of Congress's interpretations to them are discussed in later chapters.

Chapters 22 to 26 cover headings for persons, headings for geographic names, headings for corporate bodies, uniform titles, and references. With the help of the Library of Congress Name Authority Files (LCNAF), catalogers can simplify authority work substantially. But for names not found in LCNAF, catalogers will need to consult Chapters 22 to 26 to establish headings.

■ SUBJECT ANALYSIS

Catalogers analyze the content of materials to enable users to search and evaluate these materials. Subject analysis can be performed using controlled vocabulary or natural language. In the library environment controlled vocabulary such as subject headings or descriptors are regularly assigned to indicate the aboutness of materials. In addition, catalogers have used another form of controlled vocabulary, classification numbers, or codes, for this purpose. No matter which form of controlled vocabulary they use, catalogers must perform authority control on the indexing terms to control for synonyms, homographs, and variant spellings, and to represent the relationships among authorized terms.

The objectives of subject analysis are to indicate the content of a work and to collocate works on the same subject. Before choosing the language for subject indexing and deciding the extent to which an item should be analyzed, the cataloger needs to know the intended users of the catalog. Serious researchers may appreciate scientific language and in-depth indexing, while public library users will prefer less technical terminology and less exhaustive indexing. Because it covers a wide range of subjects and contains many headings, many research, academic and large public libraries have used the *Library of Congress Subject Headings. Sears List of Subject Headings* has been more prevalent in small and medium-sized public libraries and school libraries. Regardless of the specific differences between these authority lists, the same principles of subject cataloging apply. David Judson Haykin, a well-regarded chief of the Library of Congress's subject division in the 1950s, had discussed these principles,[17] and Lois Mai Chan has elaborated on the subject cataloging principles and practices of the Library of Congress.[18] These principles include user and usage, literary warrant, uniform heading, unique heading, specific entry and co-extensivity, internal consistency, and stability. If these principles are applied to a local environment in creating local subject headings, catalogers must always keep users in mind, using the terminology appropriate to the users' intellectual level. In addition, catalogers should make sure one subject is represented by one heading and address problems of synonyms, variant spellings, different phrasings, and homographs. Catalogers need to create headings that are specific to the subjects they represent, and the headings should be directly accessible. For example, if the cataloger needs to establish a heading for a particular kind of flower such as lilies, then "lilies," which is the most specific heading, should be created, not something less direct like "Botany--Flower--Lilies." In addition, catalogers need to maintain form and structural consistency among analogous headings and keep them stable within a subject system.

The first step in subject analysis is to determine the subject of a work. Catalogers examine the title, author's preface, table of contents, and the bibliography, if necessary. The containers, accompanying materials, and "README" files (for computer files only) often provide useful information on the subject of sound recordings, videorecordings, and computer files. For Internet resources, meta tags in the HTML header and "About this page" type of links often shed light on the subject of a page. Once the subject is determined, the next step is to translate the subject into authorized headings. The procedures for subject cataloging are detailed in the *Library of Congress Subject Cataloging Manual*,[19] and H180 in particular offers specific instructions. The guidelines can be summarized as follows:

> *Summative approach*: Catalogers should identify topics of a work and try to find headings that will summarize the contents. This practice has a long tradition in cataloging and is rooted in the manual environment. Due to advances in technology, many catalogers have urged the Library of Congress to provide more in-depth analysis. The guideline now allows catalogers to assign up to 10 subject headings.
>
> *Substantial treatment required*: Only topics treated substantially in a work should be assigned subject headings. The general rule is if a topic takes up at least 20 percent of a work, then it should be represented by a heading.
>
> *Specific and direct headings*: Following the principle of co-extensivity, catalogers should assign specific and direct headings to represent the content of a work. For a work about dolphins, the most specific and direct heading is "dolphins." For a work about mammals, the most specific and direct heading is "mammals." The Library of Congress also discourages catalogers from assigning specific headings and general headings at the same time, with few exceptions. So catalogers should not assign both mammals and dolphins to either of the works above.
>
> *Aspects of a topic*: Because LC subject headings are highly precoordinated, catalogers are urged to find appropriate phrase headings or subdivisions to represent aspects of a topic. In addition to the subdivisions listed in the authority list, there are pattern headings to follow and free-floating subdivisions to use. If two or more topics are in a work, catalogers should consider the relationship of these topics in choosing headings. If more than three topics are in a work and they constitute the whole of a broader subject, a heading for the broad subject is used. But if these topics do not constitute the whole of a broader subject, then catalogers should assign a heading for each topic. Assigning subject headings takes practice. Various handbooks provide good exercises.[20]

Another method to represent subject analysis work is by classification number. The *Library of Congress Classification* scheme (*LCC*) and the *Dewey Decimal Classification* scheme (*DDC*) have been the two dominant systems. Both systems are discipline-based, hierarchical, and enumerative. Based on the principle of literary warrant, *LCC* reflects the collection of the Library of Congress and continues to expand as the collection grows. *DDC* was initially based on a classification of W. T. Harris, which was based on an inverted order of Francis Bacon's classification of knowledge,[21] but has evolved to accommodate new subjects—for instance, the expansion of numbers, 004-006, for computer science. With more than 20 major classes, *LCC* has been popular in research, academic, and large public libraries. *DDC* has a more compact structure and contains only 10 major classes, but its history, reputation, and structure have made it a popular system outside the United States.

The procedure for assigning classification number is the same regardless of the format of the material being cataloged. The cataloger identifies the main thrust of the work (e.g., teaching ecology in elementary schools), determines the discipline in which the topic is treated (e.g., education [300]), then focuses on the corresponding class (e.g., elementary education in specific subjects [372.3-372.8]) to find the most specific classification number for a work (e.g., natural study [372.357]). The Library of Congress does not assign class numbers to audiovisual media and special instructional materials but has provided alternate class numbers in brackets to films, sound recordings, slide sets, and so on to aid catalogers outside of LC.[22] Nonprint materials are classified in the same manner as print materials. Table 1 of *DDC* includes provisions for some formats (e.g., encyclopedias, periodicals, handbooks) but the medium or form of a work is usually not represented in DDC numbers, rather, it is recorded elsewhere in the bibliographic record.[23] After the classification number has been assigned, the cataloger usually assigns an author number to provide further subdivision within the same subject. This author number is often called the Cutter number because the numbers are from Cutter tables. *LCC* has its own Cutter table, while *DDC* can be used with any Cutter tables. Date of publication is also added to make the call number complete. Call numbers in most American libraries serve as the addresses of works on the shelves.

■ MARC FORMAT

Bibliographic records created according to *AACR2R* and assigned subject headings and classification numbers will then be coded in the MAchine-Readable Cataloging (MARC) format to support searching and manipulation of these records. The Library of Congress developed the LC MARC format in the 1960s, which evolved into the USMARC.[24] USMARC includes five formats for the encoding of five types of data—bibliographic, authority, holdings, community information, and classification data. The Library of Congress maintains these standards and provides documentation for them. The format catalogers use most frequently is the bibliographic format. But bibliographic utilities, such as the Online Computer Library Center (OCLC) and the Research Library Information Network (RLIN), have also developed guidelines specific to their environment, and catalogers will need to consult those guidelines to conform to their input standards.

A USMARC record contains a leader, a directory, control fields, variable control fields, and variable fields.[25] The leader is the first 24 characters of the record and each position encodes information necessary for computer processing. The elements encoded include record status, type of record, bibliographic level, encoding level, and others. The directory refers to a block of data following the leader that lists the tags in the record and their respective starting positions. The directory is constructed by computer based on cataloging information. All control fields begin with the digit 0 (0XX) and are used to encode information such as Library of Congress control numbers (010), International Standard Book Numbers (020), and classification numbers (082, 050, etc.). The variable control fields are tagged 00X. They can contain a single data or a series of data. For instance, the 007 field for sound recording has more than 10 subfields. Field 008, the field of "Fixed-Length Data Elements," is very valuable because its 40 characters can be used to identify and retrieve records that meet the search criteria of the user. Field 008 is format specific and not repeatable. Bibliographic utilities like OCLC have added labels to the fixed field elements and place the block of information at the top of their bibliographic records, but others display it differently. The variable fields contain descriptive cataloging data and access points and are the parts most users see on their online catalogs, often with labels supplied by the system vendors.

Each variable field begins with a three digit tag, followed by two indicators, then appropriate subfields. The variable fields correspond closely to elements and areas specified by *AACR*. The following scheme illustrates the relationship of MARC fields to areas in *AACR*:

Variable field	*AACR*
1XX	Main entry (except for title main entry)
245	Area 1. Title and statement of responsibility
250	Area 2. Edition statement
260	Area 4. Publication place, publisher, date
300	Area 5. Extent of item
4XX	Area 6. Series
5XX	Area 7. Notes
6XX	Subject added entries
7XX	Non-subject added entries

The tags are displayed according to the first digit, but within each group (2xx, 4xx, 5xx, etc.), the order of the tags is stipulated by *AACR*. The USMARC provides the scheme for content designation, but it is *AACR* that specifies the data elements (the content) and the order of the elements in the bibliographic record. Throughout this book records will be presented in the MARC format excluding the fixed field and many of the 00X fields, except when these fields are necessary to illustrate cataloging practices.

Prior to Format Integration catalogers had seven MARC bibliographic formats from which to choose. Based on the primary characteristics of a work, the cataloger selected the appropriate format to encode the item, and secondary but important characteristics could not be represented. For instance, for a videorecording serial, the cataloger had to choose between a serials format and a videorecording format. To correct such problems, reduce the cost of maintaining seven bibliographic formats, and remove the need to create new formats when new forms of intellectual expression appear, the Library of Congress and the MARBI (Machine-Readable Bibliographic Information) Committee of the American Library Association began exploring the integration process in the early 1980s.[26] When Format Integration was completed in March of 1996, many fields and values became obsolete and new ones were added to make most of the fields and codes valid for all forms of material. Many of the changes affect serial catalogers, but changes such as the creation of field 006, "field-length data element—additional material characteristics," and the use of field 246 for variant titles affect the entire cataloging community. An appendix to Update No. 1 of the *USMARC Format for Bibliographic Data* summarizes the changes.[27]

Field 006 is probably one of the most important results of Format Integration. By using several 006 fields, catalogers are able to represent multiple aspects of a work or the characteristics of accompanying material. There are seven types of 006 fields, including 006 for books, serials, maps, music, visual materials, computer files, and archival materials. This field has 18 character positions and is optional and repeatable. Field 006 has a tree structure by which the form of the material (the first code) determines what other data elements are allowed for subsequent character positions. For instance, if the first element is coded "a" for monographs, then the following data elements are allowed:

Books Format 006 Information

| T006: a | Ills: | Audn: | Form: | Cont: | Gpub: |
| Conf: 0 | Fest: 0 | Indx: 0 | Fict: 0 | Biog: | |

This example illustrates that 006 uses the same mnemonics as the fixed field. OCLC provides prompts for data input for this field. Field 006 has no indicator values or subfield codes, and data elements are identified by their position. In the OCLC system brackets are used to present this field. For example, if a Web page is basically textual, the book format workform is used to create a record, and the 008 field for the book format will be used (with the "Type" coded as "a"). To reflect the fact that the work is a Web page, the cataloger will enter "n006 com" (without the quotation marks) and press <F11>, and a screen for 006 input will appear:

Computer Files Format 006 Information (with default values)
T006: m   Audn: File: u   GPub:

After the cataloger enters the appropriate codes—using "m" for the first element to specify computer file, and "d" for File to specify this is primarily a text file—field 006 will appear on the record this way:[28]

006   [m   d   ]

Elements in 006 use the same codes for the fixed field elements (except for "s" in T006 for serials).

In creating a MARC record the first decision catalogers must make is about the appropriate 008 field for the item being cataloged. To help catalogers make this decision a model for selecting the 008 field is provided below.

MODEL for Selecting 008 Field[29]

If an item is basically textual

Type of record (position 06 in the Leader) = a (language material), p
    (mixed material) or t (manuscript language material)

  Bibliographic level (position 07 in the Leader) = any valid code

  008 = Book, serial (depending on Leader 06/07 codes), or mixed
    material

  006 = any applicable to main item or accompanying material

If an item is basically nontextual

Type of record (position 06 in the Leader) = c (printed music), d (manu-
    script music), e (printed map), f (manuscript map), g (pro-
    jected medium), i (nonmusical sound recording), j (musical
    sound recording), k (two-dimensional nonprojectable
    graphic), m (computer file), o (kit), or r (three-dimensional ar-
    tifact or naturally occurring object)

  Bibliographic level (position 07 in the Leader) = Any valid code

  008 = Music, map, visual material, or computer file

  006 = any applicable to main item or accompanying material

So a book accompanied by a computer disk will be coded as follows:

Type of record = a   Bibliographic level = m
008 for the Book format will be used

006 for the Computer File format will be used to cover the accompanying disk.

A computer program accompanied by a manual, however, will be coded as follows:

Type of record = m   Bibliographic level = m
008 for the Computer File format will be used

006 for the Book format will be used to cover the accompanying manual.

The use of 006 fields is further discussed in Chapter Seven, where items of multiple characteristics are more common than the other chapters. It should be pointed out that 006 and 007 serve different purposes. Field 006 describes additional characteristics of an item or the characteristics of accompanying material, while field 007 describes the physical characteristics of the item or the material accompanying it. The use of field 007 is discussed in relevant chapters.

Other important changes of Format Integration include the addition of field 856 (Electronic Location and Access) for remote access electronic resources, and subfield $v (form subdivision) to designate specific kinds or genres of material. Details of field 856 are included in Chapter Seven, the chapter for Internet resources. The objective of form subdivision is to enable online catalogs to provide better display of records and assist users in searching. Subfield $v became valid after Format Integration in 1996, and the Library of Congress issued guidelines on form subdivisions and the use of subfield code $v in the fall of 1998.[30] The guidelines instruct catalogers to code a subdivision as $v (form subdivision) when it indicates what an item *is*, and to code it as $x (topical subdivision) when it characterizes what an item is *about*. See, for example,

650   0   Biology $v Periodicals.
[assigned to a journal on biology. $v indicates the form of this publication.]

650   0   Biology $x Periodicals.
[assigned to a work that discusses biology journals.]

The Library of Congress began implementing subfield $v in February, 1999 and has created authority records for subdivisions. All records include usage instruction, and two records are created for subdivisions that can be used as topical and form subdivisions. Taylor presented an educational forum[31] on subdivision $v at the 1999 ALA midwinter meeting and has maintained a site on the implementation of form subdivisions.[32] Sha has a Web page that lists free-floating form subdivisions from the *Library of Congress Subject Headings.*[33]

■ARRANGEMENT

The physical arrangement of materials, especially electronic resources, may not necessarily follow the call numbers. In fact, while many libraries assign subject headings to electronic resources to support subject collocation on their online catalogs, many of them have developed in-house systems to shelve nonprint resources. These systems are developed to address the concerns for the security and preservation of nonprint resources. But with the growth of electronic resources, the demand for easy access from users will likely become stronger. It is clearly challenging to organize sound recordings, videorecordings, computer software, multimedia, and Internet resources for easy local and remote access. Factors to consider in organizing and arranging audiovisual and electronic resources will be discussed in the chapters on these media.

■NOTES

1. Jean Weihs, "A Taste of Nonbook History: Historical Background and Review of the State of the Art of Bibliographic Control of Nonbook Materials," in *Policy and Practice in Bibliographic Control of Nonbook Media*, edited by Sheila Intner and Richard Smiraglia (Chicago: American Library Association, 1987), 3–14.

2. Sheila S. Intner, *Access to Media: A Guide to Integrating and Computerizing Catalogs* (New York: Neal-Schuman, 1984), 33–40.

3. Carolyn O. Frost, *Media Access and Organization: A Cataloging and Reference Sources Guide for Nonbook Materials* (Englewood, Colo.: Libraries Unlimited, 1989), 21–27.

4. Lucienne Maillet, *Subject Control of Film and Video: A Comparison of Three Methods* (Chicago: American Library Association, 1991), 1–34.

5. See, for example, Jean Weihs, with Shirley Lewis and Janet Macdonald, *Nonbook Materials: The Organization of Integrated Collections*, 2nd ed. (Ottawa: Canadian Library Association, 1979), 1; Jean Weihs, *The Integrated Library* (Phoenix, Ariz.: Oryx Press, 1991); and Alan L. Kaye, *Video and Other Nonprint Resources in the Small Library* (Chicago: Library Administration and Management Association, American Library Association, 1991).

6. Jay E. Daily, *Organizing Nonprint Materials* (New York: Marcel Dekker, 1972).

7. Randy Pitman, "Rockefeller Foundation Videocassette Distribution Task Force, Final Report—Library Market," unpublished report, June 30, 1989.

8. Jean Weihs and Lynne C. Howarth, "Nonbook Materials: Their Occurrence and Bibliographic Description in Canadian Libraries," *Library Resources & Technical Services* 39 (April 1995), 184–97.

9. Ingrid Hsieh-Yee, "Organization of Nonprint Resources in Public and Academic Libraries," unpublished report, May 30, 1999.

10.   See, for instance, Sheila S. Intner and Jean Weihs, *Special Libraries: A Cataloging Guide* (Englewood, Colo.: Libraries Unlimited, 1998); Alan L. Kaye, *Video and Other Nonprint Resources in the Small Library* (Chicago: Library Administration and Management Association, American Library Association, 1991); Sally Mason-Robinson, *Developing and Managing Video Collections* (New York: Neal-Schuman, 1996); and James C. Scholtz, *Video Acquisitions and Cataloging: A Handbook* (Westport, Conn.: Greenwood, 1995).

11.   Jean Weihs, 1991.

12.   Scholtz, pp. 151–52.

13.   Ingrid Hsieh-Yee, 1999.

14.   *Guidelines for Bibliographic Description of Interactive Multimedia* (Chicago: American Library Association, 1994).

15.   Nancy B. Olson, ed., *Cataloging Internet Resources: A Manual and Practical Guide*, 2nd ed. (Dublin, Ohio: OCLC, 1997).

16.   *Library of Congress Rule Interpretations*, 2nd ed. (Washington, D.C.: Cataloging Distribution Service, Library of Congress, 1990–).

17.   David Judson Haykin, *Subject Headings: A Practical Guide* (Washington, D.C.: GPO, 1951).

18.   Lois Mai Chan, *Library of Congress Subject Headings: Principles and Application*, 3rd ed. (Englewood, Colo.: Libraries Unlimited, 1995).

19.   Library of Congress. Cataloging Policy & Support Office. *Subject Cataloging Manual: Subject Headings*, 5th ed. (Washington, D.C.: Cataloging Distribution Service, Library of Congress, 1996).

20.   See, for example, Lois Mai Chan, *Cataloging and Classification: An Introduction* (New York: McGraw-Hill, 1994); Jerry D. Saye, *Manheimer's Cataloging and Classification*. 4th ed., rev. and expanded (New York: Marcel Dekker, 2000).

21.   Lois Mai Chan, *Cataloging and Classification: An Introduction* (New York: McGraw-Hill, 1994), 269.

22.   Lois Mai Chan, *Immroth's Guide to the Library of Congress Classification*, 4th ed. (Englewood, Colo.: Libraries Unlimited, 1990), 337.

23.   Lois Mai Chan, *Dewey Decimal Classification: A Practical Guide*, 2nd ed., rev. for *DDC* 21 (Albany, N.Y.: Forest Press, 1996), 47.

24.   Henriette D. Avram, *MARC: Its History and Implications* (Washington, D.C.: Library of Congress, 1975).

25.   Deborah J. Byrne, *MARC Manual: Understanding and Using MARC Records* (Englewood, Colo.: Libraries Unlimited, 1991).

26.   *Format Integration and Its Effect on Cataloging, Training, and Systems*, edited by Karen Coyle (Chicago: American Library Association, 1993).

27.   *Format Integration 1995 Change List*, available: gopher://marvel.loc.gov/00/.listarch/usmarc/ufbdfi95.cha, accessed June 2000.

28.   *OCLC Technical Bulletin 212, Format Integration Phase 2* (Dublin, Ohio: OCLC, 1996).

29.   This model was derived from a handout for Sally McCallum's presentations at a workshop on "USMARC Format Integration: Implementation Issues and Strategies," Monday, October 18, 1993, Washington, D.C. An earlier model appeared in Network Development and MARC Standards Office, *Format Integration and Its Effect on the USMARC Bibliographic Format*, 1992 ed. (Washington, D.C.: 1992), 9.

30.   "1998 Update Number 2" to the *Subject Cataloging Manual: Subject Headings* (Washington, D.C.: Library of Congress, 1998).

31.   Arlene Taylor, *Educational Forum: LCSH and Subfield v*, available: http://www.pitt.edu/~agtaylor/ala/edforum.htm, accessed June 2000.

32.   *SAC Subcommittee on Form Headings/Subdivisions Implementation*, available: http://www.pitt.edu/~agtaylor/ala/implem.htm, accessed June 2000.

33.   Vianne Sha, *Guide to the Usage of LCSH Free-Floating Form Subdivisions*, available: http://www.itcompany.com/inforetriever/form_subdivisions_list.htm, accessed June 2000.

■SUGGESTED READINGS

Chan, Lois Mai, and Theodora Hodges; revised by Giles Martin. "Subject Cataloguing and Classification." In *Technical Services Today and Tomorrow*. 2nd ed. Englewood, Colo.: Libraries Unlimited, 1998.

Coyle, Karen, ed. *Format Integration and Its Effect on Cataloging, Training, and Systems*. Chicago: American Library Association, 1993.

Furrie, Betty. *Understanding MARC Bibliographic: Machine-Readable Cataloging*. 5th ed. Washington, D.C.: Library of Congress, Cataloging Distribution Service, 1998.

Gorman, Michael. "Descriptive Cataloguing: Its Past, Present, and Future." In *Technical Services Today and Tomorrow*. 2nd ed. Englewood, Colo.: Libraries Unlimited, 1998.

McCue, Janet, with sidebar by Dongming Zhang. "Technical Services and the Electronic Library: Defining Our Roles and Divining the Partnership." *Library Hi Tech* 12 (1994): 63–70.

THREE ← SOUND RECORDINGS

Chapter 6 of *AACR2R* covers sound recordings in various formats, including disc (long playing records and compact discs), tape (open reel-to-reel, cassettes, cartridges), rolls, and sound recordings on film (excluding those designed to accompany films). Advanced technology and convenience have led to the popularity of sound cassettes and compact discs (CDs), which are noted for their sound quality and durability. Most examples in this chapter are for sound cassettes and CDs.

Sound recordings pose several challenges for catalogers:

1. Unlike print publishers, who have a fairly standard pattern for presenting information on the title page, publishers of sound recordings tend to vary in their presentation of information on the item and its label, which are designated the chief source of information by *AACR2R*.

2. Sound recordings are frequently accompanied by textual materials and come in a container. Details on sound engineers, graphic designers, illustrators, and others often appear in various parts of a sound recording, making it difficult to determine which information to transcribe.

3. Physical description of sound recordings involves more elements than print publications and requires more attention to the description of the physical characteristics.

4. The publication place is often missing in sound recordings, which means the cataloger may need to consult reference tools for the information.

Decision on access points can also be challenging because of the large number of people involved in the creation of a sound recording. Fortunately *AACR2R* offers fairly specific guidelines for these areas in Chapter 21.

■ MARC FIELDS FOR SOUND RECORDINGS

The *MARC21 Concise Bibliographic Format*[1] and OCLC's *Bibliographic Formats and Standards*[2] provide details on codes and tags and are valuable resources for creating MARC records. Because of the large number of codes for fixed field elements, records in this chapter do not include fixed field information. But field 007, required for sound recording, is introduced to illustrate how physical characteristics of sound recordings are encoded. Field 007 for the sound recording format has 13 subfields, many of them mandatory. Three subfields (j, k, and l) are for archival cataloging of sound recordings. Subfield a is coded "s" for sound recording, codes for the rest of the subfields are listed in *Bibliographic Formats and Standards*, an online version is also available.[3] Information in field 300 is the basis for coding field 007, so it is important to record field 300 correctly according to *AACR2R*. Because sound cassettes and compact discs are popular media for sound recordings, the following examples present subfields common to cassettes and compact discs.

007	s $b special material designation $d speed $e playback channels $f groove width $g dimensions $h tape width $i tape configuration $m special playback characteristics $n capture and storage technique
007	**s $b s $d l $e _ $f n $g j $h l $i c $n _**
	(subfields of standard cassettes)
	($a s = sound recording, $b s = sound cassette, $d l = 1 7/8 ips (speed), $e s = stereophonic, u = unknown configuration of playback channels, $f n = no grooves, $g j = cassette dimensions 3 7/8 x 2 1/2 in., $h l = tape width 1/8 in., $i c = 4 tracks, $m c = Doby-B encoded, $n e = analog electrical storage)
007	s $b s $d l $e u $f n $g j $h l $i c $m c $n e
300	1 sound cassette : $b analog, Dolby processed
007	s $b s $d l $e s $f n $g j $h l $i c $n e
300	1 sound cassette : $b analog, stereo
007	**s $b d $d f $e _ $f n $g g $h n $i n $m e $n _**
	(subfields of standard CDs)
	($a s = sound recording, $b d = sound disc, $d f = speed of compact digital discs, $e s = stereophonic, u = unknown configuration of playback channels, $f n = no grooves, $g g = compact disc dimensions 4 3/4 in., $h n = tape width not applicable, $i n = tape configuration not applicable, $m e = digital recording, $n d = digital storage)
007	s $b d $d f $e s $f n $g g $h n $i n $m e $n d
300	1 sound disc (63 min., 13 sec.) : $b digital, stereo ; $c 4 3/4 in.
007	s $b d $d f $e u $f n $g g $h n $i n $m e $n d
300	1 sound disc (50 min., 55 sec.) : $b digital ; $c 4 3/4 in.

Fields commonly used to code sound recordings are:

028 _ _   Publisher's stock number $b publisher's label name.

100 _   Author, composer, artist, etc., $d date.

240 _ _   A uniform title for musical work, literary work, etc.

245 _ _   Title proper $h [sound recording] : $b other title information / $c statement of responsibility ; subsequent statement of responsibility.

250   Edition statement.

260   Place of publication : $b name of publisher, $c date of publication.

300   Number of special material designation (total playing time) : $b other details ; $c dimensions + $e accompanying material.

4xx _ _   Series statement.

511 _   Performer, instrument ; performer, instrument.

518   History of recording.

500   Location of accompanying material.

520   Summary for nonmusical recordings.

505 _ _   Contents.

6xx _ _   Subject headings.

700 _   Performer(s).

710 _   Performing group(s).

730 _ _   Uniform title.

■ DESCRIPTION

Rules for Descriptive Cataloging

Chief Source and Prescribed Sources of Information

AACR2R stipulates the same chief source of information for all types of sound recordings—the physical item (the disc, the reel, the cassette, the cartridge, etc.) and the "label," which is permanently affixed to the item. If an item has labels on both sides, both labels should be treated as part of the chief source.

If no information can be found from the chief source, catalogers may take information, in this order of preference, from accompanying textual material, container, or other sources. If sound data and textual data are both available, the cataloger should use textual data.

The same eight areas of bibliographic description for print materials are used in describing sound recordings. The prescribed sources of information for each area (Rule 6.0B2) are as follows:

245 (Area 1)	Chief source of information
250, 260, 4xx (Areas 2, 4, 6)	Chief source of information, accompanying textual information and container
300, 5xx, 020, 022 (Areas 5, 7, 8)	Any source

6.1. Title and Statement of Responsibility (MARC field 245)

The title of a sound recording should be transcribed exactly as to wording, spelling, and order, but the punctuation and capitalization may vary. This rule, 6.1B1, is the same as 1.1B1. Here are a few examples:

Men are from Mars, women are from Venus

Morning aire

James Joyce's Chamber music [a book of poems by Joyce]

Diana Ross greatest hits

6 sonatas, BWV 1030-1035

The first word of the title proper must be capitalized but not necessarily the rest of the title. Proper names should be capitalized and the first word of another title, such as "Chamber music," should be capitalized.

General Material Designation (GMD): For sound recordings in all formats the GMD is "sound recording." Terms such as CD, sound cassette or LP are not used. In the physical description area the cataloger provides more details on the format, which is represented by specific material designation (SMD).

Statement of Responsibility: For this element, *AACR2R* instructs the cataloger to record only writers, composers, and collectors of field materials if these names appear prominently. "Prominently" means the names must appear in the chief source, accompanying textual materials, or container of a sound recording. Performers of popular, rock, and jazz music, who do more than perform or interpret a piece of music (for example, who also compose or arrange it), are recorded in the statement of responsibility. But performers of classical music or narrators are usually recorded in the note area. The Library of Congress has strict guidelines for this: "The rule allows performers who do more than perform to be named in the statement of responsibility. Accept only the most obvious cases as qualifying for the statement of responsibility" (CSB11). Here are a few examples:

Disc label: DIANA ROSS

               DIANA ROSS GREATEST HITS

Transcribed as:

245   10   Diana Ross greatest hits / $c Diana Ross

* * *

Disc label: BACH

               6 Sonatas, BWV 1030-1035
               Michala Petri, recorder
               Keith Jarrett, harpsichord

Transcribed as:

245   10   6 sonatas, BWV 1030-1035 / $c Bach.

511   0   Michala Petri, recorder; Keith Jarrett, harpsichord.

* * *

Cassette label: FUNNY PAPERS

               by Elaine Scott Narrated by Norman Dietz

Transcribed as:

245   10   Funny papers / $c by Elaine Scott.

511   0   Narrated by Norman Dietz.

Some sound recordings contain several works but lack a collective title. *AACR2R* allows catalogers to describe the item as a unit or create separate records for each titled work (6.1G). The Library of Congress instructs its catalogers to describe the item as a unit (CSB 11) and not to apply the other option (CSB 47).

In describing an item without a collective title, if all the works are by the same person, the cataloger should transcribe the works in the order in which they appear in the chief source and separate them with semicolons (6.1G and 1.1G3). For instance,

Disc label: Ludwig van Beethoven

Sonata No. 8 in C minor,
Op. 13 "Pathetique"
Sonata No. 23 in F minor,
Op. 57 "Appassionata"
Sonata No. 14 in C sharp minor,
Op. 27 No. 2 "Moonlight"
CLAUDIO ARRAU, piano

Transcribed as:

100   1   Beethoven, Ludwig van, $d 1770-1827.

245   10   Sonata no. 8 in C minor, op. 13 $h [sound
               recording]: $b pathetique; sonata no. 23 in F
               minor, op. 57 : appasionata ; sonata no. 14 in C
               sharp minor, op. 27 no. 2 : moonlight / $c
               Ludwig van Beethoven.

511   0   Claudio Arrau, piano.

6. 2. Edition (MARC field 250)

The edition statement of sound recordings should be recorded as instructed in 1.2B. Abbreviations and numerical notations in Appendices B and C of *AACR2R* should be consulted.

250   Remastered original sound track ed.

6.3. This area does not apply to sound recordings.

6.4. Publication, Distribution, Etc. (MARC field 260)

The prescribed sources for this area are, in the order of preference, the chief source of information, accompanying textual material, and container. Information taken from other sources must be placed in brackets. Because many sound recordings lack the place of publication, the cataloger often needs to consult reference sources for this information. The following titles are good starting points:

Billboard International Buyer's Guide. New York: Billboard Publications, 1970-

Musical America: International Directory of the Performing Arts. Great Barrington, Mass.: ABC Leisure Magazines, 1974-

Rolling Stone Encyclopedia of Rock & Roll. New York : Rolling Stone Press (current edition).

The name of a larger jurisdiction may be added to identify the name of a city if necessary. When the name of a larger jurisdiction appears with a place name in the prescribed source, Library of Congress adds it to Area 4 even though it may not be necessary for identification purpose.

Cassette label: Prince Frederick, MD 20678

Transcribed as:

260   Prince Fredrick, MD

The name of the publisher is transcribed in the shortest form possible. If the publisher's name on the item is different from that on the container, the cataloger should prefer the information on the label. If a company's name and its subdivision, trade name, or brand name appear in a sound recording, *AACR2R* instructs the cataloger to record the name of the smaller unit. But if the trade name seems to be a series title, it should be transcribed as such (6.4D3).

Disc label: Electra Entertainment Group, A Division
                          of Warner Communications, Inc. 1996

Transcribed as:

260   Beverly Hills, CA : $b Elektra Entertainment Group,
             $c p1996.

The date of publication is recorded as instructed in 1.4F. Sound recordings sometimes carry two copyright dates. "c" represents the copyright date of textual data, while "p" represents the copyright date of the sound data. The current preferred practice is to use "p" for the date of publication. If the recording date is different from the publishing date, the cataloger records the publishing date in the 260 field and the recording date in a note in field 518.

260   New York, N.Y. : $b RCA Victor, $c p1988.

518   Recorded in September, 1987 in London, England.

6.5. Physical Description (MARC field 300)

300   Number of special material designation (total playing time) : $b other details ; $c dimension. + $e accompanying material.

The prescribed source of this area is the entire work. *AACR2R* gives catalogers several terms as specific material designations: sound cartridge, sound cassette, sound disc, sound tape reel, and sound track film. Cassette and reel can be added to "sound track film" and the name of an instrument can be added to roll (such as "piano rolls").

The total playing time of a sound recording should be recorded (6.5B2). If the playing time of each part is listed, the cataloger may add the parts up and round the total to the nearest minute. If no playing time is readily available, do not record it.

The second element of Area 5, other physical details, includes several subelements (6.5C1): (1) type of recording (analog or digital), (2) playing speed, (3) groove characteristics (of analog discs), (4) track configuration (of sound track films), (5) number of tracks (on tapes), (6) number of sound channels, and (7) recording and reproduction characteristics.

"Type of recording" refers to the way the sound is encoded and the type of playback equipment needed. It is a critical element. "Analog" and "digital" are the typical terms for this subelement.

Playing speed, groove characteristics, and number of tracks are not recorded if the information is standard for a particular medium. The number of sound channels, however, is always transcribed if the information is readily available. "Mono," "stereo," and "quad" are the three most common terms for this subelement (6.5C7).

The Library of Congress instructs its catalogers to record the recording and reproduction characteristics whenever the information is necessary for selecting playback equipment (CSB 8). "Dolby processed" is one of the most common terms recorded for this subelement. Many CDs have notations such as ADD or DDD that indicate the type of recording, the type of equipment used in mixing and editing, and the type of equipment used in mastering the disc. Such information is not recorded in the 300 field. As CDs become more prevalent, some libraries are including the ADD type information in their record. Since they are not allowed to enter this information in the 300 field, some libraries have included it in the "Compact disc" note.

The dimensions for rolls, cartridges, and cassettes are not recorded if they are standard size. Discs are measured in inches, according to the standard measurement of the recording industry. An analog disc is usually 12 inches, while a CD is 4 3/4 inches. A note is provided when a sound disc is a CD.

Details of accompanying material are added to the end of Area 5. The location of the accompanying material, however, is typically recorded in the note area.

300	2 sound cassettes (60 min., 20 sec.) : $b analog, stereo. + $e 1 booklet (20 p. : ill. (some col.) ; 8 cm.)
300	1 sound disc (52 min.) : $b digital ; $c 4 3/4 in.
500	Program notes on container.
500	Compact disc (DDD).

6.6. Series (MARC field 4xx)

Details for this area can be taken from the chief source of information, accompanying textual material, or container, in that order of preference. Series title should be recorded as instructed in 1.1B1. Wording, spelling, and order of the title should be followed, but not necessarily for punctuation or capitalization. Field 440 is used to record series information if the series is traced, otherwise field 490 is used. If a series is traced in a form different from the one on the item, catalogers typically use field 490 to record the series title as it appears and field 830 to record the traced form.

6.7. Notes

Notes serve two purposes:

1. They provide additional information about a work that cannot be recorded elsewhere in the record.

2. They justify the provision of additional access points.

Notes are to be recorded in the order specified in 6.7B, but the order can be changed if one note is considered more important than others. Notes on the nature and scope of the sound recording as a whole are presented first. Other notes follow the order of the eight areas of bibliographic description.

Many types of notes are covered by 6.7B and several notes are commonly provided for sound recordings. They include variations in title, performers, time and/or place of recording, additional physical descriptions, location of accompanying material, audience, other formats, summary, contents, and publisher's numbers.

Variant Title (MARC field 246): Titles different from the title proper should be recorded in notes with added entries provided. Field 246 is used for this purpose. The first indicator specifies if a note and an added entry should be produced, and the second indicator specifies the type of variant title.

245	10	Concertos for cello.
246	18	Cello concertos ["1" "8" will create a title added entry and a note: Spine title: Cello concertos.]
245	10	Sonata no. 8 in C minor, op. 13 "Pathetique"
246	1	$i Title on container: $a Piano sonatas [subfield i encodes a display text and $a encodes the variant title.]

Performers (MARC field 511): Performers not named in the statement of responsibility area are recorded in the note area if the information is considered necessary. *AACR2R* instructs catalogers to record the names of performers, the role they play, or the medium they perform. This information is entered in field 511 and the first indicator value is "0".

511	0	Seiji Ozawa, conductor; Boston Symphony Orchestra.

History of Recording (MARC field 518): The date of recording is usually noted in field 518.

518		Recorded April 6 and 7, 1987, at St. Timothy Church, Toronto.

Physical Description (MARC field 500): *AACR2R* allows a note of "analog recording" for a digital disc made from an analog original, and a note of "digital recording" for an analog disc made from a digital original. Nowadays many CDs bear three-letter codes such as ADD and DDD. Many libraries have included this information with the "compact disc" note in the 500 field.

Other Formats (MARC field 530): If a sound recording is known to be available in other formats, the information is recorded in field 530. Catalogers may consult the Schwann catalog to find this information, but should not do extensive research to locate such information.

Summary (MARC field 520): Summary notes are usually provided for nonmusical recordings because it gives users a good idea of the item without actually playing it. Summary notes are entered in field 520.

Contents (MARC field 505): Contents of a sound recording are frequently recorded for music recordings and some nonmusical recordings. By listing the works of a recording, the cataloger offers users an understanding of the collected work and enables them to select the item. If duration of each titled work is available, the information should be included.

Publisher's number (MARC field 028): Publisher's numbers for sound recordings are useful identifiers. Although it is listed as the last type of note, this information appears as the first note in printed catalog cards. Subfield b is used for the name of the record company. The following 028 field with a second indicator 2 will generate a note saying "Publisher no.: RCA Victor 7774-2-RC."

028   0 2   7774-2-RC $b RCA Victor

6.8. Standard Number and Terms of Availability Area (field 020 or 022)

The cataloger should record international standard numbers such as International Standard Book Number (ISBN) or International Standard Serial Number (ISSN) in field 020 or 022, if the information is readily available. Other numbers should be recorded in the note area.

Enhanced CDs

Many musicians have combined video or multimedia in their recordings to present background information about their songs, concerts, and personal interests. A fairly standard practice is to create an "Enhanced CD," which is a regular audio CD with a multimedia CD-ROM track. To play an Enhanced CD, one needs an audio CD player for the audio portion of the disc and a computer for the multimedia CD-ROM track. Because an Enhanced CD involves the use of a computer, the treatment of this type of material is covered in Chapter Five.

Assignment of Access Points

Three chapters of *AACR2R* provide guidelines for assigning access points to sound recordings. Chapter 21 of *AACR2R* presents rules on how to select access points, and Rule 21.23 is devoted to sound recordings. Chapter 22 covers the construction of proper headings, and Chapter 25 focuses on formulating uniformed titles, which are commonly assigned to musical works.

21.23A. The Work of One Person

The principles of authorship specified in Chapter 21 apply to sound recordings. 21.23A states that the sound recording of a work by a single person (composer, writer, artist) should be entered under that person. Performers, readers, or narrators are assigned as additional access points.

100   1   Moyers, Bill.

245   10   Healing and the mind $h [sound recording] / $c Bill Moyers.

21.23B. Two or More Works by the Same Person(s) or Body (bodies)

Two or more works by the same person will be entered under the name of the person. Recordings of music may need uniform titles to bring various renditions of the work together. Chapter 25 focuses on uniform title and the cataloger should search OCLC Authority File to ensure proper form is used. Added entries are usually provided for principal performers.

100	1	Bach, Johann Sebastian, $d 1685-1750.
240	10	Sonatas. $k Selections. $o arr.
245	10	6 sonatas, BWV 1030-1035 $h [sound recording] / $c Bach.
511	0	Michala Petri, recorder; Keith Jarrett, harpsichord.
700	1	Petri, Michala.
700	1	Jarrett, Keith.

21.23C. Collections with Collective Title

A sound recording containing the works by two or more people is entered under the principal performer. LCRI 21.23C (CBS 45) clarifies that "performer" refers to a person or corporate body whose performance is on the sound recording. It also states that a conductor is not a member of the group he or she conducts, and a member of a performing group should not be considered a separate performer.

Disc label:

> THE PHILHARMONIC ORCHESTRA
> LESLEY GARRETT
> PRIMA DONNA
> CONDUCTED BY IVOR BOLTON

[A collection of 15 songs by various composers.]

Transcribed as:

100	1	Garrett, Lesley, $d 1955-
245	10	Prima donna $h [sound recording] / $c Lesley Garrett.
511	0	Lesley Garret, soprano; Philharmonic Orchestra; Ivor Bolton, conductor.

If a sound recording of this type has a collective title, but no principal performer can be identified or there are more than three principal performers, the item will be entered under title.

Cassette label:

>Frost, Williams, Stevens, Eberhart, Pound & Wilbur
>THE CAEDMON TREASURY OF MODERN POETS
>Read by Each Respective Author

Transcribed as:

245 04   The Caedmon treasury of modern poets $h [sound recording].

21.23D. Collections Without Collective Title

If a sound recording contains the works by two or more people and lacks a collective title, the main access point depends on the participation of the performers. If the performer goes beyond performance, execution, and interpretation, the item should be entered under the heading of the principal performer. Rock, jazz, and popular music recordings tend to belong to this category.

But if the performer's participation is limited to performance, execution, and interpretation, the item should be entered under the heading appropriate to the first work. Added entries are made for other works and performers.

21.29D. Added Entries

LCRI 21.29D (CBS 45) provides guidelines for the selection of added entries for sound recordings. It recommends that catalogers make added entries for all named performers, with six exceptions:

1. If a corporate body is selected as an access point, no added entries should be provided for individual members of the group. A conductor and accompanist should not be considered members of the body he or she conducts or accompanies. So it is acceptable to select conductors and accompanists as added entries. If a person's name appears with a corporate body, the cataloger needs to determine if the corporate name includes this person's name. If so, no added entry should be assigned. Otherwise, this person can be selected as an added entry.

2. If the chorus and the orchestra of an opera company perform in an opera and are named along with the name of the parent body, only the parent body should be selected as the added entry.

3. No added entry should be made for a performer whose role is minor or a performer who is chosen as the main entry.

4. If many performers perform the same function (e.g., actors in a drama), only those given prominence in the chief source are selected as added entries.

5. If number four does not apply, performers given prominence in other parts of the work should be selected.

6. If number five also does not apply, performers given the most important functions (the principal roles) should be selected as added entries.

■ SUBJECT ANALYSIS

In assigning subject headings, Library of Congress treats all works on the same subject in the same way regardless of their medium. Catalogers therefore analyze sound recordings in the same way they analyze print materials and assign headings—according to the general guidelines provided by LC *Subject Cataloging Manual* (H 180). Because nonprint materials are much harder to browse and users tend to rely on the catalog for subject information about them, catalogers tend to assign more subject headings to them. But no special form subdivision is assigned to bring out the format.

Juvenile Sound Recordings

The only exception is juvenile materials, which include materials intended for children and young adults from preschool through 16. For materials with the intellectual level code a, b, or c in "Audn" in the fixed field, subdivision "--Juvenile sound recordings" is added to the topical headings. For instance, a sound cassette on nutrition for teenagers will be assigned a heading: Nutrition--Juvenile sound recordings. If a work is coded f (for special audiences) and is clearly juvenile in nature, this subdivision can be assigned also. This subdivision can be used for fictional or factual treatment of a topic.

Sound recordings cover all types of topics, and music and literature are two of the more popular subject areas. So the subject cataloging practices for works of literature and works of music are briefly introduced here. The following discussion is based on the *Subject Cataloging Manual* and Chan's description of these topics.[4]

Music[5]

Many valid music headings are not listed in *Library of Congress Subject Headings* because the Library of Congress has issued standard citation patterns for catalogers to establish music headings appropriate for the item being cataloged. Catalogers should consult H1160 of the *Subject Cataloging Manual* for the citation patterns. Library of Congress also designates the phrase heading **[Medium or form for instrumental music], Arranged** as free-floating to cover a wide range of music (e.g., Piano music, Arranged). Free-floating subdivisions can be found under **Operas** (the pattern for music composition, including musical form, medium, style, music for special occasions, and others) and **Piano** (the pattern for musical instruments). (See H1161.) H1160 includes free-floating period subdivisions for headings for music compositions and explains the assignment of these subdivisions.

The practice of the Library of Congress is to treat musical sound recordings in the same way as other musical works. For instrumental music, headings are usually assigned for musical form (e.g., Sonatas; Suites), medium of performance (e.g., Flute music; Piano music), and performing group (e.g., Orchestra music; Quintets). For vocal music, headings are assigned for form (e.g., Chants; Operas), voice range (e.g., High voice; Men's voices), number of vocal parts (e.g., 4 parts), and accompanying medium (e.g., Piano). If topical headings are appropriate, they can be assigned with music subdivisions. **Keats, John, 1795-1821--Musical settings**, for instance, is assigned to a work in which the writings of Keats have been set to music.

If a sound recording includes works in different musical forms, a heading is assigned to represent the form of each work. A recording of Vivaldi's concertos for cello that includes two forms of concertos will be assigned a heading for each form: Concertos (Violoncello with string orchestra) and Concertos (Bassoon, violoncello with string orchestra).

A musical work for a specific dance form is assigned a heading for the dance form (e.g., Tangos) and headings for the medium and other appropriate topics. *SCM* H1917 details the treatment of music of ethnic groups, national groups, and non-Western art music.

Literature[6]

Library of Congress Subject Headings lists four types of headings for works of and about literature, including literary form headings (e.g., Poetry), topical headings for themes, characters, or features in literary works (e.g., Peace--Fiction), headings with form and topic combined (e.g, Mystery and detective stories), and other topical headings. Sound recordings of literature tend to include collections of literary works or individual literary works. For collections of two or more independent works by different authors, literary form headings are assigned. If a collection has a theme, a topical heading with a form subdivision is also assigned.

For instance, American poetry--19th century; and Love--Poetry are assigned to a collection of several 19th century American poets' works. Although subdivision "--Collected works" is free-floating, it *cannot* be used with literary form headings. Subdivision "--Collections" is not free-floating and can be used with very few literary form headings, including Drama, Fiction, Literature, and Poetry.

For collected works by an individual literary author, the practice is to assign *no* **literary form heading** unless the literary form headings combine form and topic (e.g., War poetry) or the form heading is highly specific (e.g., Radio stories). Topical headings with a literary form subdivision, if appropriate, are assigned.

For individual works of poetry or drama by an individual literary author, the practice is to assign no major literary forms (e.g., English poetry), but form headings that include a topic (e.g., War poetry) or highly specific form headings (e.g., Nursery rhymes) can be assigned. Appropriate topical headings with subdivisions "--Poetry" or "--Drama" can be assigned if appropriate. Children's poems or plays are assigned literary form headings for children's literature (e.g., Children's plays).

For individual works of adult fiction, children's fiction, or young adult fiction, *no form headings* are assigned. Topical headings with subdivision "--Fiction" are assigned to only three types of fiction: biographical fiction (e.g., Joyce, James, 1882-1941--Fiction), historical fiction (e.g., Holocaust--Fiction), and animal stories (e.g., Animals--Fiction; Pigs--Fiction).

The August 1998 version of *SCM* H1790 indicates that Library of Congress has begun a cooperative program with OCLC to provide increased subject access to fiction as recommended by ALA's *Guidelines on Subject Access to Individual Works of Fiction, Drama, Etc.*[7] Under this program OCLC adds headings for topic, setting, characters and genre to update LC records. Genre and form headings taken from the *Guidelines* are coded gsafd in subfield $2.

Both *Library of Congress Classification* and *Dewey Decimal Classification* classify topical sound recordings for adults and those for juveniles in the same manner as other topical materials. The most specific class number should be assigned, and Cutter numbers are used to subarrange materials. In *LCC* juvenile materials are classed with a number for "Juvenile works" under the appropriate heading, if it is available. Otherwise, the number for "General works" is used. *DDC*'s Table 1 has a provision for intended audience but the audience aspect is usually not represented by the class number.

LCC places juvenile belles lettres in PZ5-90 and juvenile fiction, folklore, etc. in English are placed in PZ5-PZ10.3, with unique Cutter numbers assigned to authors. If necessary, work letters from the title are used to subarrange works by the same author (e.g., the work letters for *Freddy the Detective* are "Fr"). The work letters include a capital letter and one or more lowercase letters. The same class number is assigned to editions of the same work, and the publication date is used to distinguish the editions. Work letters are not used if a work has a title main entry and if a work is not written in English. Except for collections of juvenile literature that are classed in 808.899282, *DDC* does not have specific numbers for juvenile belles lettres. Cutter numbers from the Cutter tables and work marks from the title are often used to subarrange materials assigned the same *DDC* number.

■ ARRANGEMENT

While subject headings provide collocation on the catalog, call numbers provide a reasonable extent of collocation on the shelves. The assignment of classification number, however, is not directly related to how sound recordings are shelved. If a library is committed to an integrated catalog, sound recordings should be shelved with other types of material. But intershelving works of different media is challenging. Weihs offers detailed instructions on intershelving, but she also acknowledges the cost of such an effort.[8] Preservation and security concerns also make intershelving all media less appealing. For these reasons libraries have developed many ways to organize sound recordings.[9] Major factors the organizer must consider are ease of browsing, ease of access, security, preservation, and equipment. Four methods and their strengths and limitations are described below.

Intershelving with Dummies

Because sound recordings come in several formats and publishers do not have standards for packaging these works, intershelving sound recordings can be difficult. One solution is to create dummies for the recordings and place them on the shelves with the rest of the collection. When a user finds the dummy, he or she can bring it to the librarian to exchange for the recording. This approach has several benefits. It collocates works on the same subject on the shelves for easy browsing. It uses only one shelving system and should cause little confusion for users. The sound recordings are less likely to be damaged because they are kept in a place only librarians can access. If special equipment is needed to play a recording, the librarian will be able to point that out to the user or provide the equipment if the library has it. As with any system, intershelving has some drawbacks. One is that the user will not have the opportunity to examine the physical item before asking for it. Another drawback is that the user will not be able to browse the entire sound recording collection. A more serious drawback is that when access to items is mediated through a librarian, full access to items may be discouraged, especially items of more controversial topics.

Case Display for Browsing

To encourage browsing, some public libraries have tried displaying cassette and CD cases without their contents. When a user desires an item, he or she will give the librarian the number on the case. This method of organization is not strongly tied to the catalog, supports browsing, and allows users to examine the cases. It also has advantages for security and preservation reasons. But the library will need to have more storage space for sound recordings—an area for the case display and an area for storing the physical items. Another challenge is that the arrangement of the cases must be logical to facilitate browsing. Because sound recordings can be arranged by title, author, composer, principal performer, type of music, etc., it is not a simple task to arrange these materials or to maintain the order of cases in the display area. Some libraries have resorted to placing cases in a locked display case to maintain the order of the cases. That method, however, limits the user's access to the cases.

Shelving by Format

Another popular approach is to shelve sound recordings by the medium, with sound cassettes in one area and CDs in another. Within each category the items are subarranged according to the nature or type. For example, music CDs are stored together and color-coded by music type (red for rock music, green for jazz, and so on); musical cassettes are similarly treated and stored in a separate area; while nonmusical cassettes are subarranged by type with "B" designating biography and subdivided by Cutter number, and other codes for different categories. This arrangement is very good for browsing and encourages direct access. The limitations are that the items tend to be touched by many users, the subgroupings within the same medium may not be very explicit, and users interested in various presentations of the same subject will have to check several media areas. Security and preservation of the items will present difficulties as well.

Shelving by Size

Although this may sound impractical, shelving by size has been used in closed stacks with success. Works are shelved according to their size and assigned an accession number. The benefits of this arrangement include space saving, easy shelf maintenance, and quick retrieval once the access number is found in the catalog. The drawback is the collection becomes unusable without the catalog. Subject collocation on the shelves and browsing are impossible, and no users can access the stacks. This approach favors the security and preservation of sound recordings at the expense of direct user access.

Each of these methods has its strengths and limitations. In devising ways to organize sound recordings for access, the organizer will need to consider the needs of the intended users first. Is browsing important to these users? Is it likely they will want to examine the physical items? Are they likely to search the catalog first? How good is the online catalog? Does the library expect heavy use of sound recordings? Can the library afford to replace damaged items frequently? Answers to these questions should guide the decision on how to organize sound recordings for access.

Cataloging Examples begin on page 50.

■ CATALOGING EXAMPLES

Cassette label:

THE SOUND OF YOUR VOICE
DR. CAROL FLEMING

TAPE 1   [Dolby System symbol]
SIDE A   79665-8
SIMON & SCHUSTER   © 1988 Carol Fleming. All rights reserved
AUDIO   p 1992 Simon & Schuster Inc. All rights
                      reserved SOUND IDEAS is an imprint of
                      Simon & Schuster Audio Division Simon &
                      Schuster Inc.

[The same label appears on three other sound cassettes.]

****

Type:	i	
007		s $b s $d l $e s $f n $g j $h l $i c $m c $n e
020		0671796658
028	02	79665-8 $b Simon & Schuster Sound Ideas
090		PN4162
092		808.5
100	1	Fleming, Carol.
245	14	The sound of your voice $h [sound recording] / $c Carol Fleming.
260		New York, NY : $b Simon & Schuster Sound Ideas, $c p1992.
300		4 sound cassettes (ca. 4 hrs.) : $b analog, stereo, Dolby processed.
500		"The essential program for communicating confidently and clearly"--Container.
511	0	Featuring the author.
520		The author takes the listener step-by-step through the fundamentals of good, confident vocal technique. Uses real-life speaking situations to demonstrate various voice characteristics.
650	0	Voice culture.

Figure 3.1   The sound of your voice.

Discussion for Figure 3.1

- Type: Code i is used for a non-musical sound recording.

- 007: Subfields common to sound cassettes are included. Code s in $e indicates stereo, code c in $i refers to 4-track which is standard, code c in $m is for Dolby processed material, and code e in $n indicates the analog format of the sound.

- 020: The ISBN is on the container.

- 028: Publisher's number is entered in subfield a, subfield b is for the label name. The second indicator 2 will produce a note for this number.

- 100: The work of a single author is entered under the author.

- 260: Although "Simon & Schuster" and "Sound Ideas" do not appear right next to each other on the cassette label, their relationship is made clear on the label. The phrase "Simon & Schuster Sound Ideas" appears with the publisher's number on the container. "Simon & Schuster Sound Ideas" is therefore used as the name of the publisher. The copyright date of the sound recording (p1992) is transcribed in subfield c.

- 300: The approximate running time, sound channel information, and the recording characteristics are on the container. Because the dimension of the cassettes is standard, subfield c is not used.

- 500: This text appears prominently on the container. Because the quotation is not from the chief source, its source is indicated.

- 511: Even though the narrator is the same as the author, this note is necessary to identify the narrator. Since the author is the main entry, no added entry needs to be created for her.

- 520: Summary note is usually provided for nonmusical recordings to inform users of the content of the work.

- 650: A topical heading for the subject content of this work. No special form subdivision is assigned to bring out the format.

Disc label:

TANGENT
STANLEY JORDAN
TOUCH SENSITIVE

SIDE 1	1001
33 1/3 RPM	STEREO

1. Renaissance Man 8:12   3. All The Children 4:38
2. Touch of Blue 4:12   4. Jumpin' Jack 2:14

All selections composed by Stanley Jordan and published
by Manifold Music (BMI) with the exception of
Havah Nagilah, which is in the public domain.
©1982 Manifold Music
p1982 Tangent Records, Inc.
134 Evergreen Place
Suite 700
E. Orange, N.J. 07018
All Rights Reserved

[Side 2 has exactly the same information except the following contents:
1. I Have A Dream 8:45   3. Orb 4:00
2. Havah Nagilah 5:22   4. A-flat Purple 5:51]

****

Type:	j	
007		s $b d $d b $e s $f m $g e $h n $i n $n e
028	02	1001 $b Tangent
090		M126
092		787.87
100	1	Jordan, Stanley.
245	1 0	Touch sensitive $h [sound recording] / $c Stanley Jordan.
260		East Orange, N.J. : $b Tangent Records, $c p1982.
300		1 sound disc : $b analog, 33 1/3 rmp, stereo ; $c 12 in.
505	0	Renaissance man (8:12) -- Touch of blue (4:12) -- All the children (4:38) -- Jump' Jack (2:14) -- I have a dream (8:45) -- Havah nagilah (5:22) -- Orb (4:00) -- A-flat purple (5:51)
650	0	Guitar music.

Figure 3.2 Touch sensitive.

Discussion for Figure 3.2

- Chief source of information: Both sides of the disc constitute the chief source.

- Type: Code j is used for a musical recording.

- 007: Subfields common to sound discs are included. Code s in $e refers to stereo sound, code e in $. indicates the dimension of the disc (12 inches), and code e in $n identifies the analog format of the sound.

- 028: Publisher's number is entered in subfield a, and label name is in subfield b.

- 260: The copyright date for the music and the copyright date for the recording are both present, but only the one for the sound recording is transcribed for subfield c.

- 505: The duration of each piece is listed on the labels, so the durations are recorded in the contents note. Only the first words of the titles are capitalized.

- 650: For instrumental music, the LC practice is to assign headings for the musical form, medium of performance, and/or performing group. Guitar music specifies the medium of performance for this work.

Cassette label:

CHARLOTTE'S WEB
E.B. White

BDD   PART ONE
410031   SIDE ONE
SR   ©1952 E.B. White
                         p1970 E.B. White
DOLBY SYSTEM   Manufactured in USA

****

Type: i
007   s $b s $d l $e u $f n $g j $h l $i c $m c $n e
028   02   410031 $b BDD
090   PZ7
092   813.54
100   1   White, E. B. $q (Elwyn Brooks), $d 1899-
245   10   Charlotte's web $h [sound recording] / $c E.B. White.
260   New York, N. Y. : $b manufactured and distributed by
                   Promotional Concept Group, $c p1970.
300   2 sound cassettes (192 min.) : $b analog, Dolby processed.
500   "A Bantam Audio cassette"--Container.
511   0   Read by E. B. White.
520   Wilbur, the pig, is desolate when he discovers that he is
                   destined to be the farmer's Christmas dinner until his spider
                   friend, Charlotte, decides to help him.
650   0   Animals $v Juvenile fiction.
650   0   Children's stories.

Figure 3.3   Charlotte's web.

Discussion for Figure 3.3

- Type: Code i indicates this is a non-musical recording.

- 007: Subfields common to sound cassettes are included. Code u in $e indicates no information about the playback channels, code c in $i refers to 4-track which is standard, code c in $m is for Dolby processed material, and code e in $n is for the analog format of the sound.

- 090 & 092: PZ7 is the *LCC* number for general juvenile belle lettres. Individual literary works for children are placed here and further subarranged by Cutter number. 813 is for American fiction, and 54 is for the period 1945–1999.

- 260: No publisher's name is found on the item, so the manufacturer and distributor are listed in subfield b. The copyright date for the recording is recorded in subfield c.

- 500: A quotation note with the source indicated.

- 520: A summary note is always provided for nonmusical recordings.

- 650: For a literary work for children a topical heading with a subdivision, "Animals--Juvenile fiction," and a literary form heading, "Children's stories," are assigned.

```
Disc label:
                        James Joyce
                        ULYSSES
        p 1994 NAXOS AudioBooks Ltd. © 1994  NAXOS AudioBooks Ltd.
        DIGITAL AUDI                          CD 1
        GEMA  Read by Jim Norton
                        with Marcella Riordan
                        NA 401112
                        DDD

[CD 2 has NA 401122, CD 3 has NA 401132, and CD4 has NA  402242.]
*Information on the container:
        Abridged and produced by Roger Marsh.
        CD1: 70:25; CD 2: 60:52; CD 3: 79:30; CD4: 79:30
        Total time:  4:49:17


*************************************************************

Type:    i
007:               s $b d $d f $e s $f n $g g $h n $i n $m e $n d
020                9626340118
028      00        NA 401112 $b NAXOS AudioBooks
028      00        NA 401122 $b NAXOS AudioBooks
028      00        NA 401132 $b NAXOS AudioBooks
028      00        NA 401142 $b NAXOS AudioBooks
090                PR6019.O9 $b U42 1994
092                823.912
100      1         Joyce, James, $d 1882-1941.
245      10        Ulysses $h [sound recording] / $c James Joyce.
260                Germany : $b NAXOS AudioBooks, $c p1994.
300                4 sound discs (4 hr., 49 min., 17 sec.) : $b digital, stereo ; $c
                   4 3/4 in. + $e 1 pamphlet ([12] p. : ill. ; 12 cm.)
500                Abridged and produced by Roger Marsh.
511      0         Read by Jim Norton with Marcella Riordan.
500                Compact disc.
500                Pamphlet in container.
520                Leopold Bloom wanders through Dublin on June 16, 1904,
                   talking to people, observing life in Dublin, and thinking of his
                   passionate wife, Molly.
500                NAXOS AudioBooks:  NA 401112, NA 401122, NA 401132,
                   NA 401142.
650      0         Bloom, Leopold (Fictitious character) $v Fiction.
650      0         Bloom, Molly (Fictitious character) $v Fiction.
650      0         Men $z Ireland $z Dublin $v Fiction.
700      1         Marsh, Roger.
700      1         Norton, Jim.
700      1         Riordan, Marcella.
```

Figure 3.4 Ulysses.

Discussion for Figure 3.4

- Type: Code i indicates a non-musical recording.

- 007: Subfields common to compact discs are included. Code s in $e indicates stereo sound and code d in $n refers to the digital format of the sound.

- 028: Normally the second indicator for field 028 is used to generate a note for the publisher's number, but when a recording has non-consecutive publisher's numbers, each number is recorded in a separate 028 field, and 0 is used for the second indicator to indicate that no note will be produced from the 028 field. The numbers are entered in field 500 so that all numbers will be included in one note. Notice the connection between the 028 fields and the last 500 field.

- 090 & 092: PR6019.O9 is the number for James Joyce, and U4-79 is for Ulysses. 823 is for English fiction, and 912 refers to the 20th century.

- 100: The original author of a literary work is used as the main access point.

- 300: The total time is on the back of the container.

- 500: A note on statement of responsibility is listed first.

- 511: Participants of the recording are noted.

- 500: The nature of the sound disc is specified in a note.

- 500: The location of the accompanying pamphlet is noted.

- 520: A summary of the contents of a non-musical recording is usually provided to help users understand the subject of the item.

- 650: For a literary work, no form headings are assigned, but topical headings with the subdivision "--Fiction" are appropriate. Both characters are fictitious ones and are listed in *Library of Congress Subject Headings*. No form subdivision is used to bring out the format.

- 700s: The producer and the readers are traced.

Disc label: [a red label "RCA VICTOR Red Seal" appears on the left side of the disc]
Vivaldi
Concertos for Cello
Ofra Harnoy, Cello
Toronto Chamber Orchestra
Paul Robinson, Conductor
7774-2-RC

COMPACT DISC
DIGITAL AUDIO
1988 BMG Music
TMK(S)   RCA Corp.
& BMG Music
Made in U. S. A.

1-3 Concerto in D Minor, RV 405
4-6 Concerto in C Minor, RV 401
7-9 Concerto in B-Flat, RV 423
10-12 Concerto in C, RV 399
13-15 Concerto for Cello and Bassoon in E Minor, RV 409 James McKay, Bassoon
16 Concerto Movement in D Minor, RV 538
****

Type:	j	
007:		s $b d $d f $e s $f n $g g $h n $i n $m e $n d
028	02	7774-2-RC $b RCA Victor Red Seal
090		M1117
092		784.274
100	1	Vivaldi, Antonio, $d 1678-1741.
240	10	Concertos $k Selections
245	10	Concertos for cello $h [sound recording] / $c Vivaldi.
246	1	$i Title on container: $a Cello concertos
260		New York, NY : $b BMG Music, $c p1988.
300		1 sound disc (53 min., 53 sec.) : $b digital, stereo ; $c 4 3/4 in.
546		Program notes in English, German, French and Italian in container.
511	0	Ofra Harnoy, cello; James McKay, bassoon; Toronto Chamber Orchestra; Paul Robinson, conductor.
518		Recorded April 6 and 7, 1987, at St. Timothy Church, Toronto.
500		Compact disc.
505	0	D minor, RV 405 (10:18) -- C minor, RV 401 (12:07) -- B-flat, RV 423 (10:02) -- C, RV 399 (8:27) -- E minor, RV 409 (8:52) -- D minor, RV 538 (3:37).
650	0	Concertos (Violoncello with string orchestra).
650	0	Concertos (Bassoon, violoncello with string orchestra).
700	1	Harnoy, Ofra, $d 1965-
700	1	McKay, James, $d 1944-
700	1	Robinson, Paul, $d 1940-
700	12	Vivaldi, Antonio, $d 1678-1741. $t Concertos, $m violoncello, string orchestra, $n RV 405, $r D minor. $f 1988.
700	12	Vivaldi, Antonio, $d 1678-1741. $t Concertos, $m violoncello, string orchestra, $n RV 401 $r C minor. $f 1988.
700	12	Vivaldi, Antonio, $d 1678-1741. $t Concertos, $m violoncello, string orchestra, $n RV 423, $r B-flat major. $f 1988.
700	12	Vivaldi, Antonio, $d 1678-1741. $t Concertos, $m violoncello, string orchestra, $n RV 399, $r C major. $f 1988.
700	12	Vivaldi, Antonio, $d 1678-1741. $t Concertos, $m violoncello, bassoon, string orchestra, $n RV 409, $r E minor. $f 1988.
700	12	Vivaldi, Antonio, $d 1678-1741. $t Concertos, $m violoncello, string orchestra, $n RV 538, $r D minor. $f 1988.
710	2	Toronto Chamber Orchestra.

Figure 3.5   Concertos for cello.

Discussion for Figure 3.5

- Type: Code j indicates a musical sound recording.

- 007: Subfields common to compact discs are included. Code s in $e refers to stereo sound and code d in $n refers to the digital format of the sound.

- 028: Publisher's number is entered in subfield a, and the label is in subfield b.

- 090 & 092: M1117 is for string orchestra with a single instrument. 784.274 is for violoncello with orchestra.

- 100: Vivaldi is the composer of these musical works and is therefore selected as the main entry.

- 240: A uniform title is created to bring recordings of various selections of Vivaldi's cello concertos together.

- 246: The source of the variant title is entered in subfield i and the variant title is entered in subfield a. The first indicator (1) specifies a note and a title added entry will be produced and the blank second indicator is used with a special display.

- 300: The total playing time is on the container.

- 511: Performers are recorded in field 511 and separated by semicolons.

- 518: The date and place of recording are recorded.

- 505: The contents note lists titles included in this work and includes playing time for each piece.

- 650: For instrumental music, subject headings are assigned for musical form, medium of performance, and performing group. When a recording includes more than one form, each form of presentation is assigned a heading.

- 700s: Added entries are created for principal performers. Following LCRI 21.29, the entries are arranged in the order in which the names appear in the bibliographic description.

- 700s: The name-title added analytical added entries are provided for each work in this collection. The uniform titles are created according to Chapter 25 of *AACR2R*, and Rule 25.30 in particular. For musical work the typical pattern is: title, medium of performance, numerical identifying element, key. "Date" is the last element. The subfield codes can be found in OCLC-MARC Code List.

- 710: An added entry for the chamber music group, which is treated as a corporate body.

Disc label:

Walt Disney PICTURES PRESENTS
Beauty and the Beast
Original Motion Picture Sound track

60618-2   Walt Disney
Music by Alan Menken   Records
Lyrics by Howard Ashman   p 1991 Buena Vista Pictures
                                           Distribution, Inc.   ©1991
                                           Walt Disney Music Company
                                           (ASCAP)/Wonderland Music
                                           Company, Inc.
Total time: 50:55   (BMI)

1. Prologue (2:27) 2. Belle (5:07) 3. Belle (reprise) (1:03) 4. Gaston (3:37) 5. Gaston (reprise) (2:01) 6. Be our guest (3:42) 7. Something there (2:16) 8. The mob song (3:28) 9. Beauty and the beast (2:44) 10. To the fair (1:55) 11. West wing (4:22) 12. The beast lets Belle go (2:19) 13. Battle on the tower (5:26) 14. Transformation (5:47) 15. Beauty and the beast (duet) (4:03).

II   ©The Walt Disney company
Printed in U.S.A.

****

Type:	j	
007:		s $b d $d f $e u $f n $g g $h n $i n $m e $n d
028	02	60618-2 $b Walt Disney Records
090		M1505
092		782.14
100	1	Menken, Alan.
245	10	Walt Disney Pictures presents Beauty and the beast $h [sound recording] : $b original motion picture soundtrack / $c music by Alan Menken ; lyrics by Howard Ashman.
246	30	Beauty and the beast
260		Burbank, CA : $b Walt Disney Records : $b [distributed by] Buena Vista Pictures, $c p1991.
300		1 sound disc (50 min., 55 sec.) : $b digital ; $c 4 3/4 in.
511	0	Robby Benson as Beast; Paige O'Hara as Belle; end title duet "Beauty and the beast" performed by Celine Dion and Peabo Bryson.
500		Compact disc.
500		Program notes on insert.
505	0	Prologue (2:27) -- Belle (5:07) -- Belle (reprise) (1:03) -- Gaston (3:37) -- Gaston (reprise) (2:01) -- Be our guest (3:42) -- Something there (2:16) -- The mob song (3:28) -- Beauty and the beast (2:44) -- To the fair (1:55) -- West wing (4:22) -- The beast lets Belle go (2:19) -- Battle on the tower (5:26) -- Transformation (5:47) -- Beauty and the beast (duet) (4:03).
650	0	Motion picture music $v Excerpts.
700	1	Ashman, Howard.
700	1	Benson, Robby.
700	1	O'Hara, Paige.
700	1	Dion, Celine.
700	1	Bryson, Peabo.
730	0	Beauty and the beast (Motion picture : 1991)

Figure 3.6   Beauty and the beast.

Discussion for Figure 3.6

- Type: Code j indicates a musical recording.

- 007: Subfields common to compact discs are included. Code u in $e indicates no information on playback channels and code d in $n refers to the digital format of the sound.

- 028: Publisher's number is entered in subfield a, and the label is in subfield b.

- 090 & 092: M1505 is for vocal music excerpts for a movie; 782.14 is for musical plays.

- 245: Record the wording of the title proper as presented on the disc label. Separate the first statement of responsibility from the second one by a semicolon.

- 246: A variant title is made because this title is better known than the title proper. Indicator 3 will produce an added entry but not a note, indicator 0 explains the variant title is part of the title proper.

- 260: Place of publication is on the container. Information on the distributor is entered into a separate subfield b.

- 511: Performers are listed in the program notes; only the principal performers are included in this note.

- 505: The total playing time of the disc is included in field 300, and the duration of each song is listed in the contents note.

- 700s: Personal name added entries are made for all named performers and the entries are arranged in the order in which the names appear in the bibliographic description.

- 730: A uniform title for the motion picture is used to bring together related works.

Disc label: LINDA RONSTADT
                          Dedicated to the One I Love

        Produced by GEORGE MASSENBURG & LINDA RONSTADT
p1996 Elektra Entertainment Group, A Division of Warner Communications
Inc. for the United States and WEB International Inc. for the world outside of
the United States. A Time Warner Company.
                          All Rights Reserved.
        Unauthorized duplication is a violation of applicable laws.
                Made in U.S.A. by WEB Manufacturing Inc.
                                61916-2

****

Type:	j	
007:		s $b d $d f $e s $f n $g g $h n $i n $m e $n d
028	02	61916-2 $b Elektra
090		M1630.18
092		781.63
100	1	Ronstadt, Linda.
245	10	Dedicated to the one I love $h [sound recording] / $c Linda Ronstadt.
260		Beverly Hill, CA : $b Elektra Entertainment Group, $c p1996.
300		1 sound disc : $b digital, stereo ; $c 4 3/4 in.
518		Recorded September, 1995 through January, 1996 at The Simplex, San Francisco.
500		Compact disc.
500		Lyrics and program note on insert.
505	0	Dedicated to the one I love -- Be my baby -- In my room -- Devoted to you -- Baby I love you -- Devoted to you (instrumental) -- Angel baby -- We will rock you -- Winter light -- Brahm's lullaby -- Good night.
650	0	Popular music $y 1991-2000.
650	0	Lullabies

Figure 3.7   Dedicated to the one I love.

Discussion for Figure 3.7

- Type: Code j indicates a musical recording.

- 007: Subfields common to compact discs are included. Code s in $e refers to stereo sound and code d in $n refers to the digital format of the sound.

- 028: Publisher's number is entered in subfield a, and the label name is in subfield b.

- 100: Works of several composers performed by one vocalist (Rule 21.23C1), so the performer is selected as the main entry.

- 260: The division name is treated as the publisher's name (6.4D2).

- 518: A note is provided for the date and site of recording.

- 650s: A heading for the type of music is assigned with a period subdivision. A second subject heading indicates the nature of the songs.

```
Disc information:
09026-61228-2                    BOCCHERINI
                          1-3  Concerto for Cello and Orchestra
                                in B-Flat
RCA VICTOR                       MYSLIVECEK
RED SEAL                  4-6  Concerto for Cello
                                and Orchestra in C
p 1993, BMG Music               VIOTTI
TMK(S) ® G.E. Co., USA    7-9  Concerto for Cello
& BMG Music                     and Orchestra in C
Made in U.S.A.

                          OFRA  HARNOY
                          TRILOGY

                          BOCCHERINI . MYSLIVECEK . VIOTTI
                            I SOLISTI VENETI
                          CLAUDIO SCIMONE
                            conductor

*************************************************************

Type:   j
007:
                s $b d $d f $e s $f n $g g $h n $i n $m e $n d
028     02      09026-61228-2 $b RCA Victor Red Seal
090             M1117
092             784.274
100     1       Harnoy, Ofra, $d 1965-
245     10      Trilogy $h [sound recording] / $c Ofra Harnoy.
260             New York, NY : $b BMG Music, $c p1993.
300             1 sound disc (63 min., 13 sec.) : $b digital, stereo ; $c 4 3/4 in.
511     0       Ofra Harnoy, cello; I Solisti Veniti; Claudio Scimone, conductor.
518             Recorded digitally on June 4, 6 & 7, 1991, in La Chiesa di San
                Francesco in Schio, Italy.
500             Compact disc.
500             Program notes on insert.
505     0       Concerto for cello and orchestra in B-flat / Boccherini
                (20:16) -- Concerto for cello and orchestra in C / Myslivecek
                (19:06) -- Concerto for cello and orchestra in C / Viotti (23:41).
650     0       Concertos (Violoncello with orchestra).
700     1       Scimone, Claudio.
700     12      Boccherini, Luigi, $d 1743-1805. $t Concertos, $m violoncello,
                orchestra, $n G. 482, $r B-flat major. $f 1993.
700     12      Myslivecek, Josef, $d 1737-1781. $t Concertos, $m violoncello,
                orchestra, $r C major. $f 1993.
700     12      Viotti, Giovanni Battista, $d 1755-1824. $t Concertos, $m
                violoncello, orchestra,  $r C major. $f 1993.
710     2       I Solisti Veneti.
```

Figure 3.8   Trilogy.

Discussion for Figure 3.8

- Type: Code j indicates a musical recording.

- 007: Subfields common to compact discs are included. Code s in $e refers to stereo sound and code d in $n refers to the digital format of the sound.

- 100: The recording has a collective title and contains the works of three composers. According to Rule 21.23C1, the recording is entered under the principal performer, Ofra Harnoy.

- 511: Performers are noted.

- 518: The recording date and site are from the program notes.

- 505: The duration of each work is from the program notes.

- 650: For instrumental music, a subject heading for the form of music is assigned.

- 700s: An added entry is provided for the conductor. Name-title analytical added entries are provided for the composers to make the individual works searchable.

- 710: An added entry is provided for the performing group.

Cassette label:

Walt Disney's FANTASIA
Leopold Stokowski and the Philadelphia Orchestra
REMASTERED ORIGINAL SOUNDTRACK EDITION

VOL. 1   600074
SIDE 1
DOLBY SYSTEM
Printed in U.S.A.

Toccata and Fugue in D Minor (John Sebastian Bach) * The Sorcerer's Apprentice (Paul Dukas) * The Nutcracker Suite (Peter Ilich Tchaikovsky)

© The Walt Disney Company p 1990 Buena Vista Pictures Distribution, Inc.

****

Type:	j	
007:		s $b s $d l $e u $f n $g j $h l $i c $m c $n e
090		M1527
092		784.21542
110	2	Philadelphia Orchestra.
245	10	Walt Disney's Fantasia $h [sound recording] / $c Leopold Stokowski and the Philadelphia Orchestra.
246	10	Fantasia
250		Remastered original soundtrack ed.
260		Burbank, CA : $b Buena Vista, $c p1990.
300		2 sound cassettes : $b analog, Dolby processed.
500		Program notes by David R. Smith.
511	0	Philadelphia Orchestra ; Leopold Stokowski, conductor.
500		Originally released in 1940.
505	0	Toccata and fugue in D minor / Bach -- The sorcerer's apprentice / Dukas -- The nutcracker suite / Tchaikovsky -- Symphony no. 6 "Pastoral" / Beethoven -- Rite of spring / Stravinsky -- Dance of the hours / Ponchielli -- A night on Bald Mountain / Moussorgsky -- Ave Maria, op. 52, no. 6 / Schubert.
650	0	Motion picture music.
650	0	Orchestra music.
700	1	Stokowski, Leopold, $d 1882-1977.
730	0	Fantasia (Motion picture)

Figure 3.9   Fantasia.

Discussion for Figure 3.9

- Type: Code j indicates a musical sound recording.

- 007: Subfields common to sound cassettes are included. Code u in $e indicates no information on the playback channels, code c in $m indicates Dolby processing, and code e in $n indicates the analog format of the sound.

- 090 & 092: M1527 is for specific sound track movie. 784.21542 is built from 784.2 for orchestra music and 1542 for film music.

- 110: The orchestra is selected as the main entry, according to Rule 21.23C1.

- 245: Record the information as instructed in 1.1B1.

- 246: A variant title added entry is provided to lead users to this item. This added entry is necessary because the title proper is not as well known as this variant title.

- 250: Record the exact edition statement except for the use of the abbreviation "ed."

- 511: Performing body and person are recorded.

- 500: The history of the movie and the music is from the program notes.

- 505: Contents of the item are taken from the cassettes. The titles are listed in the order of their appearance in the item; only the last names of the composers are included because these are well-known composers.

- 700: Conductor is traced.

- 730: A uniform title added entry brings this item together with related works.

Cassette label: Frost, Williams, Stevens, Eberhart, Pound & Wilbur
              THE CAEDMON TREASURY OF MODERN POETS
              Read by Each Respective Author

              Caedmon   Side 1
              CPN 2006   25:35
              © 1957 HarperCollins Publishers, Inc., 10 East 53rd Street,
                  New York, N.Y. 10022. All rights reserved.
                  Made in the U.S.A. DOLBY SYSTEM®

[Sides 2-4 have the same information except the durations:
Side 2: 22:50   Side 3: 24:50   Side 4: 22:13]
Case insert: Library of Congress card #: R57-256
Copyright © 1957, 1988 Caedmon, 1995 Broadway, New York, N.Y. 10023

****

Type:	i	
007:		s $b s $d l $e u $f n $g j $h L $i c $m c $n e
010		r57-256
020		0694503703
028	02	CPN 2006 $b Caedmon
090		PR1225
092		821.91
245	04	The Caedmon treasury of modern poets $h [sound recording]
246	1	$i Title on container: $a Modern poets reading their own poetry
260		New York, N. Y. : $b Caedmon, $c c1957, c1988.
300		2 sound cassettes (1 hr., 35 min.) : $b analog, Dolby processed.
500		In one container.
520		Twenty-seven poems, read by each respective author, by T. S. Eliot, W.B. Yeats, W.H. Auden, Dylan Thomas, Louis MacNeice, Robert Graves, Gertrude Stein, Archibald MacLeish, e.e. cummings, Marianne Moore, William Empson, Stephen Spender, Conrad Aiken, Robert Frost, William Carlos Williams, Wallace Stevens, Richard Eberhart and Ezra Pound.
650	0	English poetry $y 20th century

Figure 3.10   The Caedmon treasury of modern poets.

Discussion for Figure 3.10

- Type: Code i indicates a non-musical recording.

- 007: Subfields common to sound cassettes are included. Code u in $e indicates no information on playback channels, code c in $m refers to Dolby processing, and code e in $n indicates the analog format of the sound.

- 010: This field is for Library of Congress card number.

- 020: The ISBN of this item is on the back of the container.

- 090 & 092: PR1225 refers to 20th century English poetry general work. 821.91 is built from 821 (English poetry) and 91 is for the period 1900-1999.

- 245: This item is entered under its title because it contains works by several authors, and no principal author can be identified.

- 246: The title on the container is different from the title proper, so indicator 1 is used to create a note and a title added entry. Subfield i indicates the source of this title, and subfield a lists the title.

- 500: This note indicates the two cassettes are in one container.

- 520: This note summarizes the contents and the nature of the recording.

- 650: This is a collection of works, so form headings are assigned. But the subdivision "--Collection" is not used because it is not a free-floating subdivision and can only be used with very few headings such as Drama, Literature, and Poetry.

■NOTES

1. Available: http://www.loc.gov/marc/marc.html, accessed June 2000.

2. Available: http://www.oclc.org/oclc/bib/about.htm, accessed June 2000.

3. *007 Physical Description Fixed Field (Sound Recording)*, available: http://www.oclc.org/oclc/bib/007sound.htm, accessed June 2000.

4. Lois Mai Chan, *Library of Congress Subject Headings: Principles and Applications*, 2nd ed. (Englewood, Colo.: Libraries Unlimited, 1995).

5. Chan, 301–21.

6. Chan, 272–301.

7. *Guidelines on Subject Access to Individual Works of Fiction, Drama, Etc.* (Chicago: American Library Association, 1990).

8. Jean Weihs, *The Integrated Library* (Phoenix, Ariz.: Oryx Press, 1991).

9. See for example, Alan L. Kaye, *Video and Other Nonprint Resources in the Small Library* (Chicago: Library Administration and Management Association, American Library Association, 1991).

■SUGGESTED READINGS

ACRL Media Resources Committee. "Guidelines for Media Resources in Academic Libraries." *College & Research Libraries News* 60 (April 1999): 294–302.

Hoban, Michi S. "Sound Recording Cataloging: A Practical Approach." *Cataloging & Classification Quarterly* 12, no. 2 (1990): 3–26.

Holzberlein, Deanne, with assistance of Dolly Jones. *Cataloging Sound Recordings: A Manual with Examples.* New York: Haworth Press, 1988.

FOUR ← VIDEORECORDINGS

Like the treatment of print resources, the cataloging of videos involves taking data from the chief and prescribed sources for the description of eight areas, assigning access points, and the analysis of subject contents. There are several major challenges in cataloging videos:

1. Video producers do not present information in a standard format, which makes it hard for catalogers to determine where the title frames begin and end. This lack of a standard frequently means that catalogers must check beginning frames and end frames to make sure appropriate information is included.

2. Many people are often involved in the creation of a video. The authorship is so diffuse that it can be difficult to select access points.

3. Containers of videos generally present a great deal of information. Some of this information is different from the information on the video, which makes it necessary for catalogers to determine what to record and how to accommodate the differences.

4. Some videos are now presented on videodiscs or DVD and require special equipment.

5. Production information is usually provided, and catalogers often have to make a judgment call as to what types of notes to provide for this type of information. The subject analysis of videos also requires a slight variation in how subject headings are assigned, which makes it difficult for catalogers not familiar with the use of format headings.

These challenges can be addressed through a careful examination of the video and its container. Videorecordings tend to contain plenty of information. To assist readers in finding information useful for cataloging purposes, the next section describes areas with pertinent information.

■ TECHNICAL READING OF VIDEORECORDINGS

1. *Title frames and end credits frames*: These areas usually provide information on the people involved in the creation of the videorecording, including production firm, title proper, producers, directors, lead actors, supporting actors and technical staff. Catalogers should keep in mind that only people with "overall responsibility" for the work should be included in the statement of responsibility area (field 245, $c). These people will also be assigned as access points. In addition, lead actors will be recorded in field 511, while important technical staff will be recorded in field 508. These names are usually used as added entry headings.

2. *Container label*: This area often presents information on title, production firm, distributor, catalog number, series information, playing time, rating, sound, and copyright information. The information on the label can be useful for fields 245, 028, 260, and 300.

3. *Box or case of the videorecording*: Because the box or case is not the preferred chief source of information, the information presented on the box or case should be verified in the chief source. This area, however, usually captures important information on the item and can be used to speed up the cataloging process. For example, in film videos, the lower part of the back of a box/case usually presents information that is almost identical to that presented on the title and credit frames. Producer, distributor, rating, sound, captioning, and playing time are usually included in this area also. In the front of the box/case, lead actors are usually listed. The spine of the box has publisher information and stock number. This information is typically recorded in field 028.

   While the information in this area cannot be transcribed without verification, it does provide catalogers a short list of very important data. After these data are verified in the prescribed sources, they should be transcribed.

4. *DVD main menu*: The latest medium, DVD, has a main menu that provides several choices. The "CAST" entry can be used to verify people responsible for the work. Lead characters, director, screenplay writers, and other key people are usually listed here.

The "Language" entry will show the languages in which the video is dubbed. This information should be transcribed in a 546 note. The "subtitles" entry will show in which languages the caption can appear. The main menu also lists additional materials on the disk, such as documentary or director's commentary.

Similar to the box/case of a film video, the back of a DVD box often has the information presented on the DVD's main menu. This can speed up the process of cataloging. This area tends to include information on rating, color, playing time, sound characteristics, and closed-captioning.

■ MARC FIELDS FOR VIDEORECORDINGS

The MARC fields commonly used to encode videorecordings are listed below. Field 007 is required for all types of videorecordings, and 028 is used to present a publisher's number.

MARC fields often used to encode videorecordings are:

028	42	number $b production firm
245	_ _	Title $h [videorecording] / $c statement of people responsible for the overall production of the video.
246	_ _	Title variation
250		Edition statement.
260		Publication place : $b publisher name, $c date of publication.
300		No. of special material designation (playing time) : $b sound, color ; $c dimensions.
4XX	_	Series statement
511	_	Cast members
508		Creation/production credits
538		Technical information (e.g., VHS hi-fi)
520		Summary
6XX	_ _	Subject headings.
700	_	Performers, contributors.

710   _   Corporate bodies.

007 field: This field is required for all videorecordings. It has eight subfields:

007         $a category of material $b specific material designation $d color $e format $f sound $g medium of sound $h dimension $i playback channel configuration

Examples:

A videocassette in color, VHS format, with stereo sound

007         $a v $b f $d c $e b $f a $g h $h o $i s

A videodisc in black and white, VHS format, with Dolby surround

007         $a v $b d $d b $e b $f a $g i $h z $i q

Code values for field 007 are available from the MARC21 site[1] and OCLC Input Standard site.[2]

■ DESCRIPTION

Rules for Descriptive Cataloging

Chief Source of Information

AACR2R stipulates the chief source of information for videos should be the title and credit frames, or the labels on the container (cassette, disc, etc.) if the container is an integral part of the item. If the desired information cannot be found in these sources, other sources can be used, including accompanying material, container (case), and other sources. In such instances a source note should be provided.

[title frame]: NORTHERN EXPOSURE

[cassette label]: NORTHERN EXPOSURE

"The First Episode"

Transcribed as:

245 00   Northern exposure $h [videorecording] : $b the first episode

246 30   First episode

500   Title from cassette label.

Since the information on the cassette label is more complete, it is transcribed for the title field. When the title proper is not taken from the preferred chief source (i.e., title frame), a note is provided to clarify this point.

Prescribed Sources of Information

The prescribed sources of information for each of the seven areas of the description of videorecordings are summarized below:

245 (Area 1)	Chief source of information
250, 260, 4xx (Areas 2, 4, 6)	Chief source, accompanying material, container
300, 5xx, 02X (Areas 5, 7, 8)	Any source

Information taken from non-prescribed sources should be recorded in square brackets.

7.1. Title and Statement of Responsibility (MARC field 245)

A common problem in transcribing title proper is that the title frames are usually preceded or followed by the names of performers, producers, and so on. In such cases, LCRI 7.1B1 (CSB 13) recommends that these names not be considered part of the title proper.

[beginning screens]:

ORION HOME VIDEO
AN ORION PICTURES RELEASE
A STRONG HEART/DEMME PRODUCTION
JODIE FOSTER
ANTHONY HOPKINS
SCOTT GLENN
THE SILENCE OF THE LAMBS
TED LEVINE ...
SCREENPLAY BY
TED TALLY

PRODUCED BY
EDWARD SAXON
KENNETH UTT
RON BOZMAN

DIRECTED BY
JONATHAN DEMME

Transcribed as:

245   04   The silence of the lambs $h [videorecording]

Similarly, if a video begins with "So and so present," this phrase is in general not considered part of the title proper.

[beginning screens]

Warner Home Video
Warner Bros-Seven Arts
present
A Phil Feldman Production
The Wild Bunch
William Holden ...

Transcribed as:

245   04   The wild bunch $h [videorecording]

If a parallel title appears in the chief source, it is transcribed after the general material designation.

245   00   Como agua para chocolate $h [videorecording] =
               $b Like water for chocolate

General Material Designation (GMD): The GMD for videorecordings, regardless of the physical carriers, is "videorecording."

Statement of Responsibility: Many people are involved in the creation of a video or a film. LCRI 7.1F1 (CSB 36) indicates that only person(s) or body(ies) with **overall responsibility for the work** should be entered in the statement of responsibility area. People in this category typically include producers, directors, and writers. People responsible for part of the work are covered by notes. In the *Silence of the Lamb* example, actors with major roles are recorded in a note, while the screenplay writer, the producers, and the director are entered in Area 1.

245 04   The silence of the lambs $h [videorecording] / $c Orion Pictures ; screenplay by Ted Tally ; produced by Edward Saxon, Kenneth Utt, Ron Bozman ; directed by Jonathan Demme.

511 1   Jodie Foster, Anthony Hopkins, Scott Glenn.

Another common practice of film and video producers is to present credit information at the end of the product.

[title frame]: Pathways
              to Better Living with Arthritis
              and related conditions
[End credits]
Produced for the
Arthritis Foundation by
MOBILITY LIMITED
Written by
SHOOSH CROTZER
Directed by THOMAS WALTERS ...
Arthritis Foundation
Pittsfield, MA 01202-4284

Transcribed as:

245 00   Pathways to better living with arthritis and related conditions $h [videorecording] / $c written by Shoosh Crotzer ; directed by Thomas Walters.

260   Pittsfield, MA : $b Produced for the Arthritis Foundation by Mobility Limited, $c 1997.

[comment: Note that in field 245 the transcription of the statement of responsibility follows that of the original to simplify the transcription activity. In field 260, the phrase indicating the function of the producer is also included, following Rule 1.4D3.]

When many individuals are listed in the credit area, it can be difficult to determine who has the overall responsibility and should be recorded in Area 1. It can also be challenging to determine which actors play "major roles" in a video. Fortunately the label or the container often provides some clues on this matter. Especially for actors, the container tends to list only the major characters, suggesting that these individuals should become access points.

[beginning frames]: The X-Files

> Starring DAVID DUCHOVNY
> GILLIAN ANDERSON

> WRITTEN BY
> CHRIS CARTER
> DIRECTED BY
> ROBERT MANDEL

[container]: STARRING DAVID DUCHOVNY GILLIAN ANDERSON

Transcribed as:

245	04	The X-Files $h [videorecording] / $c written by Chris Carter ; directed by Robert Mandel.
511	1	David Duchovny, Gillian Anderson.
700	1	Duchovny, David.
700	1	Anderson, Gillian.

7.2. Edition (MARC field 250)

The prescribed sources for Area 2 are the chief source, the accompanying material, and the container. Only formal edition statements should be recorded. If an item has known, significant differences from other editions, the cataloger may provide a brief statement to that effect (optional rule, applied by LC per LCRI 1.2B4, CSB 47).

250	Letterboxed ed.
250	Widescreen ed.

7.4 Publication, Distribution, Etc. (MARC field 260)

The prescribed sources for this area are the chief source, the accompanying material and the container. The name of the publisher and that of the distributor, if known, are recorded in this area. If several dates appear on an item or different dates are listed for different parts of an item, catalogers should use a date that covers the entire work if possible. If this is not possible, the latest date is used. If distributor information is available, the name and place of the distributor, releasing agency, etc. can be recorded in this area also (1.4D, 7.4D). Subfields a and b can be repeated for this area.

260	Universal City, CA : $b MCA Universal Home Video, $c c1996.
260	Alexandria, Va. : $b Distributed by PBS Home Video, $c c1995.
260	Boston, Mass. : $b Blackside ; $a Alexandria, Va. : $b PBS Video [distributor], $c c1989.

For videos of feature films, the publication date of the video is recorded in subfield c of field 260, while the date of the original film is recorded in the edition and history note (7.7B7).

7.5 Physical Description (MARC field 300)

300	$a number of specific material designation (playing time or frames for "still images"[see 7.5B2]) : $b sound, color ; $c dimensions. + $e accompanying material.

In addition to videocassettes and videorecordings, other videomediums include videodisc and DVD. Videodisc has two distinct formats, CAV (constant angular velocity) and CLV (constant linear velocity). CAV is the preferred format for interactive videodisc applications because the frames are laid down in concentric circles and each frame has its own 360-degree track on the videodisc, making it possible for laser readers to randomly access the frames.[3] Information on CLV is laid down in one continuous spiral, making the format appropriate for long, continuous video plays.[4] DVD stands for digital videodisc. It expands the optical storage capacity of CD-ROM into the multi-gigabyte range to support applications such as digital video. The DVD Forum identifies three levels of DVD storage capacity: a 4.7 GB standard for single-layer DVD, an 8.5 GB standard for dual-layer, and a 17 GB standard for floppy disks designed to record on both sides of a dual-layer system.[5] Major film studios have released feature films on

DVD. Encyclopedias and games with video and surround sound are also popular applications of DVD. DVDs require their own player. The attraction of such a player is that it can read both CD-ROM titles and audio CDs.

Data for this area can be taken from any source. The information usually appears on the label or the container. For videodiscs (CAV and CLV) and DVD, the specific material designation is "videodisc." Information about the type of player, special sound effects, and so on are usually recorded in field 538 as system requirements. The "sound" element indicates whether a video has sound, but it does not indicate the quality of the sound, such as "stereo" or "Dolby surround," which is typically recorded in a note.

300	1 videocassette (1 hr., 55 min.) : $b sd., col. ; $c 1/2 in.
300	1 videocassette (52 min.) : $b sd., col. with b&w sequences ; $c 1/2 in.
300	4 videodiscs (4 hrs.) : $b sd., col. ; $c 12 in.
538	CAV, standard play; THX digital sound, Dolby system, stereo.

7.6 Series (MARC field 4xx)

The prescribed sources for this area are the chief source, the accompanying material, and the container. This information usually appears prominently on the container or the first few frames of a video.

440	0	Eyewitness video series
440	0	Storyteller's classics
440	0	Yoga with Linda Arkin
440	0	At time of diagnosis

When an item belongs to a series, it is typically cataloged for itself, with an added entry created for the series. This practice is sometimes applied to multiple-part items, and should be done according to the library's policy.

Joseph Campbell and the Power of Myth, for instance, includes six parts, each with its own title. Catalogers have at least two ways to treat these items. Option one is to catalog these six items as a set under the collective title, provide a content note listing the six parts, and provide analytical added entries for the six titles. This practice is common for parts with a collective title.

A second way to catalog this item for libraries that do not own all parts of a work, is to catalog each item and use the collective title as a series title to link the parts owned by the library together. While both approaches are acceptable, a rule of thumb is to see if the second approach would result in six records with nearly identical information. If so, Option One should be applied.

Option One (one record)

245	00	Joseph Campbell and the power of myth ...
246	30	Power of myth
505	0	1. The hero's adventure -- 2. The message of the myth -- 3. The first storytellers -- 4. Sacrifice and bliss -- 5. Love and the goddess -- 6. Masks of eternity.
740	01	Hero's adventure.
740	01	Message of the myth.
740	01	First storytellers.
740	01	Sacrifice and bliss.
740	01	Love and the goddess.
740	01	Masks of eternity.

[comment: Field 246 is used to record a variant title, and 740 fields are used for analytics. OCLC input guidelines recommend that initial articles not be used in fields 246 and 740.]

Option Two (each part has its own record)

245	04	The hero's adventure ...
440	0	Joseph Campbell and the power of myth ; $v 1

7.7 Notes

Fields 546, 500, 508, 511, 538, 520, 505, and 521 are frequently used in the cataloging of videorecordings. Information for Area 7 can be taken from any source. The rules of 7.7 specify the order of these notes.

Language (MARC field 546): Languages can be associated with videorecordings in many ways. Subtitling and closed captioning are common. Some videos include signing or audio description on a second audio track of the video. Such information is usually listed on the container and/or on the main menu. Such information should be recorded in 546 field and coordinated with the fixed-field element "Lang" and field 041.

Example: For a bilingual program presented in Italian and English

Transcribed as: Lang: ita

041	itaeng
546	A bilingual program in Italian and English.

* * *

Example: For a DVD video with subtitles in "English, Francais, Espanol"

Transcribed as: Lang: eng

041	engfrespa
546	Subtitles in English, French, and Spanish.
546	Closed-captioned.

Source of Title Proper (MARC field 500): If the title proper is not taken from the chief source of information, a 500 note should be provided to indicate the source.

Variant Title (MARC field 246): Titles other than the title proper are recorded in field 246, and the first indicator can be coded to produce a note and a title added entry.

245	00	My first green video $h [videorecording]
246	1	$i Subtitle on cassette and container: $a kids' guide to ecology and environmental activities

Most videos have title frames, but the information on the title frames may not be the same as that on the container labels. When that happens, the title from the title frame is recorded in field 245 and the other titles are recorded in 246 fields.

[title frame]:   YOGA

FOR RELAXATION

WITH LINDA ARKIN

[cassette label]:   YOGA

WITH LINDA ARKIN

FOR RELAXATION & REJUVENATION

Transcribed as:

245 00   Yoga with Linda Arkin for relaxation $h [videorecording]

246 3   Yoga with Linda Arkin for relaxation & rejuvenation

246 3   Yoga for relaxation and rejuvenation

[comment: the cassette box lists other titles in "Yoga with Linda Arkin Series," that is why the title proper and the first variant title use the wording "yoga with Linda Arkin"]

* * *

[title frame]:   EYES ON THE PRIZE

AMERICA AT THE RACIAL CROSSROADS

POWER!

1967 - 1968

[cassette label]:

EYES ON THE PRIZE II: America at the racial crossroads

Power 1967 - 1968

Transcribed as:

245 00   Eyes on the prize $h [videorecording] : $b America at the racial crossroads. $p Power, 1967-1968.

246 3   Eyes on the prize II

Statement of Responsibility (MARC field 511, 508): Two major notes for statement of responsibility include field 511, which records players, performers, narrators, hosts or presenters of a videorecording, and field 508, which records people who contribute to the artistic or technical production of a videorecording. People named in field 511 should play major roles in a video, and those listed in field 508 should have major contribution to the production of the video. The wording and the order in which names appear in the credit frames suggest the importance of these names. Information on the carrier (cassette or videodisc) and the container may be helpful, too.

245	00	High blood pressure $h [videorecording]
508		C. Everett Koop, medical director.
511	0	Host, Boyd Matson.

Edition and History (MARC field 500): This type of note describes the edition being cataloged or the history of a videorecording. Many videos or feature films contain information on the original movie release.

500	Originally produced for PBS television in 1986.
500	Based on the Mary Poppins books by P. L. Travers.
500	A 1990 episode of the television series.
500	Videocassette release of the 1982 motion picture.
500	Remake of a 1977 motion picture of the same name

Physical Description (MARC fields 500, 538): Several physical characteristics of a videorecording should be noted. "Sound characteristics" and color information are typically recorded in field 500, while videorecording system information is recorded in field 538.

500	Dolby stereo.
500	Technicolor.
538	VHS.
538	VHS Hi-fi.
538	CAV

Accompanying Material (MARC field 500): This note is mainly used to indicate the location of accompanying material. It is also used to described accompanying material that is not described elsewhere in the record.

500 Program no. on insert

Audience (MARC field 521): If the intended audience or the intellectual level of a videorecording is found in the iter its container, or accompanying material, a 521 note should be provided. Rating information is also recorded in 521. If the first indicator is blank, a print constant "Audience" will be displayed; if it is 8, no print constant will be displayed.

521 Suitable for Grades 4-8.

521 8 For age 8+

521 8 Rated PG.

521 8 MPAA rating

Other Formats (MARC field 530): If the item also appears in other physical formats, the information is presented in a 530 note.

530 Also available on videodisc.

Summary (MARC field 520): To inform users of the content of an item, catalogers should prepare a brief, objective summary. The *Subject Cataloging Manual* instructs catalogers to use summaries to determine which topics will be assigned subject headings, so it is important to prepare an informative and unbiased summary for each item cataloged.

Contents (MARC field 505): The parts included in a videorecording can be presented in a formal note in field 505 or an informal note in field 500. If each part has its own statement of responsibility, the statement can be added. To make the parts searchable, an enhanced contents note can be created, with the second indicator coded "0."

245 04 The X-Files $h [videorecording] : $b Pilot/Deep throat

505 0 Pilot / directed by Robert Mandel -- Deep throat / directed by Daniel Sachheim.

Publisher's Number (MARC field 028): The publisher's number for a videorecording should be entered in field 028. The first indicator is 4 for videorecording, and the second indicator can be used to produce a note.

028   42   Publisher number $b Source.

028   42   51328-3 $b WarnerVision Entertainment

7.8 International Standard Numbers
(Fields 020, 022)

The international standard numbers are recorded in field 020 or field 022.

020   1568324928

Assignment of Access Points

The assignment of access points to videorecordings is the same as that to print materials, except for musical videorecordings. Videorecordings usually do not have a personal author as the main entry because they tend to include the intellectual and artistic work of many people. In addition, videorecordings also tend not to have a corporate body as the main entry because a work will have to be emanated from the body and belong to one of the six categories of material named in Rule 21.1B2. Most videorecordings have title as the main entry.

LCRI 21.23C (CSB 45) recommends that Rules 21.23C1 and 21.23D be applied to videorecordings that are "collections of music performed by a principal performer." *Sarah Brightman in Concert*, for instance, contains performances by Brightman of a selection of songs. Applying Rule 21.23C1 to this video, the cataloger will select Sarah Brightman as the main entry. Rule 21.23D covers videos containing works by several people without collective title.

LCRI 21.29 (CBS 45) also provides guidance on the selection of added entries for videorecordings. These guidelines are similar to those for sound recordings and are summarized below:

1. Catalogers should make added entries for all openly named persons or corporate bodies that contributed to the creation of the work.
    a. But if a production company, unit, etc., has been made an added entry, no entries should be made for persons such as producers, directors, and writers unless their contributions are significant. If no production company is present, added entries should be made for producers, directors, and writers. Added entries are made for other persons only if they made significant contribution to the work.
    b. If a person is the main entry heading, make no added entries for other people unless they are true collaborators.

2. All corporate bodies named in the publication, distribution, etc., area should be traced.

3. All featured players, performers, and narrators should be traced, but not group members. If a person's name appears with a group, do not consider him a member of the group. If several players are involved, make added entries for those given prominence in the chief source. If this criterion does not apply, make added entries for each if there are no more than three.

4. Make added entries for persons serving as interviewers, interviewees, lecturers, etc., who are not selected as the main entry.

■ SUBJECT ANALYSIS

Library of Congress Subject Headings

Catalogers have been concerned about the limitations of authority lists such as the *Library of Congress Subject Headings* and the *Sears List of Subject Headings* for the subject analysis of nonprint materials. Weihs pointed out in 1987 that *LCSH* did not incorporate new topics fast enough and the terms were not specific enough for the indexing of nonprint materials.[6] Intner stated in 1992 that precision and retrieval remained problematic because many LCSH terms could be used as topical headings and form headings.[7] Furthermore, LC's principle of literary warrant, a principle to use LC collection as the basis for establishing headings, also precluded LC from adding new terms for works it did not own.[8] The National Moving Image Database Standards Committee of the National Center for Film and Video Preservation at the American Film Institute published *Moving Image Materials: Genre Terms* (*MIM*) in 1988;[9] and Miller described the use of *MIM* and *LCSH* in their catalog to illustrate the compatibility concerns.[10] As Intner pointed out, *LCSH* has remained the main source for subject headings because of a strong interest in integrating nonprint resources into the catalog, the benefit of record sharing, LC's effort to revise and augment the tool, and the high cost of developing and maintaining a new list.[11] Intner and Studwell extracted descriptors pertaining to motion pictures, television, and videorecordings from the 13th edition of *LCSH* (1990) and made it easier for catalogers to use the terms and to decide if new terms ought to be developed locally.[12]

The cataloging policy has also been a matter of concern. ALA published *Guidelines on Subject Access to Individual Works of Fiction, Drama, Etc.* in 1990.[13] The ALA *Guidelines* recommend four types of subject access that are valuable for searchers, including form/genre access, access for characters or group of characters, access for setting, and topical access. The current Library of Congress policies for visual materials have similar treatments for motion pictures that can be extended to videorecordings. These policies are summarized below.

Fiction Films (*SCM* H2230)

Videos that are feature films are assigned:

1. topical headings with the subdivision "--Drama" (use the subdivision "--Juvenile films" for juvenile fiction films),

2. form headings indicating genre (e.g., Western films) or technique (e.g., Silent films), and

3. either the form heading "Feature films" (for films at least 40 minutes long) or "Short films" (for films less than 40 minutes long).

The first two types of headings are assigned if appropriate, while the third heading is required. If all three types of headings are assigned to a work, the headings should be arranged in the order presented above.

245	00	Get Shorty $h [videorecording]
520		Loan shark Chili Palmer had done his time as a gangster. So when "business" takes him to Los Angeles to collect a debt from down-and-out filmmaker Harry Zimm, Chili pitches Harry a script idea and is immediately swept into the Hollywood scene. All would be smooth for this cool new producer, if it weren't for the drug smugglers and an angry mobster who won't leave him alone.
650	0	Gangsters $z United States $v Drama.
650	0	Motion picture producers and directors $z California $z Los Angeles $v Drama.
650	0	Comedy films.
650	0	Feature films.

Films prepared with captions or sign language for viewing by the hearing impaired should also be assigned the heading, "Films for the hearing impaired" or "Videorecordings for the hearing impaired." But films with subtitles in other languages should not be assigned such headings if the subtitles are meant as translation and not as an aid for the hearing impaired.

Films prepared with audio description for the visually handicapped should be assigned either "Films for the visually handicapped" or "Videorecordings for the visually handicapped."

For foreign-language teaching films, Library of Congress advises that the heading [...] language--Films for [...] speakers be assigned as the first heading, and other special topics be assigned as appropriate. Thus, a film teaching German language to English speakers will be assigned: German language--Films for English speakers.

Nonfiction Films

Topicals: For topical films all important topics mentioned in the summary statement are assigned headings. The form subdivision "--Pictorial works" is never used.

520		Step-by-step video instructions: layout and installation of fence posts and rails; how to build and install a gate; installation of a chain link fence.
650	0	Fences $v Amateurs' manuals.
650	0	Gates $v Amateurs' manuals.

Person & profession: Films about a person as illustrative of a profession are assigned headings for the person and the profession.

520		Alfred I. Maleson, Professor Emeritus of the Suffolk University Law School, discusses his career in legal education, from his first teaching position in Toledo, Ohio to Suffolk University in Boston.
600	10	Maleson, Alfred I., $d 1922-
650	0	Law teachers $z Massachusetts $z Boston.
610	20	Suffolk University. $b Law School. $x Faculty.

Topic & place: Films that present a topic in a particular place are assigned headings for the topic and the place.

520		Follows three international stars Laurent Fignon of France, Pedro Delgado of Spain, and Greg LeMond of the U.S. as they pedal across the French countryside and mountains in a battle for victory in the 1989 Tour de France.
600	10	LeMond, Greg.
650	0	Tour de France (Bicycle race)
650	0	Bicycle racing $z France.
651	0	France $x Description and travel $y 1975-

Commercials: Commercials advertising a particular product are assigned the generic name of the product and a heading for the advertising medium.

520		A commercial for Taster's Choice.
650	0	Instant coffee.
650	0	Television advertising.

Films on foreign language teaching are assigned, as the first heading, a heading based on the pattern: [Language]--Films for [group] speakers.

For example, Japanese--Films for Chinese speakers

Juvenile works with topical headings should have the free-floating subdivision "--Juvenile films" added to them. "Juvenile videorecordings," however, is not a form subdivision.

245	00	Beating and bleeding
520		Examines and explores the workings of the heart with its lifelong movement of blood.
650	0	Heart $v Juvenile films.
650	0	Blood $v Juvenile films.

Classification Numbers

In assigning numbers from *DDC* and *LCC*, the cataloger should focus on the content of the videorecordings instead of the format. Topical videorecordings should be assigned the most specific number available in the classification schedule for the topics and no special number is assigned to bring out the format. Videorecordings of feature films and literary works intended for entertainment are classed with PN1997 A2-Z8 in *LCC*, and subarranged by Cutter number from title. Special topics for motion pictures are classed under 1995.9 A-Z, with .C55 for comedy, .F36 for fantastic films, and .S26 for science fiction films. Videorecordings of juvenile belles lettres are classed in PZ5-PZ90, and those written in English are classed in PZ5-PZ10.3. PZ7 is for American and English juvenile belles lettres, 1870-, PZ8 for fairy tales, PZ8.1 for folklore, PZ8.3 for verses for children and stories in rhyme, and PZ 10.3 for animal stories. PZ5-PZ10.3 includes unique Cutter numbers assigned to literary authors to subarrange materials. Work letters from the title (ignoring the initial article) can be added to subarrange works by the same author.[14] Date can also be added to distinguish editions of the same work.

In *DDC* topical videorecordings are also assigned the most specific number available in the schedule. Table 1 of *DDC*, the standard subdivision, supports catalogers to add numbers to represent some forms (e.g., dictionaries, directories), but in general the form aspect of a work is usually ignored when one assigns a classification number.[15] For videorecordings of feature films, *DDC* has a number (791.4372) for single films, which can be subarranged by Cutter number of film title. Videorecordings of literary works are classed in the literature class. Works by and about individual literary authors are grouped together. Class numbers for such works usually consist of numbers for the main class, language, form, and period. For instance, Fitzgerald's *Great Gatsby* will be classed in 813.54 [813.54 = 8 (literature) + 1 (American literature in English) + 3 (Fiction) + 54 (1945-1999)]. 808.89 is designated for collections for and by specific kinds of persons. With the help of Table 3-C, catalogers can build a number for collections of juvenile literary works (808.899282).

■ ARRANGEMENT

The use of classification numbers does not necessarily affect the physical arrangement of a video collection. Although shelving videorecordings with the other types of material makes it easier for users to browse and access the collection, security and preservation concerns cause many libraries to separate videorecordings from other types of material. Here are a few popular approaches for arranging videorecordings.

Closed Stacks

The "closed stacks" arrangement is popular among academic libraries for several reasons. First, some of the videorecordings are educational materials that would be expensive to replace. Second, the major function of academic media centers is to support curricula, so these centers are strongly interested in ensuring the condition, security, and availability of materials for educators. Many, in fact, do not circulate videorecordings to students because of licensing restrictions. In closed stacks, because materials are stored in a secure and controlled environment, it becomes easier to take inventory of the collection, to maintain and preserve the materials, and to control access. But users cannot browse the stacks, and the collection cannot be used without the catalog.

Libraries using DDC or LCC numbers often add "Video" to their classification numbers to remind users that the items are videorecordings. In such libraries, items in the closed stacks will be arranged by classification numbers. But closed stacks tend to encourage arrangement by accession number, size, or type, resulting in libraries creating full bibliographic records for videorecordings but assigning special numbers (e.g., Video A12) to them. The reason is that shelving by accession number is more efficient for inventory control and retrieval but wastes space. Shelving by size, on the other hand, saves space and supports quick retrieval if the catalog is good. Some libraries arrange items by format, so videocassettes, videodiscs, and films are stored in separate areas, and items within each group are arranged with its own sequence of accession numbers. This approach also requires strong support from the catalog.

Shelving by Format, Type, Etc.

Many public libraries encourage browsing by storing videorecordings in an area separate from the other materials. The video collection is still fully searchable in the catalog. These libraries put a special term (e.g., video, videocassette) on top of the call number to identify them, and use some kind of classification number to subarrange them. Depending on the nature and size of the collection, some libraries use standard classification schemes such as *DDC* and *LCC*, while others devise their own categories (e.g., "B" for biography; "F" for feature films), and subarrange materials by Cutter numbers. This method collocates materials and supports browsing.

A variation to this approach is to arrange videorecordings by their type. That means documentaries, videos of feature films, juvenile videos, and topical videos are arranged separately. This method is appropriate if a library has many items of each type. But if the videos are not classified and items of each category are arranged by title, as in some libraries, browsing becomes somewhat limited. For example, although it is fine to browse feature film videos by title, it is not easy to browse topical videos by title—*Saving Our Environment* and *Green Earth* cover the same subject but are far apart alphabetically. Users will have to rely on the catalog to collocate these videos. One may wonder if public libraries would take this approach a step further and subarrange feature film videos by genre. A common response to this inquiry is that the videos public libraries purchase are selected to meet the needs of their community and they have no intention to compete with video stores. Indeed, many videos in public libraries are educational and topical videos.

Other Possibilities

The method of "intershelving with dummies" discussed in Chapter Three is also a possibility for arranging videorecordings because the size of videorecordings is fairly standard. The same benefits and drawbacks also apply. Interested readers may turn to Chapter Three for a discussion of this method.

Cataloging Examples begin on page 94.

■ CATALOGING EXAMPLES

QUESTAR
HOME VIDEO
THE STORY OF
YELLOWSTONE
NATIONAL PARK
[END CREDITS]
DIRECTOR
Dale Johnson
CINEMATOGRAPHY
Bob Landis
Dale Johnson
NARRATION
Stanley Wessel
EDITING
Dale Johnson
Caron Pepper ...
DISTRIBUTED BY
Questar Video, Inc.
P.O. Box 11345
Chicago, Illinois 60611

Also on container label:
Filmed & Produced by: Dale Johnson and Robert Landis
Distributed by: Questar Video, Inc.
              P.O. Box 11345
              Chicago, IL 60611
****

Type: g	Audn:	BLvl: m	TMat: v	Time: 065

007		v $b f $d c $e b $f a $g g $h o
020		0927992329
028	42	QV2233 $b Questar Video
090		F722
092		917.8752
245	04	The story of Yellowstone National Park $h [videorecording] / $c filmed and produced by Dale Johnson and Robert Landis.
260		Chicago, IL : $b Questar Video, $c c1991.
300		1 videocassette (65 min.) : $b sd., col. ; $c 1/2 in.
538		VHS format.
520		Presents the wonders of Yellowstone, including rare footage of dramatic wildlife action, the fire of 1988, and the charred land in full bloom.
651	0	Yellowstone National Park $x Description and travel $x Views.
700	1	Johnson, Dale.
710	1	Landis, Robert.
710	2	Questar Video, Inc.

Figure 4.1   The story of Yellowstone National Park.

Discussion for Figure 4.1

- Fixed field elements: Code g in Type indicates projected media, code m in BLvl indicates a nonserial item, code v in TMat refers to videorecording, and the playing time of the item is recorded in Time.

- 028: This field is used for the publisher's number. The first indicator value is 4 for videorecordings, the second indicator 2 will generate a note for this number.

- 245: The statement of responsibility is taken from the container label.

- 538: The video format is transcribed.

- 651: A place name is the main heading, so field 651 is used.

- 700s: According to LCRI 21.29, when a production company is not present, added entries are made for producers. These added entries are arranged in the order in which the names appear in the bibliographic description.

- 710: LCRI 21.29 recommends making added entries for corporate bodies named in Area 4.

SONY KIDS' VIDEO
MY FIRST GREEN VIDEO

[End Credits]
Dorling Kindersley Vision
Demonstrator
EVA MARIE BRYER
Script
ANGELA WILKES ...
Director
DAVID FURNHAM
© 1993 SONY Music Entertainment, Inc.

****

Type: g   Audn: c   BLvl: m   TMat: v   Time: 040   Tech: l
007   v $b f $d c $e b $f a $g h $h o $i s
020   1564066908
090   TD170.15
092   363.7
245   00   My first green video $h [videorecording] / $c Dorling
             Kindersley Vision ; script, Angela Wilkes ; directed by David
             Furnham.
246   1 $i Subtitle on cassette and container: $a Kids' guide to ecology
             and environmental activities
260   New York, N.Y. : $b Sony Kids' Video, $c c1993.
300   1 videocassette (40 min.) : $b sd. , col. ; $c 1/2 in.
546   Closed-captioned.
511   0   Demonstrator: Eva Marie Bryer.
538   VHS Hi-fi stereo, Dolby system on linear tracks.
521   For ages 5 years and older.
520   Step-by-step instructions for carrying out experiments and
             activities that deal with the environment.
500   "LV 49572"--Cassette label.
650   0   Video recordings for the hearing impaired.
650   0   Pollution $x Experiments
650   0   Conservation of natural resources
650   0   Environmental protection
650   0   Ecology
700   1   Wilkes, Angela.
700   1   Furnham, David.
710   2   Dorling Kindersley, Inc.
710   2   Sony Kids' Video (Firm)

Figure 4.2   My first green video.

Discussion for Figure 4.2

- Fixed field: In addition to the typical codes for videorecordings, the codes for Audn and Tech are added. Code c in Audn indicates the item is intended for young people in grades four through eight; code l for Tech indicates live action.

- 090 & 092: TD170.15 is for juvenile works on environmental protection, and 363.7 is for environmental protection. *DDC* does not have a category for juvenile works under this number.

- 245: The statement of responsibility is taken from the end credits. Only people with overall responsibility for the work are included in this area, and the demonstrator is entered in field 511.

- 246: A variant title is recorded in field 246. Subfield i indicates the source and subfield a the variant title. The first indicator 1 means a note and an added entry will be produced.

- 546: If a video is closed-captioned, the information is recorded in field 546. A subject heading needs to be assigned to reflect this fact.

- 511: Demonstrator's name is taken from the end credits. Since she is not well-known, the demonstrator is not traced.

- 538: The format of the video and the sound quality are entered in a note. This note complements the information in field 300.

- 521: The intended audience is listed on the container and transcribed in field 521. With the first indicator blank, a print constant "Audience" will precede this information.

- 650s: A form heading is assigned to indicate the film is closed-captioned for the hearing impaired. Because "juvenile videorecordings" is not a form subdivision, the topical headings are not subdivided.

- 700s: People who made significant contributions to the video are traced.

- 710s: The corporate bodies listed in the statement of responsibility area and the publication area are traced.

a
mystic fire
video
VOICES
&
VISIONS
A
NEW YORK
CENTER FOR VISUAL HISTORY
PRODUCTION

Emily Dickinson

[END CREDITS]
Director
Veronica Young
Producer
Jill Janows
Editor
Lisa Jackson ...

For Voices & Visions
Executive producer: Lawrence Pitkethly.

© 1988 New York Center for Visual History, Inc.

****

Type: g	Audn:	BLvl: m TMat: v Time: 060
007		v $b f $d c $e b $f a $g h $h o
020		156176308X
028	42	MYS-76308 $b Mystic Fire Video
090		PS1541
092		811.4
245	00	Emily Dickinson $h [videorecording] / $c A New York Center for Visual History Production ; director, Veronica Young ; producer, Jill Janows.
260		New York, NY : $b Mystic Fire Video, $c c1995.
300		1 videocassette (60 min.) : $b sd., col. ; $c 1/2 in.
440	0	Voices & visions
500		Executive producer of Voices & visions: Lawrence Pitkethly.
538		VHS.
520		Examines the life and work of American poet Emily Dickinson. Richard B. Sewall, Adrienne Rich, Anthony Hecht, and Joyce Carol Oates discuss her achievement, separating the facts of her life from the myths around her.
600	10	Dickinson, Emily, $d 1830-1886.
650	0	Poets, American $y 19th century $v Biography.
700	1	Sewall, Richard Benson.
700	1	Rich, Adrienne Cecile.
700	1	Hecht, Anthony, $d 1923-
700	1	Oates, Joyce Carol, $d 1938-
710	2	New York Center for Visual History.

Figure 4.3   Emily Dickinson.

Discussion for Figure 4.3

- 020 & 028: The ISBN and the publisher number are taken from the container.

- 090 & 092: PS1541 is for 19th century American poets; 811.4 is a number for works by and about literary authors. 811.4 is built from 811 (American poetry) and 4 (1861-1899).

- 245: The video has a title screen stating simply "Emily Dickinson." The statements of responsibility are taken from the opening credits and the end credits. Young and Janows are transcribed here because they have overall responsibility for the creation of this work.

- 260: The place of publication is taken from the container. The date of publication requires reconciliation. While the program was produced in 1988, the date on the cassette is 1986, and the video-cassette was produced in 1995. Since what we have in hand is the video, the 1995 copyright date is used.

- 440: "Voices & visions" is prominently listed on the container and the item itself. The end credits indicate that this is a series.

- 538: The format of the video is always included in this field. Some libraries include the format information in the first element of field 300 (e.g., 1 videocassette (VHS)). That is a local decision.

- 500: Lawrence Pitkethly is well-known for his series, so the fact is noted.

- 520: A brief and objective summary of a video gives users an idea of its content. Information on the container is usually useful for this purpose.

- 600 & 650: Since Dickinson is the subject of this video, she is entered in field 600, and a topical heading for her occupation is also provided and subdivided by Biography.

- 700s: LCRI to 21.29 recommends that when a production company is an added entry, no added entries are made for producers, directors, writers, etc. Since the production company is traced in 710, the director and the producer are not traced. If a library chooses to trace the producers and the director, it could justify that decision if the contribution of these people is believed to be significant. The same LCRI also recommends that added entries be made for people serving as interviewees, delivering lectures or discussing their ideas. So the four poets are traced in the order in which their names appear in the bibliographic description.

- 710 fields: The production firm and the video distribution firm are traced.

RANDOM HOUSE
HOME VIDEO
CHILDREN'S
TELEVISION
WORKSHOP
MY
SESAME STREET
HOME VIDEO

SING ALONG

[end credits]
Executive Producer
Jon Stone
Directed by Jon Stone
Lisa Simon
Writers
Jon Stone
Cathi Rosenberg
Tony Geiss ...

[container information]
Featuring Jim Henson's Sesame Street Muppets
and the Sesame Street Live Cast

Executive Producer: Jon Stone
Director: Jon Stone
Writers: Jon Stone and Cathi Rosenberg-Turow

****

Type: g	Audn:	BLvl: m TMat: v Time: 030 Tech: 1
007		v $b f $d c $e b $f a $g h $h o $i u
020		0394889320
090		M1990
092		782.7
245	00	Sing along $h [videorecording] / $c Children's Television Workshop.
260		New York : $b Random House Home Video, $c c1987.
300		1 videocassette (30 min.) : $b sd., col. ; $c 1/2 in.
440	0	My Sesame Street home video
546		Closed-captioned.
511	1	Featuring Jim Henson's Sesame Street Muppets and the Sesame Street live cast.
508		Executive producer/director, Jon Stone; writers, Jon Stone and Cathi Rosenberg-Turow.
538		VHS.
520		The whole family will want to join in when Big Bird and his friends get together for a sing-along.
650	0	Video recordings for the hearing impaired.
650	0	Children's songs.
710	2	Children's Television Workshop.
710	2	Random House Video.
730	0	Sesame Street (Television program)

Figure 4.4   Sing along.

Discussion for Figure 4.4

- 245 & 508: The statement of responsibility includes the production company only because a long list of individuals is included in the end credits, and information on the people with overall responsibility is not exactly the same as that on the container. Because of this uncertainty, information on the producer, director, and writer is included in field 508 instead of field 245.

- 440: The series information appears on the tape and the container. Several titles of this series are listed on the container suggesting that "Sesame Street home video" is a series title.

- 650s: Form headings are assigned. Closed-captioning is represented by a heading.

- 700s & 710s: LCRI 21.29 recommends that when a production company is made an added entry, no added entries are made for the producers, directors, writers, etc. So no personal names are traced, but the production firm, Children's Television Workshop is traced. Authority work is done on all access points.

- 730: The television series is traced to link related works.

THE AMERICAN EXPERIENCE
with David McCullough

THE ORPHAN TRAINS
Produced & directed by
JANET GRAHAM AND
EDWARD GRAY
Written by
EDWARD GRAY
Narrated by
STACEY KEACH

[end credits]
Edited by
Joshn Waletzky ...
A production of Edward Gray Films, Inc.
© 1995 Janet Graham and Edward Gray
For
THE AMERICAN EXPERIENCE
© 1995 WGBH Educational Foundation
A production of WGBH Boston [voice announcement]

****

Type: g	Audn: e	BLvl: m TMat: v Time: 057 Tech: 1
007		v $b f $d m $e b $f a $g h $h o $i u
028	42	AMEX-804 $b PBS Video
043		n-us---
090		HV985
092		362.734
245	04	The orphan trains $h [videorecording] / $c produced and directed by Janet Graham and Edward Gray ; written by Edward Gray ; a production of WGBH.
260		[Alexandria, Va.] : $b Distributed by PBS Home Video, $c c1995.
300		1 videocassette (57 min.) : $b sd., col. with b&w sequences ; $c 1/2 in.
546		Closed-captioned.
511	3	Stacey Keach.
500		Originally produced as an episode of the television series: The American experience.
538		VHS.
520		An examination of the results of the Children's Aid Society in New York which from 1853 to 1929 sent over 100,000 unwanted and orphaned children from the city to homes in rural America.
650	0	Orphan trains.
610	20	Children's Aid Society (New York, N.Y.)
650	0	Adopted children $z United States $x History.
650	0	Video recordings for the hearing impaired.
700	1	Graham, Janet.
700	1	Gray, Edward, $q (Edward S.)
700	1	Keach, Stacey.
710	2	WGBH (Television station : Boston, Mass.)
710	2	PBS Home Video.
730	0	American experience (Television program)

Figure 4.5   The orphan trains.

Discussion for Figure 4.5

- 028: Publisher's number is entered in field 028, the first indicator 4 indicates video and the second indicator 2 will produce a note for this number.

- 245: The statement of responsibility was taken from the beginning screens and the end credits.

- 300: The playing time on the cassette label is "57 min." but it is described as 60 minutes on the container. Since the cassette label is considered a more preferable source for information, "57 min." is used in this field. The phrase, "b&w sequences," is included with the second element to indicate that the video is not entirely colored. The playing time is encoded in the fixed field element, Time.

- 500: A note of publishing history indicates this video was originally a television episode. It clarifies the nature of this work, links it to the original series, and provides an explanation for an added entry for the original series.

- 520: The summary states that this video is an examination of the Children's Aid Society's success and failure in relocating orphaned children. It clarifies the nature of the video and justifies the provision of an added entry for the society.

- 700s: Directors, producers, and the narrator are traced in the order they appear in the bibliographic description.

- 710s: The production firm and the corporate body mentioned in Area 4 are traced, according to LCRI 21.29.

- 730: A uniform title for the original television series is traced to link this item to the series.

EYEWITNESS

WEATHER
[end credits]
Director
Edwina Vardey
Producer
Richard Thomson
Writer
Lynette Singer
Music
Guy Dagul ...
A CAFE PRODUCTION
for
BBC WORLDWIDE AMERICAS
DORLING KINDERSLEY VISION
in association with
OREGON PUBLIC BROADCASTING
© Dorling Kindersley Vision Ltd. and BBC Worldwide Americas
MCMXCVI

****

Type: g	Audn:	BLvl: m TMat: v Time: 035 Tech: c
007		v $b f $d c $e b $f a $g h $h o $i s
020		0789407191
028	42	5-71663 $b DK Vision
090		QC863.4
092		551.5
245	00	Weather $h [videorecording] / $c a CAFE production for BBC Worldwide Americas, Dorling Kindersley Vision in association with Oregon Public Broadcasting ; director, Edwina Vardey ; producer, Richard Thomson ; writer, Lynette Singer.
260		[S.l.] : $b DK Vision, $c c1996.
300		1 videocassette (35 min.) : $b sd., col. ; $c 1/2 in.
490	0	Eyewitness videos
490	0	Eyewitness II series
546		Closed-captioned.
511	3	Martin Sheen.
538		VHS Hi-fi stereo.
520		A mixture of animation and live footage serves as a background for a narrated introduction to a portrayal of weather and climate and their influence on human life and activities.
650	0	Video recordings for the hearing impaired.
650	0	Weather.
650	0	Climate.
700	1	Vardey, Edwina.
700	1	Thomson, Richard.
700	1	Singer, Lynette.
700	1	Sheen, Martin.
710	2	CAFE Productions.
710	2	Dorling Kindersley Vision.
710	2	BBC Worldwide Americas, Inc.
710	2	Oregon Public Broadcasting.

Figure 4.6   Weather.

Discussion for Figure 4.6

- Fixed field: Code c in Tech indicates this video includes animation and live action.

- 245: Statement of responsibility is taken from the end credits. The corporate bodies' role in the creation of this item was copied and presented first. Individuals with overall responsibility are entered next.

- 490s: Items in these series seem to relate to each other only by common physical characteristics (videos) and the numbering suggests stock control, so the series are not traced (Rule 21.30L1).

- 511: Indicator 3 will produce a print constant, "Narrator:" for this note.

- 650s: The first 650 field is required for videos that are closed-captioned. The other two topical headings reflect the contents of the video. No appropriate form subdivisions are available to bring out the format.

- 700s: The contribution of these individuals is significant, so they are traced.

- 710s: Corporate bodies contributing to the production of this work are also traced.

[Same information on all three volumes]
GoodTimes
Home Video
Fisher-Price
Home Entertainment Library
Fisher-Price
Presents
PIPHER FILMS
Presents
touchpoints
The Brazelton Study
Created & Hosted by
T. Berry Brazelton, M.D.

[end credits]
Creator & Host
T. Berry Brazelton, M.D.
Producer and Director
Joseph Pipher
Writers
T. Berry Brazelton, M.D.
Joseph Pipher

A Pipher Films Inc. Production
© 1991
[cassette label for volume 1]
Fisher-Price
touchpoints   volume 1
One Year through Toddlerhood
© 1991 Pipher Films Inc. Production
Color 3148   GOODTIMES   Approx. 50 min.
© 1992 GoodTimes Home Video. All Rights Reserved.
VHS   16 East 40th St., NY, NY 10016
[volumes 2 and 3 vary from this label only in the volume number, the title for the volume, and
the number for the volume.]

****

Type: g	Audn: e	BLvl: m TMat: v Time: 150 Tech: l
007		v $b f $d c $e b $f a $g h $h o $i u
020		1555114954 (vol. 1)
020		1555114962 (vol. 2)
020		1555114970 (vol. 3)
043		n-us---
090		HQ792.U5
092		649.1
245	00	Touchpoints $h [videorecording] : $b the Brazelton study / $c A Pipher Films Inc. production.
246	1	$i Container title: $a Touchpoints, the definitive video series on parenting
260		New York, NY : $b GoodTimes Home Video, $c c1992.
300		3 videocassettes (ca. 50 min. each) : $b sd., col. ; $c 1/2 in.
511	0	Creator and host, T. Berry Brazelton.
508		Producer and director, Joseph Pipher.
500		Videocassette release of a 1991 production.
538		VHS.
520		By watching a dozen families in unique situations, Dr. Brazelton shows how and why children develop the way they do. Touchpoints are defined as periods of time that precede rapid growth in learning for parent and child.
505	0	v. 1. Pregnancy, birth and first 4 weeks of life -- v. 2. First month through first year -- v. 3. One year through toddlerhood.
500		On containers: 3146, 3147, 3148.
650	0	Parenting.
650	0	Child rearing.
650	0	Child development $z United States.
650	0	Infants $z United States $x Development.
650	0	Child psychology $z United States.
650	0	Infant psychology $z United States.
700	1	Brazelton, T. Berry, $d 1918-
710	2	GoodTimes Home Video (Firm)
710	2	Pipher Films, Inc.

Figure 4.7   Touchpoints.

Discussion for Figure 4.7

- Fixed field: The video is intended for adults, so code e is used in Audn.

- 020: Each volume has its own ISBN, which is entered in its own 020 field.

- 043: When a work has a geographic focus, which is represented by the subject headings, an 043 field can be added. The country code is taken from the OCLC-MARC code list.

- 245: This is a three-volume work and each volume has its own title. This work can be cataloged as a multi-volume set or each volume can be cataloged for itself and be linked to other volumes in this work by a series title. Because the information on the chief source is the same on all the volumes, it is better to catalog this work as a three-volume set. Since field 511 is for information about performers and field 508 for people who contribute to the production of the video, the information about the creator and the producer are entered in these fields instead of in the statement of responsibility.

- 246: A variant title is provided because it appears on the container and users are likely to search for this item by it. The first indicator 1 will generate a note and an added entry for the title. The subtitle of the title proper is also a likely candidate for variant title. If it is traced, the indicators for 246 should be 10 and the initial article is not entered, according to OCLC input guidelines.

- 260: The program was produced in 1991 and copyrighted by Pipher Films, Inc., but the video was produced in 1992 and copyrighted to GoodTimes Home Video, so 1992 is used as the date of publication.

- 500: A production history note is entered in field 500.

- 505: If parts of a work have their own titles, those titles can be listed in a formal contents note, 505. If it is desirable to make these titles searchable, an enhanced 505 field can be used, with a second indicator 0.

- 710s: The production company and the corporate body mentioned in Area 4 are traced.

TURNER HOME ENTERTAINMENT
Closed Captioned for the hearing impaired
TBS PRODUCTIONS

A CENTURY OF WOMEN

PART 1
Work & Family

...

Directed by Sylvia Morales
Written by Jacoba Alta & Heidi Schulman
=============
[Part 2 has the same information except for the title, "Sexuality & social justice," and the director, Judy Korin.]

[cassette label for part 1]
TURNER HOME ENTERTAINMENT
A CENTURY
OF WOMEN

WORK AND FAMILY
color, Hi-Fi Stereo
Appx. 95 mins.
Cat. No. 3145
Closed Captioned
© 1994 TBS PRODUCTIONS

[The labels for the other parts are essentially the same except for the part-titles and the catalog numbers.]

[container information]

TBS PRODUCTIONS, INC. AND VU PRODUCTIONS, INC. PRESENTS "A CENTURY OF WOMEN"
NARRATED BY JANE FONDA starring JUSTINE BATEMAN OLYMPIA DUKAKIS JASMINE GUY
TALIA SHIRE ...
executive producer JACOBA ATLAS writers JACOBA ATLAS LYNN ROTH HEIDI SCHULMAN

****

Type: g	Audn:	BLvl: m TMat: v Time: 285 Tech: 1
007		v $b f $d m $e b $f a $g h $h o
020		0780605209 (v. 1)
020		0780605365 (v. 2)
020		0780605373 (v. 3)
043		n-us---
090		HQ1426
092		305.4
245	02	A century of women $h [videorecording] / $c TBS Productions.
260		Atlanta, Ga. : $b Turner Home Entertainment, $c c1994.
300		3 videocassettes (95 min. each) : $b sd., col. ; $c 1/2 in.
546		Closed-captioned.
511	3	Jane Fonda, $d 1937-
511	1	Justine Bateman, Olympia Dukakis, Jasmine Guy, Talia Shire.
508		Executive producer, Jacoba Atlas; producer, Lynne Tuite; writers, Jacoba Atlas, Lynn Roth, Heidi Schulman.
538		VHS; hi-fi stereo.
520		Tells the story of women in the 20th century--how they lived, loved, worked, played and, most importantly, changed the course of American history.
505	00	$g v. 1. $t Work and family -- $g v. 2. $t Sexuality and social justice -- $g v. 3. $t Image and popular culture.
650	0	Women $z United States $x History.
650	0	Women $z United States $x Social conditions.
650	0	Videorecordings for the hearing impaired.
700	1	Fonda, Jane.
700	1	Atlas, Jacoba.
700	1	Tuite, Lynne.
700	1	Roth, Lynn.
700	1	Schulman, Heidi.
710	2	TBS Productions, Inc.
710	2	Turner Home Entertainment (Firm)

Figure 4.8   A century of women.

Discussion for Figure 4.8

- 245: This work consists of three volumes and the same actors appear in each of them, but each volume has its own director and production team. Since the three volumes constitute one work, subfield c of field 245 transcribes only the information that is common to the volumes. The containers highlight persons whose contributions are more significant than others, and that information is transcribed in field 508.

- 300 & 538: The sound information is recorded in subfield b of field 300, but the characteristics of the sound are entered in field 538 together with the video format.

- 511s: The first 511 field uses indicator 3 to explain the role of Fonda as the narrator. The second 511 field list the cast members, so indicator 1 is used.

- 505: An enhanced contents note is created, with the second indicator 0, the numbering encoded in $g and the title encoded in $t to make each title searchable.

- 700s: The producers and writers are traced for their contribution to the entire work, and the narrator is traced also. These added entries are arranged in the order in which the names appear in the bibliographic description.

- 710s: The production company and the corporate body mentioned in area 4 are traced according to LCRI 21.29.

WARNER HOME VIDEO

WARNER BROS. PICTURES
A TIME WARNER ENTERTAINMENT COMPANY
The Ladd Company
IN ASSOCIATION WITH SIR RUN RUN SHAW
THROUGH WARNER BROS., A TIME WARNER ENTERTAINMENT
COMPANY

JERRY PERENCHIO
AND
BUD YORKIN
PRESENT

HARRISON FORD

BLADE RUNNER

RUTGER HAUER
SEAN YOUNG
EDWARD JAMES OLMOS
M. EMMET WALSH
DARYL HANNAH
WILLIAM SANDERSON
BRION JAMES
JOE TURKEL
AND
JOANNA CASSIDY
SUPERVISING EDITOR
TERRY RAWLINGS

Figure 4.9   Blade runner (DVD version).

MUSIC
COMPOSED, ARRANGED, PERFORMED AND PRODUCED BY
VANGELIS
ASSOCIATE PRODUCER
IVOR POWELL
PRODUCTION DESIGN BY
LAWRENCE G. PAULL
DIRECTOR OF PHOTOGRAPHY
JORDAN CRONENWETH
SCREENPLAY BY
HAMPTON FANCHER
AND
DAVID PEOPLES

PRODUCED BY
MICHAEL DEELEY

DIRECTED BY
RIDLEY SCOTT

****
END CREDITS
A MICHAEL DEELEY -
RIDLEY SCOTT PRODUCTION

[MANY CREDIT FRAMES: on executive producers Brian Kelly Hampton Fancher ...
Special photographic effects supervisor ... art director, and so on.]
BASED ON THE NOVEL
"DO ANDROIDS DREAM OF ELECTRIC SHEEP"
BY PHILIP K. DICK

© 1991 THE BLADE RUNNER PARTNERSHIP
ALL RIGHTS RESERVED

DISTRIBUTED BY WARNER BROS.
A TIME WARNER ENTERTAINMENT COMPANY

Figure 4.9 continues on page 112.

```
****************************************************************
```

Type: g   Audn: e   BLvl: m   TMat: v   Time: 117 Tech: l

007		v $b d $d c $e g $f a $g i $h z $i q
020		0790729628
028	42	12682 $b DVD Video
090		PN1997
092		791.4372
245	00	Blade runner $h [videorecording[/ $c Warner Bros., ; Ladd Company ; screenplay by Hampton Fancher and David Peoples ; produced by Michael Deeley ; directed by Ridley Scott.
260		Burbank, CA : $b Warner Home Video, $c c1991.
300		1 videodisc (117 min.) : $b sd., col. ; $c 4 3/4 in.
546		Subtitles in English, French, and Spanish; closed-captioned.
511	1	Harrison Ford, Rutger Hauer, Sean Young, Edward James Olmos, Daryl Hannah.
508		Music by Vangelis; photography, Jordan Cronenweth.
500		Videodisc release of the 1982 motion picture.
500		Based on "Do androids dream of electric sheep?" by Philip K. Dick.
500		"The director's cut"--Disc.
500		"The original cut of the futuristic adventure"--Container.
538		DVD format, Dolby surround.
521	8	R Rated.
520		Los Angeles, 2019: Deckard, a "blade runner," must identify and execute four replicants, which have illegally returned to earth from their off-world slave duty.
650	0	Science fiction films.
650	0	Feature films.
650	0	Video recordings for the hearing impaired.
700	1	Fancher, Hampton.
700	1	Peoples, David Webb.
700	1	Deeley, Michael.
700	1	Scott, Ridley.
700	1	Ford, Harrison, $d 1942-
700	1	Hauer, Rutger, $d 1944-
700	1	Young, Sean.
700	1	Olmos, Edward James.
700	1	Hannah, Daryl.
700	1	Vangelis.
700	1	Dick, Philip K. $t Do androids dream of electric sheep?
710	2	Warner Bro. Pictures.
710	2	Ladd Company.
710	2	Warner Home Video (Firm).

Discussion for Figure 4.9

- Fixed field: Because this work is R rated, code e (adults) is used in Audn.

- 245 & 508: One of the major challenges in cataloging films is to determine which corporate bodies and individuals among the many listed in the credits should be transcribed in Area 1. The practice is to record those with overall responsibility for the work. If there are others whose contribution is important, they are recorded in field 508.

- 300: The specific material designation for DVD is videodisc. The presence of sound is recorded in subfield b, but the quality of the sound is recorded in field 538.

- 546: Two language notes are combined.

- 511: Only lead performers are recorded in field 511. Indicator 1 is for cast members.

- 508: This field records people whose contribution to the film is important but not important enough for them to be recorded in Area 1. Catalogers can exercise their judgment in determining if these persons should be traced.

- 500s: These two notes are about the history of this work. They are typical of videos of feature films.

- 500s: The quotation notes explain how this work differs from the others. Since the quotations are not from the title screens, their sources are indicated.

- 521: Rating information is recorded in field 521, indicator 8 is used so that no print constant will be displayed with this information.

- 650s: Following *SCM* H2230, a genre heading, a required form heading, and a heading for closed-captioned films are assigned to this work.

- 700s: The writer, producer, director, cast members, and other contributors are traced. They are presented in the order in which their names appear in the bibliographic description. The name-title added entry is the last of this group because of the order of added entries specified by LCRI 21.29 (CBS 45).

Walt Disney
Masterpiece Collection
Digitally mastered
for optimal video
and audio performance
LUCASFILM LTD
THX
Walt Disney
Pictures

Walt Disney
Presents

Julie Andrews
Dick Van Dyke
David Tomlinson
Glynis Johns
In
Mary Poppins
co-starring
Hermione Baddeley
Karen Dotrice
Matthew Garber
Elsa Lanchester
Arthur Treacher
Reginald Owen
Ed Wynn

Figure 4.10   Mary Poppins.

Director of Photography
Edward Colman
Technicolor
Music and Lyrics by
Richard M.   Robert B.
and
Sherman   Sherman
Music Supervised, Arranged and Conducted by
Irwin Kostal ...
Screenplay by
Bill Walsh
Don DaGradi

Based on the "Mary Poppins" books by
P.L. Travers
Co-producer
Bill Walsh
Directed by
Robert Stevenson

Figure 4.10 continues on page 116.

```
*************************************************************
```

Type: g   Audn: g   BLvl: m   TMat: v   Time: 139   Tech: c
DtSt: p   Dates: 1997,1964

007		v $b f $d c $e b $f a $g h $h o $i q
020		078880684X
028	42	9871 $b Walt Disney Home Video
090		PZ7
092		791.4372
245	00	Mary Poppins $h [videorecording] / $c Walt Disney Company.
250		Fully restored limited ed.
260		[United States] : $b Walt Disney Home Video ; $a Burbank, Calif. : $b Distributed by Buena Vista Home Video, $c [1997?], 1964.
300		1 videocassette (139 min.) : $b sd., col. ; $c 1/2 in.
440	0	Walt Disney masterpiece collection
546		Closed-captioned.
511	1	Julie Andrews, Dick Van Dyke, David Tomlinson, Glynis Johns.
508		Music and lyrics, Richard M. and Robert B. Sherman; music supervisor/conductor, Irwin Kostal; screenplay, Bill Walsh, Don DaGradi; co-producer, Bill Walsh; director, Robert Stevenson.
500		Video release of a 1964 motion picture.
500		Based on the Mary Poppins books by P.L. Travers.
538		VHS; digitally mastered hi-fi stereo; Dolby surround.
521	8	Rated G.
520		An irrepressible nanny soars out of the London skies, bringing a carpetbag of magical adventures into the lives of the Banks family on Cherry Tree Lane. Blends live-action and animation.
650	0	Musical films.
650	0	Animated films.
650	0	Fantasy films.
650	0	Children's films.
650	0	Video recordings for the hearing impaired.
650	0	Feature films.
700	1	Andrews, Julie.
700	1	Van Dyke, Dick.
700	1	Tomlinson, David.
700	1	Johns, Glynis.
700	1	Stevenson, Robert, $d 1905-1986
700	1	Travers, P. L. $q (Pamela Lyndon), $d 1899-1996.
710	2	Walt Disney Company.
710	2	Walt Disney Home Video (Firm)
710	2	Buena Vista Home Video (Firm)

Discussion for Figure 4.10

- Fixed field: Since this film is of interest to many age groups, code g is used in Audn for an item of general interest. The date of the video was inferred from a accompanying material, so code p (multiple date) is used in DtSt and two dates are entered in Dates, the first is the publication date and t e second the original date.

- 028: The publisher's number is enter . in field 028 with first indicator 4 for video and second indicator 2, which will generate a note.

- 090 & 092: PZ7 is used for juvenile belles lettres since 1870. A complete call number will include a Cutter number by the author, P.L. Travers, work letters from the title word, Mary, and a date of publication. In *DDC* single films can be classed in 791.4372 and further arranged alphabetically by film title.

- 245: Because many individuals were mentioned in the item, it is appropriate to list the name of the production company in subfield c and leave the names of these people in field 508. The name of the company, Walt Disney Company, is recorded here to indicate this is a corporate body.

- 250: The edition statement is taken from the container.

- 260: The production firm and the distributor are listed on the box, but the location of Walt Disney Home Video is not provided, so the place is presented in square brackets. The publication date of the video is inferred from an accompanying material, so it is entered with a question mark in square brackets.

- 440: The series information appears on the item, the container, and the box.

- 538: The format and sound characteristics are on the box.

- 511: Major cast members are recorded in field 511.

- 508: Several people who contributed to this work are recorded in field 508 but not all of them are traced.

- 521: The rating information is entered in field 521 with an indicator 8 so that no print constant will be displayed with the information.

- 650s: This film represents several types of films, all of which are represented by subject headings.

- 700s: Only people with overall responsibility for the creation of this film and the lead actors are traced.

- 710s: The original production firm, the producer of the video and the distributor of the video are traced.

■NOTES

1. Available: http://www.loc.gov/marc/marc.html, accessed June 2000.

2. Available: http://www.oclc.org/oclc/bib/toc.htm, accessed June 2000.

3. Patrick M. Dillon and David C. Leonard, *Multimedia and the Web From A to Z,* 2nd ed. (Phoenix, Ariz.: Oryx Press, 1998), 31.

4. Dillon and Leonard, p. 43.

5. Dillon and Leonard, pp. 84–85.

6. Jean Weihs, "Access to Nonbook Materials: The Role of Subject Headings and Classification Numbers for Nonbook Materials," in *Policy and Practice in Bibliographic Control of Nonbook Media*, Sheila S. Intner and Richard P. Smiraglia, eds. (Chicago: American Library Association, 1987), 53–63.

7. Sheila S. Intner and William E. Studwell, with the assistance of Simone E. Blake and David P. Miller, *Subject Access to Films and Videos* (Lake Crystal, Minn.: Soldier Creek Press, 1992), 6.

8. Intner, et al., p. 8.

9. Martha M. Yee, comp., *Moving Image Materials: Genre Terms* (*MIM*) (Washington, D.C.: Library of Congress, Cataloging Distribution Service, 1988).

10. David P. Miller, "Level of Compatibility Between Moving Image Materials: Genre Terms and Library of Congress Subject Headings in a General Library Catalog" in Sheila S. Intner and William E. Studwell, with the assistance of Simone E. Blake and David P. Miller, *Subject Access to Films and Videos* (Lake Crystal, Minn.: Soldier Creek Press, 1992), 17–30.

11. Intner, et al., pp. 4–5.

12. Intner, et al.

13. *Guidelines on Subject Access to Individual Works of Fiction, Drama, Etc.*, prepared by the Subject Analysis Committee, Association for Library Collection & Technical Services, American Library Association (Chicago: American Library Association, 1990).

14. Lois Mai Chan, *Immroth's Guide to the Library of Congress Classification*, 4th ed. (Englewood, Colo.: Libraries Unlimited, 1990), pp. 340–42.

15. Lois Mai Chan, *Dewey Decimal Classification: A Practical Guide*, 2nd ed., rev. for *DDC* 21 (Albany, N.Y.: Forest Press, 1996).

■ SUGGESTED READINGS

Guidelines on Subject Access to Individual Works of Fiction, Drama, Etc., prepared by the Subject Analysis Committee, Association for Library Collection & Technical Services, American Library Association. Chicago: American Library Association, 1990.

Intner, Sheila S., and William E. Studwell, with the assistance of Simone E. Blake and David P. Miller. *Subject Access to Films and Videos*. Lake Crystal, Minn.: Soldier Creek Press, 1992.

Maillet, Lucienne G. *Subject Control of Film and Video: A Comparison of Three Methods*. Chicago: American Library Association, 1991.

Weihs, Jean. "Access to Nonbook Materials: The Role of Subject Headings and Classification Numbers for Nonbook Materials," in *Policy and Practice in Bibliographic Control of Nonbook Media*, Sheila S. Intner and Richard P. Smiraglia, eds. Chicago: American Library Association, 1987, 53–63.

FIVE ← COMPUTER FILES

Library collections of computer files have grown by type and number since the 1960s, and the development of microcomputers in the 1980s contributed to rapid proliferation of computer programs and data files.[1] A recent survey found that 100 percent of the academic library respondents collect computer files, and 93 percent of the public library respondents collect computer files.[2] As computer files become increasingly popular among users, the need to organize them for access becomes stronger. One of the major challenges in cataloging computer files is the lack of uniformity in the information that comes with the work. Some computer files have extensive documentation and tip sheets, while others keep all information on the files and the cataloger needs to install or decompress the files to locate bibliographic information. A related problem is the lack of equipment to read the files. While most libraries will not purchase computer files not readable on their existing machines, some files carry introductory materials in portable data format (PDF) that requires the use of Adobe Acrobat. If this software is not available, the cataloger will have to download it from the Internet and install it on his or her machine. Some knowledge of computer applications and file structure, therefore, becomes important to catalogers. A more serious consideration for catalogers is the need to reconcile information from various sources. The title screen(s), disk label, container, and accompanying material may carry similar information, thus catalogers often need to determine which source to use for the necessary information. For instance, a "README" file may list the system requirements of a program, while the container highlights some of the machinery needed to run it. Similarly, a file may carry a publication date, while its documentation carries a different date, and the container has a third date. Cataloging rules cover problems like these, but it is also a challenge to keep up with the changing standards.

Cataloging rules for computer files have evolved with technology. The second edition of the Anglo-American Cataloguing Rules was published in 1978 when data and program files were stored and manipulated in mainframe computers. As collections of microcomputer files grew in the early 1980s, catalogers realized the inadequacy of the rules designed for machine-readable data files. In 1984, in response to the need for guidance in cataloging microcomputer files, ALA published the *Guidelines for Using AACR2 Chapter 9 for Cataloging Microcomputer Software*[3] and the British Library published a report, *Study of Cataloguing Computer Software: Applying AACR2 to Microcomputer Programs.*[4] The recommendations were subsequently debated and revised into Chapter 9 of the 1988 revision of *AACR2.* Olson's report on how the rules were developed and approved by various national and international bodies illustrates the thoughtful process of rule revision.[5] The rationale for the major changes in Chapter 9 is explained by Weihs.[6] In 1990 the first edition of the *ISBD (CF) International Standard Bibliographic Description for Computer Files* was published by its sponsor, the International Federation of Library Associations' Sections on Cataloguing and on Information Technology. It focused on software programs and machine-readable databases.[7] Many of its recommendations have been incorporated into the latest *AACR2R.*

Technology in the late 1980s made it possible for creators to combine text, sound, music, graphics, video, and other forms to present their ideas. Multimedia applications have soared in the 1990s, and catalogers, once again, realized rules for microcomputer files could not cover multimedia properly. As a result, in 1994, ALA published the *Guidelines for Bibliographic Description of Interactive Multimedia.*[8] A bigger challenge presented itself in the 1990s when the World Wide Web, with its user-friendly graphical interface, became widely popular. The here-today-and-gone-tomorrow nature of Web resources caused serious concerns about their organization. Some have questioned the wisdom in cataloging the Web[9] while others have affirmed the role of libraries in providing access to information.[10] A set of guidelines were developed for the InterCat project, an experiment to determine whether cataloging rules and MARC format could accommodate Web resources, and Olson's *Cataloging Internet Resources: A Manual and Practical Guide*[11] (2nd ed.) has become the standard for cataloging Web resources. In the international arena the International Federation of Library Associations' Sections on Cataloguing and on Information Technology decided in 1994 to review *ISBD (CF)* to determine how well it could cover interactive multimedia, remote electronic files, new developments in optical technology, and files in various formats. The result is the 1997 publication of ISBD for Electronic Resources (ER).[12] Many recommendations of *ISBD (ER)* are likely to be incorporated into cataloging standards in the future.

In this chapter the cataloging rules for computer files are discussed. Rules for multimedia are covered in Chapter Six and rules for remote access files are described in Chapter Seven.

■ MARC FIELDS FOR COMPUTER FILES

The MARC fields commonly used to encode computer files are listed below. Field 006 is required if the Type element is not coded "m." It is also required for electronic serials. Field 007 records additional physical characteristics and is required for all computer files.

Common MARC fields for encoding computer files are:

Type:	m (or others)
File:	Nature of file
007	$a computer file $b SMD $d color $e dimensions $f sound
245 _ _	Title proper $h [computer file] : $b other title information / $c statement of responsibility.
246 _ _	Variant title
250	Edition statement.
256	File characteristics (e.g., computer data, computer programs).
260	Place of publication : $b name of publisher, $c date of publication.
300	Number of special material designation : $b sound, illustration ; $c dimensions. + $e accompanying material.
4XX _ _	Series title ; $v number
538	System requirements.
500	Source of title proper.
521	Audience.
520	Summary.
505 _	Contents.
6XX _ _	Subject headings.
700 _	Contributors.
710 _	Corporate bodies.

Since the completion of format integration in the spring of 1996 catalogers are able to code bibliographic information consistently across formats. OCLC's *Bibliographic Formats and Standards* (http://www.oclc.org/oclc/bib/toc.htm) contains changes that resulted from format integration. Two major changes are related to computer files and deserve attention.

In the USMARC Update no. 3, code "m" for Type of Record ("Type" in OCLC fixed field) was substantially narrowed to cover only computer software, numeric data, computer-oriented multimedia, and online systems or services. Such computer files will have a Type code "m" and the "Type of Computer File" ("File" in OCLC fixed field) element will indicate the nature of the file. Thirteen values have been defined for the "Type of Computer File" element, including code a for numerical data, code b for computer program, code c for graphic data, code d for text documents, code e for bibliographic data, code f for font, code g for game, code h for sound, code i for interactive multimedia, code j for online system or service, code m for combination of files and others. OCLC announced in February 1998 that it would implement the changes, and issued *OCLC Guidelines on the Choice of Type and BLvl for Electronic Resources*[13] in March 1998 to assist catalogers in coding electronic resources. These guidelines were revised in October 1999 and became *Cataloging Electronic Resources: OCLC-MARC Coding Guidelines*.

Another change is the addition of field 006, one of the results of MARC format integration. Field 006 is an optional field that can be used to code items that have material in more than one format—a book accompanied by a CD-ROM, for instance. In such a case, the MARC format for monograph will be used and a 006 field is added to code the electronic aspect of the CD-ROM.

[on the monograph format]

245 00   Web page design cookbook / $c William Horton ... [et al.]

300   xx, 649 p. : $b ill. ; $c 28 c,. + $e 1 computer optical disc (ill : 4 3/4 in.).

and this item will have an 006 com field as follows:

T006: m   AuDn: g   File: c   GPub:

Code m in T006 indicates computer file, code g in AuDn indicates general audience, and code c in File indicates graphic files. Because of this 006 field, searchers qualifying their search statement to computer file format will be able to retrieve this item.

Field 006 has been defined for books, serials, visual materials, mixed materials, maps, scores, sound recordings, and computer files.

006 and electronic serials: Field 006 is also used with electronic serials. Since February 1998 the national standards recommend that the serial format be used for language-based electronic serials and that the computer aspect be represented by a field 006. For instance,

> [on a serial format, with code a (language material) in Type, code s (serial) in Blvd]
>
> 245 00   Proceedings of the ... ACM Conference on digital libraries ...

This item will have an 006 com field:

> T006: m   AuDn: File: d   GPub:

These codes indicate the item being cataloged is a computer file ("m"), no audience is specified ("blank"), and the file is textual in nature ("d").

Field 007 is for additional physical characteristics. After format integration field 007 is **required** for computer files. The subfields and codes include (see OCLC bibliographic format for details) five elements:

Subfield a: computer file	Code: c
Subfield b: physical format	Codes: 11 codes (e.g., disks (j), discs (o))
Subfield d: color characteristics	Codes: 7 codes (e.g., multicolored (c), grey scale (g))
Subfield e: size	Codes: 10 codes (e.g., 3 1/2 in. (a), 4 3/4 in. (g), 5 1/4 in. (o))
Subfield f: sound characteristics	Codes: 3 codes (e.g., silent (blank), sound (a))

Examples:

> A CD-ROM database with grey scale and sound
>
> file: j
>
> 007 $a c $b o $d g $e g $f a
>
> A game file on disk with multicolor and sound
>
> file: g
>
> 007 $a c $b j $d c $e a $f a

■ DESCRIPTION

Rules for Descriptive Cataloging

Rules in Chapter 9 cover published and unpublished computer files, which include computer programs and data files of all types. These files can be encoded on any types of physical carriers, including magnetic disks, optical discs, cartridges, cassettes, reels, and many others. These rules cover computer files that are accessible directly on a workstation, on a local area network, or on the Internet. This chapter focuses on the cataloging of computer files that are accessible locally.

Chief Source of Information

In the course of revising cataloging rules, catalogers learned that cataloging records based on title screen(s) and those based on external sources were quite different, so it was decided that internal sources should be preferred. According to Chapter 9, the title screen(s) is the chief source of information for computer files. If no title screens are available, catalogers may take information from other internal sources such as the main menus, the "about" sub-menu, or program statements. If different amounts of information are presented in these sources, *AACR2R* recommends that the source with the most complete information be used as the chief source.

Disc label:

WAVE-Saver

WATER MANAGEMENT SYSTEM

Version 2.0 for Windows

First screen: Welcome to WAVE●Saver

Transcribed as:

245   00   Wave-saver $h [computer file] : $b water management system.

500   Title from disc label.

If no internal sources present the information needed, the following sources can be used, in order of preference: the physical carrier or its labels, information provided by the publisher or creator (often referred to as "documentation"), or information on the container. The source of the title proper is always recorded as a 500 note.

245 00   Dictionary of organic compounds $h [computer file]

500   Title from disc label.

If a work consists of several physical parts that do not contain a collective title, but the container or its label has a collective title, catalogers may use the container or its label as the chief source. If the information needed is not found in the chief source or the alternate sources described above, catalogers may use, in the order of preference, other published description of the file or other sources to describe the item.

Prescribed Sources of Information

The prescribed sources for each of the eight areas of the bibliographic record are summarized below:

245, 250, 260, 4xx   Chief source (the internal sources),
(Areas 1, 2, 4, 6)   the carrier or its labels, information
                         from the publisher, and the
                         container

256, 300, 5xx, 02x   Any source
(Areas 3, 5, 7, 8)

Information taken from outside the prescribed sources is to be enclosed in square brackets.

9.1. Title and Statement of Responsibility (MARC field 245)

Title proper is transcribed as instructed in 1.1B. The source of the title is a required note (in the 500 field). Catalogers need to keep in mind that there are several possible sources of title proper. If a work has a title screen, a title proper is usually presented there. For works without a title screen, likely sources include the "README" file, "VolInfo" file, the "About this program" option from the pull down menu of the "HELP" page, and many others. When a file is open in Macintosh machines the Apple icon has an option for "About [this file]" which often provides the title screen or similar information. When internal sources are not helpful, catalogers can rely on external ones such as the disc label, documentation, container, etc., to locate information needed for this area.

When a title begins with the phrase "Welcome to ..." catalogers need to consider if the phrase is an integral part of the title. If it is not, the phrase is not included in the title proper.

Title screen: Welcome to Clinical Practice Guidelines on CD-ROM

Transcribed as:

245 00   Clinical practice guidelines on CD-ROM $h
             [computer file]

But when a title is preceded by a phrase that indicates the involvement of a corporate body or a person, that phrase is included in the title proper transcription, according to LC Rule Interpretation 7.1B (CSB 13). A variant title is typically provided for the part following this phrase.

Title screen: Microsoft presents Dragon Games

Transcribed as:

245 00   Microsoft presents dragon games $h [computer file]

246 30   Dragon games

General Material Designation (GMD): The general material designation for all computer files is "computer file" regardless of the type or size of the carrier or the location of the file. The only exception is that "interactive multimedia" is the GMD for interactive multimedia because it is so designated by the 1994 ALA Guidelines. Many catalogers have expressed a need for a better GMD for Internet resources, and *ISBD (ER)* has recommended "electronic resource." Some libraries have adopted "electronic resource" locally, but the term has yet to be approved by the Joint Steering Committee for Revision of *AACR*.

Statement of Responsibility: Statement of responsibility is recorded only if it is prominently presented in the chief source. Persons or bodies responsible for the content of the file should be recorded in Area 1. Persons contributing to the preparation or production of the file and those sponsoring the creation of the file are usually recorded in notes. Such notes are useful in justifying the provision of added entries. Information not taken from the chief source should be enclosed in square brackets.

100 1   Hoffman, J. D. $q (James D.)

245 10   National geochemical data base $h [computer file]
             / $c by J.D. Hoffman and Kim Buttleman.

| 500 | | "MAPPER display software by Russell A. Ambroziak"--Container insert. |

| 100 | 1 | Alverson, David P. |

| 245 | 00 | ZTerm $h [computer file] |

| 500 | | Author: David P. Alverson. |

[Author information is not on the chief source, so it is not transcribed in Area 1.]

9.2. Edition (MARC field 250)

When a file experiences changes in the intellectual or artistic content, a separate bibliographic record is created. To determine the presence of an edition statement, catalogers should look for words such as "edition, issue, version, release, level, update" (9.2B2). Appropriate abbreviations and numerals from Appendices B and C in *AACR2R* should be used to transcribe an edition statement.

It is important to distinguish the edition of a computer file from the edition of an operating system. Only formal edition statements of computer files are recorded, and multiple edition statements are recorded in one 250 field. If the source of an edition statement is different from that of the title proper, a note should be provided. This is because information on the disk label, container, or accompanying material may be different from internal information. Sometimes publishers update a file without updating the documentation, sometimes the other way around. So if the source of an edition is different from that of the title proper, *AACR2R* recommends a note be given.

| 250 | | Version 1.0B3., public Beta test version. |

| 245 | 00 | VendorFACTS $h [computer file] |

| 250 | | [version] 1.0 |

| 500 | | Ed. statement from disk label. |

Some computer files are available for IBM PCs and Macintoshes. A statement such as "Macintosh version" is considered an edition statement. But if a file simply states "Poetry writing for Macintosh," no edition statement should be inferred.

9.3. File Characteristics (MARC field 256)

Area 3 records the content information of the file(s) being cataloged. If information on the type of files, number of records, number of statements, or bytes that constitute the content of the files is readily available, it should be recorded.

Currently acceptable file designations include computer data, computer program(s), and computer data and program(s). These statements are obviously not specific enough. They can be enhanced by terms listed for the "Type of Computer Files" element. For example, if a file is basically textual, "computer text data" can be used.

| 256 | Computer text data and program. |

| 256 | Computer program (1200 statements) |

| 256 | Computer data (10 files : 250 records each) |

CONSER participants do not use field 256, but LC has used this field in its non-serial records. If the information is available, it is a good practice to include it. Catalogers should know that for computer files that are accessed remotely, field 256 is required. *ISBD (ER)* has developed a long list of new terms for this area.[14] If *ISBD (ER)* is incorporated into *AACR*, more descriptive terms such as computer newsletter, computer game, and computer spreadsheet program will be available.

9.4. Publication, Distribution, Etc. (MARC field 260)

The formal publishing statement found in the item is transcribed. Rules for this area are the same as Rules 1.4. Catalogers record the first place of publication, use the shortest possible form for the publisher's name (as long as the shortest form does not cause any confusion), and record the date of publication that applies to the item being cataloged. Distributor information, if available and important, is recorded in Area 4, and catalogers may add a term to clarify the role of a distributor. If several dates are found on a computer file, the date that applies to the item as a whole is used. If several copyright dates are present, the latest one is recorded. For unpublished files, the place of publication and the publisher's name are left blank and only the date of creation is recorded.

| 260 | Kirkland, WA : $b Ars Nova, $c c1992. |

| 260 | [Reston, Va.] : $b U.S. Dept. of Interior, U.S. Geological Survey ; $a [Denver, Colo. : $b USGS Distribution Branch], $c 1995. |

9. 5. Physical Description (MARC field 300)

300	Extent of item : $b sound, color ; $c dimensions + $e accompanying material.

The first element records the number of physical units of the carrier. These specific material designations include computer cartridge, computer cassette, computer disk (for magnetically encoded disks), computer optical disc (for optically encoded discs such as CD-ROM), and computer reel. The 1998 revision of the *Anglo-American Cataloguing Rules* uses "computer optical disc" instead of "computer laser optical disc" for CD-ROM.

If a file contains sound or color, "sd." and "col." are recorded for the second element. The dimension of the physical carrier is recorded in inches. The size of floppy disks is either 5 $\frac{1}{4}$ in. or 3 $\frac{1}{2}$ in., while the standard size of optical discs is in 4 $\frac{3}{4}$ in.

300	2 computer disks ; $c 3 1/2 in.

300	1 computer optical disc : $b sd., col. ; $c 4 3/4 in.

Libraries vary in the amount of information they provide for accompanying materials. Generally, details about an accompanying material are provided if the material is substantial. The following practices are common.

300	1 computer disk : $b sd., col. ; $c 3 1/2 in + $e 1 user's manual.

300	1 computer optical disc ; $c 4 3/4 in. + $e 1 user's guide (35 p. : ill. ; 20 cm.) + 1 installation card.

9.6. Series (MARC field 4xx)

The transcription of this area is straightforward and very similar to that for other types of material.

440	0	U.S. Geological Survey digital data series ; $v DDS-15
440	0	Junior adventures
440	0	Davidson Learning Center series

9.7. Notes

Notes are important to computer files because they help users assess the files without running the files. *AACR2R* stipulates the order in which notes should be recorded, whereas *CONSER* Guidelines instruct participants to enter notes by field number in numerical order. Libraries can select the approach that is most helpful to their users. In this section *AACR2R* prescribed order for notes is followed.

9.7B1a. Nature and Scope Note (MARC field 500): Information about the nature and scope is always presented first. If this information is not clear from the rest of the record, a note should be provided.

> 500   Statistical program with graphic capabilities.

9.7B1b. System Requirements (MARC field 538): This information is critical because it helps users decide if they have the right setup to run a file. This note usually includes the following data elements in the order given:

> 538   System requirements: Make or model of computer;
> memory required; operating systems; software
> requirements; required or recommended character-
> istics of peripherals.

> 538   System requirements: IBM PC compatible; 4 MB
> RAM; Windows 3.1 or later; double-drive CD-ROM.

This string of data may seem confusing, but the note is actually easy to prepare. Information on system requirements often appears on the container, the user's guide, or internal sources such as the "README" file. Publishers usually list the system requirements somewhere in the item. Catalogers may need to rearrange the order of the elements to conform to the order listed above.

If the requirements for several platforms are the same, only one note is needed:

> 538   System requirements: Windows or Macintosh; 8 MB
> RAM; CD-ROM.

But if the requirements are platform specific, a note is provided for each platform:

> 538   System requirements for Windows: 133 MHz Pentium
> computer; 24 MB RAM; Windows 95 or 98; high
> color (65,535 colors) capable 2 MB video card; 8X
> CD-ROM drive ; sound card and mouse.

> 538   System requirements for Macintosh: Power MAC
> 100 MHz; 32 MB RAM; OS 7.6; thousands of colors/
> 640x480 screen resolution.

9.7B1c. Mode of Access (MARC field 538): This note is especially important for remote access files. Previous cataloging practice included the host site of the files. Current practice presents only the information on how the files can be accessed.

538   Mode of access: Company intranet.

538   Mode of access: World Wide Web.

9.7B3. Source of Title Proper (MARC field 500): The source of title proper is always recorded for computer files.

500   Title from title screen.

500   Title from disc label.

9.7B4. Variant Title (MARC field 246): After format integration, title variants are entered in field 246. Such titles can appear in different parts of the chief source or other parts of an item (such as cover title, spine title, running title, and caption title). The first indicator dictates the production of a note and an added entry, and the second indicator specifies the type of variant title.

245 00   History of ships & navies $h [computer file].

246 30   History of ships and navies

246 30   Ships and navies

To produce a special display for a variant title, catalogers should enter the source in subfield i and the variant title in subfield a.

246 1 $i Container title: $a Web publishing with HTML

will produce a note: Container title: Web publishing with HTML and a title added entry: Title: Web publishing with HTML.

9.7B6. Statement of Responsibility (MARC field 500): People and corporate bodies involved in the creation of the file but not included in Area 1 are entered here.

500   Developed by Pixel Technology.

500   Designed by Iris Magic, Inc.

9.7B7. Edition and History (MARC field 500): The source of the edition statement, if different from that of the title proper, should be presented in a note.

500   Ed. statement from container.

The basis of a file's content, if available, should be cited in this note.

500	Based on: Possessing the past: treasures from the National Palace Museum, Taipei (1996).

Publishing history of an item is also recorded.

500	Data and program first released in 1997.

9.7B8. File Characteristics (MARC field 516): Any important characteristics not recorded in Area 3 (field 256) should be given here.

516	Files available in two formats, a multimedia Macintosh file and an NCSA Mosaic hypertext file; all images are in GIF format.

516	Files in ASCII and PDF formats.

9.7B14. Audience (MARC field 521): Audience information is recorded in field 521 if the information is formally presented. Information can appear in a formal statement or an image indicating the age groups intended. If the rating source is present, it can be included. Catalogers should not use personal evaluation as audience note.

521	Ages 9+

521　8	ESRB rating: ages 13+

When the first indicator is blank, a print constant "Audience:" is displayed with the data. When indicator 8 is used, no print constant is displayed.

9.7B17. Summary (MARC field 520): A succinct, objective statement of the contents of a file can be very useful for users. If a description in the file summarizes the contents well, quote it as the summary.

520	A shareware telecommunications program for the Macintosh. It supports ZModem, YModem, Xmodem, Kermit and CIS B-Plus/Quick-B file transfers, VT100 & ANSI-BBS emulation, including colors, and an efficient scroll back buffer.

9.7B18. Contents (MARC field 505): The title of parts of an item can be listed in field 505 if they can help users understand the contents of the item. If there are too many parts, a partial list can be provided. If it is desirable to make the individual titles searchable, a second indicator 0 can be used to create an enhanced content note.

505	0	Disc 1. Reading basics -- Disc 2. Reading adventure.
505	0	1. Painting. Drawing -- 2. Sculpture. Objects d'art -- 3. Near and Middle Eastern antiquities. Egyptian antiquities. Greek and Roman antiquities.

9.7B19. Numbers (MARC field 500): Numbers on an item can be useful for identification purposes. If a number is a publisher's stock number, it can be entered into field 037. If that is difficult to determine, a quotation note is given. If the source of the quotation is not the chief source, it is indicated in this note.

500	"CD92-TGR-42."
500	"ACPHR no. 95-DP10"--Container.

9.8. Standard Numbers (MARC fields 020, 022)

The International Standard Book Number (ISBN) is entered in field 020. If different parts of a work carry their own ISBN, field 020 can be repeated to encode the numbers. The International Standard Serial Number (ISSN) is entered in field 022.

Enhanced CD

Many vocal artists have combined video or multimedia in their recordings to present background information about their songs, concerts, and personal interests. A fairly standard practice is to create an "Enhanced CD," which is a regular audio CD with a multimedia CD-ROM track. To play an Enhanced CD, one needs an audio CD player for the audio portion of the disc and a computer for the multimedia CD-ROM track. Publishers usually label Enhanced CDs prominently on the disc, the case, or the documentation to encourage sale. Because audio CD players cannot access the multimedia CD-ROM track, some publishers include a warning on the disc or the case: "Don't play track one. Track one will play silence or static on audio CD players. Macintosh System 7 or Microsoft Windows 3.1 required (or greater)." Details of the system requirements for the multimedia track and installation instructions are usually included in the "READ ME" file on the Enhanced CD.

The cataloging of Enhanced CDs is the same as that of regular CDs, except for the following parts. First, the cataloger usually provides a note to indicate the item is an Enhanced CD. It can be a 500 note (e.g., An Enhanced CD.), a 520 note (An Enhanced CD of ten songs and a CD-ROM multimedia presentation), or a 505 note (1. CD-ROM Multimedia presentation -- 2. Elsewhere -- 3. Plenty.). Second, the cataloger records the system requirements of the multimedia track in a 538 field, following Rule 9.7B1b. Third, the cataloger records the characteristics of the multimedia CD-ROM track in a computer file 006 field so that the item can be retrieved as a computer file. Finally, the cataloger uses a computer file 007 field to record the physical characteristics of the multimedia CD-ROM. Field 007 is required for all computer files. For example,

Type: j

BLvl: m

006		[m h]
007		s $b d $d f $e u $f n $g g $h n $i n $m e $n d
007		c $b o $d c $e g $f a
028	02	07822-18970-2 $b Arista
100	1	McLachlan, Sarah.
245	10	Surfacing $h [sound recording] / $c Sarah McLachlan.
260		New York : $b Arista, $c p1997.
300		1 sound disc (41 min.) : $b digital ; $c 4 3/4 in.
511	0	Sarah McLachlan, vocals, piano, keys, acoustic and electric guitar ; with vocal and instrumental accompaniment.
508		Recorded, mixed and produced by Pierre Marchand.
500		Enhanced CD.
500		Program notes on container insert.
538		System requirements for CD-ROM multimedia presentation: Macintosh System 7.0 or greater or Windows 95 compatible computer; 6 MB of available RAM; monitor capable of displaying 640x480 screen resolution and at east 256 colors; double speed or faster CD-ROM drive that is multisession enabled.
505	0	Building a mystery / Sarah McLachlan ; Pierre Marchand (4:07) -- I love you / Sarah McLachlan (4:44) -- Sweet surrender / Sarah McLachlan (4:40) -- Angel / Sarah McLachlan (4:30) -- Witness / Sarah McLachlan ; Pierre Marchand (4:45) -- Do what you have to do / Sarah McLachlan (3:47) -- Adia / Sarah McLachlan ; Pierre Marchand (4:05) -- Black & white / Sarah McLachlan (5:02) -- Full of grace / Sarah McLachlan (3:41) -- Last dance / Sarah McLachlan (2:33).
650	0	Rock music $y 1991-2000.

Because this CD is musical, a workform for musical sound recording is used. The code in "Type" is "j" (musical sound recording), and code "m" (a nonserial item) is used in "Blvl." Code "j" in "Type" enables this item to be searched as a musical sound recording.

Field 006 represents the computer characteristics of this item, with "m" specifying this is a computer file, and code "h" in "File" indicating sound file. Because of code "m" in the 006 field, this item can be retrieved as a computer file. The first 007 field (a sound recording 007 field) records the characteristics of the sound recording, and the second one (a computer file 007 field) describes the physical characteristics of the computer aspect of this item. A 500 note identifies the item as an Enhanced CD. Field 538 records the system requirements, listing the elements according to the order specified by Rule 9.7B1b—model, memory, operating system, software, peripherals.

Electronic Serials

Serial publications have appeared in CD-ROM and computer disk formats, but more and more publishers are placing their serials on the Internet. According to a standard directory for serials on the Internet, electronic journals have increased from 27 titles in 1991 to 2,459 titles in 1997.[15] Some of these titles have print counterparts, while others are available online only. The *CONSER Cataloging Manual* provides authoritative guidance for the cataloging of remote access serial files,[16] and the treatment of such files are included in Chapter Seven of this book. For serials on CD-ROM or other types of electronic carriers, catalogers need to consult Chapter 9 (for computer files) and Chapter 12 (for serials) of *AACR2R*. There are many complex cases in serial cataloging. The following section summarizes the most typical approach. Readers interested in more examples should consult Liheng and Chan's excellent guide for serial cataloging.[17]

The chief source of information for printed serial is the title page, or title page substitute, of the first issue, or the earliest available issue. Similarly, in cataloging direct access electronic serials, catalogers begin with the title screen of the first issue or the earliest available issue. If no title screen is available, other internal sources such as main menu or program statements can be used. If no internal sources present the information needed, the following sources can be used, in order of preference: the physical carrier or its labels, information provided by the publisher or creator (often referred to as "documentation"), or information on the container. The source of the title proper is always recorded in a 500 note.

The description of direct access electronic serials is more similar to the description of monographic computer files than different, and many rules discussed above can be applied to such electronic serials. The differences, however, should be noted. First, *CONSER* participants do not use field 256. Second, as typical to printed serials, the frequency of a serial is entered in field 310 and its numeric or chronological designation is entered in field 362. If the description is based on the earliest available issue, a 500 note: "Description based on: ..." is provided. A typical MARC record for a direct access computer file serial without print counterpart therefore looks as follows:

[on a serial format, with Type coded "a," Blvd coded "s"]

T006: m   AuDn: File: GPub:

007	Physical characteristics of computer file
245 _ _	Title proper $ h [computer file]
260	Place of publication : $b publisher, $c date-
300	SMD : $b sound, color ; $c dimension.
310	Frequency.
362 _	Numerical/chronological designation
500	Source of title proper.
538	System requirements.
6XX _ _	Subject headings.
710 _	Corporate body traced.

Two examples of direct access computer file serials are included at the end of this chapter to illustrate this practice.

But if a print counterpart of the serial exists and it shares the same title with the electronic version, a uniform title with a qualifier is used to distinguish the title of the electronic version from the print title:

245	00	Multimedia technology.	<= for the print title
130	0	Multimedia technology (CD-ROM)	<= for the electronic version
245	00	Multimedia technology $h [computer file]	

In addition, a 530 note is added to indicate the existence of another version and a 776 field is used to enter the title of the print version and link the two versions. For instance,

530		Also available in print version.
776	1	$t Multimedia technology $x 2345-5467

Assignment of Access Points

Chapter 21, Choice of Access Points, applies to the selection of access points for computer files also. If a personal author is responsible for a work, the author is the main entry. If a corporate body meets the requirements of Rule 21.1B2, it is selected as the main entry. Since the creation of a computer file often involves many people, most computer files have title as the main entry.

Rules 21.29 and 21.30 provide guidelines for selecting added entries. Corporate bodies named in the publication, distribution, etc., area are usually good candidates for added entries. But no headings should be assigned for the program language, the make and model of computer for which the computer file is designed, or the operating system required for a computer file. Such information is included in the note for system requirements (field 538), which can be made searchable if a library chooses to do so. Earlier records in bibliographic utilities may include 753 fields for these elements, but that practice was discontinued by the Library of Congress in 1996.

■ SUBJECT ANALYSIS

Library of Congress Subject Headings

American Library Association published *Guidelines on Subject Access to Microcomputer Software*[18] in 1986 to aid the subject analysis of computer files. The three principles of the *Guidelines* continue to be valid:

1. The entire record (descriptive cataloging, subject cataloging, and classification) should provide the access needed by the user.

2. Sound practices of subject analysis and classification should be followed to avoid unwieldy files and useless shelf arrangements caused by grouping materials together by form alone.

3. One must ensure that adequate subject headings and linkages exist in *Library of Congress Subject Headings*, and that *Library of Congress Classification* and *Dewey Decimal Classification* have adequate provisions for the subjects covered by microcomputer software. Where standard headings are inadequate, libraries should develop and document their own according to sound principles of subject analysis.

LC's practice reflects many recommendations of the ALA *Guidelines*. *Subject Cataloging Manual* (*SCM*) instructs that the principles regarding the number of headings assigned and the specificity of headings (H180) should be applied to the subject analysis of computer files.[19] *SCM* H2070 recommends that when cataloging a computer program, catalogers should assign at least one topical heading to indicate the subject or genre of the software and add the free-floating subdivision "--Software" to the topical heading. But catalogers should not assign a heading for the named computer program. For instance,

245 00   Songworks $h [computer file]

650   0   Composition (Music) $v Software

The heading of a program should be assigned only to works **about** the program. This practice is explained later.

SCM H2070 also advises that catalogers assign **no headings** for the program language, the make or model of the computer, or the operating systems of a computer file because such information is usually recorded in the descriptive cataloging part of a bibliographic record.

Subdivisions such as "--Computer programs" and "--Software" are frequently used in describing computer files, but there is also confusion over their assignment. According to *SCM*, the free-floating form subdivision "--Software" should be used under each heading assigned to a work. Computer programs intended for children no higher than the 8th grade should be assigned "--Juvenile software." This practice applies to materials with the intellectual level code a, b, or c in Audn and those coded f (for special audiences) but is clearly juvenile in nature.

But catalogers should not assign the subdivision "--Computer programs" to software because this subdivision is **not** a form subdivision and is used only for works **about** computer programs.

In cataloging works **about** software, the practice of Library of Congress is to assign a heading (usually a uniform title) for the named computer program and a topical heading with the subdivision "--Computer programs" to indicate this is a work about the named computer program. For instance,

245 00   Beginner's guide to Songworks. [a book about this program.]

630 00   Songworks

650   0   Composition (Music) $x Computer programs.

SCM H2070 offers details on how to establish headings for named computer programs.

The subdivision "--Databases" is also frequently associated with computer files. *SCM* H1520 defines a database as "a collection of logically interrelated data stored together in one or more computerized files, usually created and managed by a database management system" (p. 1). Before assigning this subdivision catalogers need to examine the file to determine if it is truly a database. For instance,

245 00   Solutions T-PRO database $h [computer file].

650   0   Chemicals $v Databases.

650   0   Poisons $v Databases.

If a file cannot be viewed, catalogers should consider if the item has been presented as a database or if accompanying materials indicate the coding and structure of the data. To a work **about** databases on a subject, "--Databases" is assigned as a topical subdivision (entered under subfield x).

In addition, *SCM* stipulates that for two special categories of material the subdivision "--Databases" **should not** be assigned. If the computer files are "essentially textual in nature" (H1520, p. 3), catalogers are advised to assign only the subject headings appropriate for the textual material. Conference proceedings, full-text databases, literary works, and articles belong to this category. For instance,

245 00   Poetry in motion $h [computer file]

520   Includes original texts of poems by 24 contemporary poets. Also contains the poets' performance and interviews.

650   0   American poetry $y 20th century $x History and criticism.

650   0   Poetry, modern $y 20th century.

The other category includes works for reference, such as "directories, bibliographies, catalogs, dictionaries, encyclopedias, indexes, or other similar types" (H1520, p. 6). Catalogers should assign the appropriate form headings or form subdivision under the subjects. For example,

245 00   ACM electronic guide to computing literature $h [computer file].

650   0   Computer science literature $v Indexes.

Furthermore, for collections of non-textual data that are not encoded for data management, *SCM* also advises against using the subdivision "--Databases."

Classification Numbers

While many libraries use authority lists such as *LCSH* to assign subject headings, the classification of computer files is less uniform. A recent survey found 70 percent of large academic libraries classify computer files by *LCC*, while 64 percent of large public libraries classify them by *DDC*.[20] There are many other different arrangements among libraries.

Both *LCC* and *DDC* treat computer files the same as other materials, and files are classed with the area of applications. For instance, a computer program for accounting is classed with accounting instead of with computer science. The practice of the Library of Congress is to class a software "in the same number in which a book about that software would be classed" (*SCM* F710).[21] If "Special programs, A-Z" is listed under the appropriate number, computer files are classed there. In most cases, computer files are classed in the number for "Data processing" or its equivalent under the appropriate topic. *DDC* has expanded the range for computer science materials and offered instructions for the use of 004-006.

Arrangement

Weihs and Intner both advocate an integrated approach to make computer files browsable.[22] Other benefits include ease of circulation control, aid to collection selection, and support for collection evaluation. The use of the same classification scheme is also useful for closed stacks because the scheme gives users and staff an arrangement pattern to follow. Weihs details procedures to intershelve computer files with the rest of the collection[23] and suggests the use of dummies if libraries prefer to shelve computer files elsewhere. But some libraries choose to shelve them separately from other materials because computer files are subject to climatic and handling problems. For security reasons, some place computer files in closed stacks or treat them much like reserve materials.[24]

Circulation of computer files is a related concern. For books accompanied by electronic materials, public libraries tend to shelve them with the books and circulate them like books. But some academic libraries prefer to place the electronic materials in a separate area to ensure their integrity and security, and patrons need to check out the electronic materials while they check out the books. As for computer files, many large academic libraries load popular files on library computers or networks to encourage access and circulate less popular titles. Some libraries do not circulate computer files at all, and patrons have to make a request for files to be loaded on a network to be used. Similarly, some public libraries only allow in-house use of computer files so that patrons can have expert assistance if needed and the security of the file and the security of the library's network are ensured. Some libraries, however, have found success in circulating software and electronic materials that accompany books.[25]

Cataloging Examples begin on page 144.

■ CATALOGING EXAMPLES

Title screen:

Bookends Pro
3.2
Reference Management Software
© 1988-1996
Westing Software
134 Redwood Avenue
Corta Madera, CA94925

****

Type: m	BLvl: m	File: b
007	c $b j $d n $e a	
090	Z1001.A2	
092	011.0028533	
245	00	Bookends pro $h [computer file] : $b reference management software.
250		Version 3.2 for Macintosh.
256		Computer program.
260		Corta Madera, CA : $b Westing Software, $c c1996.
300		1 computer disk ; $c 3 1/2 in. + $e 1 user's guide (153 p. : ill. ; 22 cm.)
538		System requirements: Macintosh; at least 2 MB RAM (4 MB for System 7); a hard disk with at least 2.5 MB free; System 7 or later.
500		Title from title screen.
500		Ed. statement from disc label.
520		A program for organizing references, citations, and notes. Has several journal specifications built in and can automatically generate bibliographies for a specified style.
650	0	Bibliographical citations $v Software.
710	2	Westing Software.

Figure 5.1   Bookends Pro.

Discussion for Figure 5.1

- File, 007: Code b in File indicates this is a computer program. Field 007 is required for all computer files. The codes specify that this is a computer file ("c") on a magnetic disk ("j") with no color ("n") and is 3 $\frac{1}{2}$ in. in diameter.

- 245: Like most computer files this item has a title main entry. The general material designation "computer file" follows the title proper immediately, so the other title information is recorded after the subfield h for GMD.

- 250: This is an example of edition statements that include information on the type of computer for which a file is intended. Because the source of this statement is different from that of the title proper, a 500 note is created and included below.

- 300: The file is on a magnetically encoded disk, so "computer disk" is used to describe the physical carrier. Because the user's guide is substantial, details of this item are provided.

- 538: Information on system requirements is one of the first notes to be presented. The information appears on the container and the user's guide, but these two sources do not have exactly the same information. Since the user's guide provides fuller information, it is used as the source for the information on system requirements. The source does not list the information in the order specified by *AACR2R*, and the elements are rearranged to conform to that order.

- 500: The source of the title proper is a required note.

- 500: This note is provided because the source of the edition statement is different from that of the title proper.

- 650: *LC Subject Cataloging Manual* advises that when cataloging a software program, catalogers should assign a topical heading for the program with "software" as the form subdivision. No headings for the name of the program should be assigned. Following the latest guidelines in encoding form subdivision, "software" is entered under subfield v.

- 710: Publisher of the program is traced per 21.1B3.

Disc label:

StatView 5
for Macintosh & Windows
1992-98 SAS Institute Inc.

==

Title screen:

Stat View

5.0
3/29/98
Free mem: 95%
PowerPC Version
****

Tell All
****

© 1992-98 SAS Institute Inc.   SAS
****

Type:	m		BLvl: m	File: b
007			c $b o $d u $e g	
090	00		QA276.3	
092	10		519.5	
245	00		StatView 5 $h [computer file] : $b for Macintosh & Windows.	
246	3		Stat View 5	
250			PowerPC version.	
256			Computer program.	
260			Cary, N.C. : $b SAS Institute, $c c1998.	
300			1 computer optical disc ; $c 4 3/4 in. + $e 1 installation instruction + 1 StatView Shortcuts + 1 manual (288 p. : ill. ; 23 cm.)	
538			System requirements for Windows: Minimum CPU 80486; 8 MB for Windows 3.1 or Windows 95; 12 MB for Windows NT; 16-32 MB RAM recommended; 18 MB hard disk space, 20 MB hard disk space for Win32s; Windows 3.1 (requires Win32s, which is provided), Windows 95, or Windows NT version 3.5 or 4.0.	
538			System requirements for Macintosh: Any Macintosh or Power Macintosh (68040 or higher recommended); Minimum 4 MB free RAM (8 MB free RAM recommended); System 7.1; fully compatible with Mac OS 8; math coprocessor recommended but not required.	
500			Title from disc label.	
500			Ed. statement from title screen.	
520			A statistical graphics program that analyzes data and creates reports and graphs.	
650	0		Statistics $x Graphic methods $v Software.	
650	0		Computer Graphics $v Software.	
710	2		SAS Institute.	

Figure 5.2   StatView 5.

Discussion for Figure 5.2

- File, 007: Code "b" specifies this is a software program. Field 007 describes the physical characteristics of this item: computer file ("c"), optical disc ("o"), and 4 ¾ in. ("g").

- 245: When a title appears in different forms in different sources, the fuller form is used. On the disc label "for Macintosh & Windows" follows the title proper closely, so it is transcribed as the other title information in subfield b.

- 250: The edition statement appears on the title screen and is transcribed accordingly. "5.0" on the title screen may be interpreted as an edition statement. But since this information is transcribed as part of the title proper, it is not treated as an edition statement here.

- 260: Publisher information is found in the pull-down menu from the title screen, so it is not bracketed.

- 300: When there are several accompanying materials, all of them are recorded in one subfield e. There is no prescribed order for entering accompanying materials.

- 538: Since the system requirements are platform specific, two 538 notes are provided. The information is taken from the installation instruction and the elements are rearranged so that computer type is presented first, followed by memory requirements, operating systems, software requirements, and peripherals. "Recommended" system information is included in this note.

- 650: Two topics describe the purpose of this program, so two topical headings are assigned, with "software" as the form subdivision.

- 710: Publisher is traced per 21.1B3.

Disc:

Slackware linux 3.0
2 DISC SET. includes ELF BINARIES!
October 1995

DISC 1
Installation & ready-to-run applications

In MSDOD, type
VIEW to start

Walnut Creek
CDROM
suite 260, 1547 Palo Verdes Mall
Walnut Cree, CA 94596 USA
Sales +1 510 674-0783
Made in the USA

compact
DISC
DATA STORAGE
ISO 9660 Format
with Rock Ridge
Extensions

The Internet's
favorite 32-bit
multiuser
operating
system

Shareware requires payment to author if found useful.
Copyright 1995 Walnut Creek CDROM

****

Type: m		BLvl: m	File: b
007		c $b o $d n $e g	
090		QA76.76.O63 $b S43 1995	
092		005.43	
245	00	Slackware linux $h [computer file].	
250		[Version] 3.0.	
256		Computer program.	
260		Walnut Creek, CA : $b Walnut Creek CDROM, $c 1995.	
300		2 computer optical disc ; $c 4 3/4 in. + $e 1 installation booklet (12 p.).	
538		System requirements: 4 MB RAM (8 recommended); 12 MB of hard disk space. Compatible with most Intel PC hardware, from PCI/Pentium motherboard to 386, & supports all modern CDROM drives, sound, ethernet, and mice.	
500		Title from disc label.	
500		"Includes ELF Binaries."	
500		"Includes KERNET 1.2.13 & 1.3.18"--Booklet.	
500		"ISO 9660 format with Rock Ridge Extensions."	
500		"October 1995."	
630	00	Linux.	
650	0	Operating systems (Computers) $v Software.	
710	2	Walnut Creek CDROM (Firm).	

Figure 5.3   Slackware linux.

Discussion for Figure 5.3

- File, 007: Code "b" indicates computer program. Codes in field 007 specify the file is on an optical disc with a diameter of 4 ¾ in.

- 245: Although "3.0" appears with the title proper on the disc label, the file is referred to elsewhere as "Slackware Linux." So the title proper is transcribed without "3.0."

- 250: Version is added to clarify the edition statement.

- 538: Information about this operating system's compatibility with hardware is important, so it is recorded. An alternative treatment is to present this information in a 500 note.

- 500: Because the title and the edition statement are from the same source, no note on the source of the edition statement is provided.

- 500: Several 500 notes are used to record additional files in this package, the technical format, and the publication date of this item.

Title Screen

THE
ENGINEERING
HANDBOOK

CD-ROM Version
Editor-in-Chief
Richard C. Dorf

CRC Press

ISBN 0-8493-8576-8

****

Type: m	BLvl: m	File: m

007		c $b o $d u $e g
020		0849385768
090		TA151
092		620
245	04	The engineering handbook $h [computer file] / $c editor-in-chief, Richard C. Dorf.
250		CD-ROM version.
256		Computer data and program.
260		Boca Raton : $b CRC Press, $c c1998.
300		1 computer optical disc : $b ill. ; $c 4 3/4 in. + $e 1 guide (21 p.)
538		System requirements: IBM or compatible computer with 80486-25 MHz processor; 8 MB RAM; 6 MB available hard disk space; Windows 3.1 or higher; 2x CD ROM drive; VGA monitor with 16 colors.
500		Title from title screen.
520		An electronic version of the Handbook of engineering, with search capabilities, zoom option, hypertext links, line drawings, photographs, bookmark and notebook functions. Users can print, save, and copy information into word processing programs.
650	0	Engineering $v Handbooks, manuals, etc.
700	1	Dorf, Richard C.

Figure 5.4 The engineering handbook.

Discussion for Figure 5.4

- This computer file employs texts and images to illustrate its subjects and connects related information with hypertext links. But it is not considered an interactive multimedia file because the navigation patterns are essentially linear. It has a "tree-and-branch" structure that requires users to explore each level sequentially. As a result, this item is treated as a computer file.

- File: Code "m" stands for combination of file types and is used because the item has text, graphics, and a limited search program.

- 260: The information is located within the file, so it is not presented in brackets.

- 520: The note indicates the source of this file's content and new features provided in the electronic version. This information should help users to determine if the electronic version is useful to them.

- 650: The subject is easy to determine. Form subdivision is entered in subfield v.

- 700: The editor is traced.

Disc label:
**MARVEL
CD-ROM
COMICS**

SPIDER-MAN

© 1995 Marvel Entertainment Group, Inc.
All rights reserved.
Distributed by TOY BIZ, Inc.

****

Type: m	BLvl: m	File: m
007		c $b o $d c $e g $f a
090		PS6728
092		741.5
245	00	Spider-man $h [computer file].
246	3	Spiderman
256		Computer data and program.
260		[S.l.] : $b Marvel Entertainment Group ; $a New York, NY : $b Distributed by Toy Biz, $c c1995.
300		1 computer optical disc : $b sd., col. ; $c 4 3/4 in. + $e 1 installation instructions sheet.
440	0	Marvel CD-ROM Comics
538		System requirements for Windows: MPC compatible 486 SX, 33 MHz; 4 MB RAM free; 2 MB free on hard disk; Windows 3.1; SVGA card and monitor (256-color mode); Sound Blaster 8 or 16 or equivalent sound card; Microsoft mouse or 100% compatible; double-speed CD-ROM drive.
538		System requirements for Macintosh: 68030 processor or higher; 4 MB RAM (8 MB recommended); System 7.0; 640 x 480 screen, 256 color mode; double-speed CD-ROM.
500		Title from disc label.
500		"Developed by Pixel Technologies"--Container.
500		"Interactive CD-ROM comic book!"--Container.
520		Includes a video introduction by Marvel creator, Stan Lee, an electronic version of a Spider-Man story, a Marvel Trivia game, video clips of television shows, and biographical pages of heroes and villains. The "zoom-in zoom-out" feature allows readers to read the book at their own pace.
650	0	Spider-man (Fictitious character) $v Fiction.
710	2	Marvel Entertainment Group.
710	2	Pixel Technologies.
710	2	Toy Biz (Firm)

Figure 5.5   Spider-Man.

Discussion for Figure 5.5

- Similar to the previous title, this item uses multimedia (sound, text, image, and video) to present information. Although the container states that this is an "interactive CD-ROM comic book," the parts of the file are not interconnected, nor can users explore the file at will. Because of the linear paths provided, this item is treated as a computer file.

- File, 007: Code "m" indicates several file types are included. The codes of 007 specify that this computer file ("c"), on an optical disc ("o"), multicolored ("c"), on a 4¾ in. disc ("g"), and has sound ("a").

- 245: The title proper is transcribed as stated by Rule 1.1B1, with the wording recorded exactly but not the capitalization. Because users may look for this item under "spiderman," a 246 field is provided for it.

- 260: The place of publication cannot be located, so "s.l." (sino loco) is used. Information on the distributor is included. Since the location of the distributor is available, it is coded in field 260.

- 440: The container lists X-Men, Fantastic Four, and Iron Man as the other CD-ROM comic books available and urges potential buyers to "get them all." "Marvel CD-ROM Comics" is therefore interpreted as a series title. In case of doubt, an alternative treatment is to present it as a quotation note.

- 538: Two notes are provided because the system requirements are platform specific. The elements are rearranged to follow the order specified by *AACR2R*.

- 500: The company developing the product is quoted here. Because the information is not taken from the chief source, its source is recorded. This note will make it clear to users why Pixel Technologies is traced.

- 500: This statement appears in large print on all sides of the container. Since it seems important, it is presented as a quotation note with the source noted.

- 710: The corporate bodies are traced per 21.1B3 for their involvement in the production of this item.

Disc label:

SMART GAMES
Challenge
1

MAC/PC CD-ROM

© 1996 Smart Games, Inc. Smart Games, Smart Games Challenge 1, the excited nerd cartoon character, and the names and logos of the 20 puzzle categories are trademarks of Smart Games, In. All Rights Reserved. P/N:SGC1CD0001.

****

Type: m	Audn: e BLvl: m File: g	
007	c $b o $d c $e g $f a	
090	GV1493	
092	793.73	
245	00	Smart games $h [computer file] : $b challenge 1.
246	30	Smart games challenge 1
256		Computer data and program.
260		Marblehead, MA : $b Smart Games : $b Distributed by RandomSoft, $c c1996.
300		1 computer optical disc : $b sd., col. ; $c 4 3/4 in. + $e 1 booklet (20 p.)
538		System requirements for Macintosh: Macintosh (030 processor or higher) or Power Macintosh; 4 MB RAM; 5 MB of hard disk space; System 7.0 or higher; CD-ROM drive.
538		System requirements for Windows: 386 SX or higher processor; 4 MB RAM; 5 MB of hard disk space; Window 3.x or above; Sound card; 640 x 480 256-color SVGA graphics; CD-ROM drive.
500		Title from disc label.
500		"MAC/PC CD-ROM."
500		"P/N:SGC1CD0001."
500		"Over 300 games for people with brains!"--Container.
521		Ages 14 to adult.
520		Contains more than 300 games and puzzles of word, mathematics, perception, and strategy, with multiple levels of difficulty and optimization scoring.
650	0	Computer games $v Software.
710	2	Smart Games (Firm)
710	2	RandomSoft (Firm)

Figure 5.6   Smart games.

Discussion for Figure 5.6

- This item is a collection of computer games. Although it makes use of sound and graphics and gives players scores, players have to explore the games in a linear fashion. So this item is cataloged as a computer file.

- File, 007: Code "g" indicates the file contains games. The codes of field 007 shows that this is a computer file ("c"), on an optical disc ("o"), multicolored ("c"), 4 ¾ in. in diameter ("g"), and includes sound ("a").

- 245: Because "smart games" and "challenge 1" appear in different font sizes, they are transcribed as title proper and other title information. A variant title is provided to enable users to find this item under a similar title.

- 260: Information about Area 4 is found in the file. The distributor's information is added and encoded in the second subfield b.

- 538: Two notes are provided because the system requirements are specific to the type of computers. The elements in the source have to be rearranged to follow the order specified by *AACR2R*.

- 500: A 500 note is provided for this "MAC/PC CD-ROM" because it appears on the disc.

- 500: The statement about "over 300 games ..." appears prominently on three sides of a container. It is presented as a quotation note to help users identify this item.

- 521: The intended audience is clearly identified on the container, so the statement is recorded in this note. The audience group includes secondary ("d") and adult ("e"), two of the audience groups listed for the Audn element in the fixed field. Following the OCLC input standards, the code for the higher level is used for the Audn element.

- 500: The "P/N ..." number is on the disc and seems important, so it is presented in a 500 note. If it can be determined that this number is the publisher's stock number, the information can be presented in field 037. According to 9.7B, the note for number is one of the last notes in a record.

- 650: This is a software of computer games, so form subdivision --Software is used.

- 710: The publisher and distributor are traced per 21.1B3.

Disc label:

POETRY
in
MOTION

by Ron Mann

COMPACT
DISC
DIGITAL DATA
QT 11
CDRM1176910

VOYAGER
© Software design. The Voyager Company. 1992, 1994.

****

Type: m	BLvl: m	File: m
007		$a c $b o $d c $e g $f a
020		1559404361
090		PN6101
092		811.5
100	1	Mann, Ron.
245	00	Poetry in motion $h [computer file] / $c by Ron Mann.
256		Computer data and program.
260		New York, N.Y. : $b Voyager, $c c1994.
300		1 computer optical disc : $b sd., col. ; $c 4 3/4 in. + $e 1 user's guide (5 p.)
538		System requirements for Macintosh: Any Macintosh; 2,500K of available RAM (at least 4 MB installed); System 6.0.7 or higher; 13-inch (640 x 480 resolution) or greater color monitor; CD-ROM drive (double-speed recommended).
538		System requirements for Windows: 486SX-25 or higher CPU; 4 MB RAM (8 MB recommended); Windows 3.1, DOS 5.0 or later, MSCDEX; 640 x 480 256-color display; MPC-compatible CD-ROM drive; sound card with speakers or headphones.
500		Title from disc label.
520		Presents the performances of twenty-four contemporary poets such as Amiri Baraka, William S. Burroughs and Alan Ginsberg. Features original texts and the poems as performed. Includes some interviews.
500		"CDRM176910."
650	0	American poetry $y 20th century $x History and criticism.
650	0	Poetry, Modern $y 20th century.
650	0	Poets $y 20th century $v Interviews
710	2	Voyager Company.

Figure 5.7   Poetry in motion.

Discussion for Figure 5.7

- "Type" and "File": This item employs texts and videos to illustrate the beauty and power of poetry. Users select a poet and are able to access the poet's reading, the text as performed, the text as published, and an interview with the poet. Users can play and pause the video clips as desired. The navigation routes, however, are predetermined and linear. For this reason the item is cataloged as a computer file. To reflect the fact that the item contains text data, moving images, and programs for navigation, the "File" element is coded "m."

- 007: The codes indicate the characteristics of the optical disc, which is multicolored and has sound.

- 020: More and more computer files have been assigned ISBN and the number often can be found on the container, as this one was.

- 245: Ron Mann, the person who developed and directed this project, appears prominently on the disc label and is therefore recorded in subfield c of the 245 field and assigned as the main access point (field 100). The names of the selected poets appear on the table of content screen, but such information is not recorded in a 500 note because there are 24 of them. Many people associated with the technical production of the work are listed on the "credits" screens but are not recorded in a note because there are too many of them.

- 256: "Computer data and program" is used to indicate that the item contains data and a program to exploit the data.

- 260: Information on the place of publication and publisher appears at the end of the credits screens. Copyright information on the credits screen includes:

    ©Text of each poem by its author

    ©Motion picture footage, Sphinx Production, 1982, 1992, 1994

    ©Software design, The Voyager Company, 1992, 1994

    Since the computer file brought the texts and videos together, the latest copyright date for the software design is used as the publication date.

- 300: "Computer optical disc" indicates the carrier is an optically encoded disc. The user's guide is included in this field as an accompanying material.

- 538: Two notes are provided because the system requirements are specific to the type of computers. The elements in the source have to be rearranged to follow the order specified by *AACR2R*.

- 500: The note for numbers borne by a file is usually one of the last notes given.

- 650: As a collection of literary works, this item is assigned literary form headings.

- 710: The publisher is traced per 21.1B3.

Disc:

Agency for Health Care Policy and Research
clinical practice guidelines

AHCPR
CD-ROM

===

Additional information about the item:
Container: AHCPR Clinical Practice Guidelines
AHCPR No. 95-DP10
Guide:
AHCPR Information Resources Center
Executive Office Center, Suite 501
2101 East Jefferson Street
Rockville, MD 20852

****

Type: a		
T006: m	Audn:	File: d	GPub: f
007		c $b o $d u $e g
043		n-us---
086	0	HE 20.6520/3:1-15
090		RC46
092		362.1
245	00	Clinical practice guidelines $h [computer file] / $c Agency for Health Care Policy and Research.
246	1	$i Title from container: $a AHCPR clinical practice guidelines
256		Computer text data.
260		Rockville, MD : $b The Agency, $c [1995].
300		1 computer optical disc ; $c 4 3/4 in. + $e 1 guide (8 p.).
490	1	AHCPR ; $v no. 95-DP10
538		System requirements: IBM PC, XT, AT, or compatible; 500 KB RAM; minimum of 2 MB free hard disk space, 300 KB of free disk space (necessary for images only); MS DOS e.1 or higher; a CD-ROM with MS-DOS extensions 2.0 or later capable of reading ISO 9660 format.
500		Title from disc label.
520		Created to enable health care providers to access clinical information on patient assessment and management by the clinical conditions selected. Includes 15 clinical practice guidelines.
505	0	1. Acute pain management -- 2. Urinary incontinence in adults -- 3. Prevention of pressure ulcers -- 4. Cataract in adults -- 5. Depression inprimary care -- 6. Sickle cell disease in infants -- 7. Early HIV infection -- 8. Benign prostatic hyperplasia -- 9. Management of cancer pain -- 10. Unstable angina -- 11. Heart failure -- 12. Otitis media with effusion in children -- 13. Quality determinants of mammography -- 14. Acute low back problems in adults -- 15. Treatment of pressure ulcers.
500		"AHCPR no. 95-DP10"--Container.
650	0	Clinical medicine $x Standards $z United States.
650	0	Medical care $z United States.
710	1	United States. $b Agency for Health Care Policy and Research.
830	0	AHCPR pub. ; $v no. 95-DP10

Figure 5.8   Clinical practice guidelines.

Discussion for Figure 5.8

- Type, File, GPub: Because this item is mainly textual, Type is coded "a" and an 006 field is added to represent the computer aspect, with code d in File indicating textual data and code f in GPub indicating the file is produced by a federal agency.

- 043: When a geographic name is used in the subject heading, field 043 can be added to indicate the geographic focus of the item. The seven-character code is taken from the OCLC-MARC geographic area codes list.

- 086: The SuDocs number of an item, if known, is presented in field 086. The "0" value for the first indicator explains that the source of the Government Document number is the Superintendent of Documents Classification system.

- 245 & 246: The title proper is recorded according to the layout of the information on the disc label. Since an alternative title is found on the container, a 246 field is used to record that title. Subfield i specifies the source of the title and subfield a the form of the alternative title.

- 256: The guidelines are mainly textual, so "computer text data" is used.

- 260: The date of publication is derived from the publication number on the container, so it is bracketed.

- 490 & 830: LC name authority file confirms this is a series, so the series title on the item is recorded in field 490, and the authorized form is entered in 830.

- 520 & 505: Field 520 summarizes the contents while field 505 lists the parts of the file. A medical library may find both notes useful, whereas a public library or an academic library may find field 520 adequate.

- 710: The issuing agency is traced as per 21.1B3.

Disc label

T·H·E
DAEDALUS
ENCOUNTER

MECHADEUS   ONE
TEEN
AGES 13+   mac cd-rom

[around the rim of the disc:
Copyright © 1995 Virgin Interactive Entertainment, Inc. All rights reserved.
Created by Mechadeus. The Daedalus Encounter is a trademark of Virgin Interactive
Entertainment, Inc. Virgin is a registered trademark of Virgin Enterprises, Ltd.]

****

Type: m	Audn: e BLvl: m	File: g

007		c $b o $d c $e g $f a
090		GV1202
092		793.932
245	04	The Daedalus encounter $h [computer file] / $c Mechadeus.
256		Computer program.
260		Irvine, CA : $b Virgin Interactive Entertainment, $c c1995.
300		3 computer optical discs : $b sd., col. ; $c 4 3/4 in. + $e 1 instruction manual (17 p.).
538		System requirements: Macintosh 68040/25 MHz; 8 MB RAM; 4 MB free hard drive; System 7.x; 640 x 480 256 color video; double-speed CD-ROM drive. For best performance: Power Macintosh PowerPC 601/60 or better; 25 MB free hard drive; 640 x 480 thousands of colors; powered external stereo speakers; triple or quad-speed CD-ROM drive.
500		Title from disc label.
500		"mac cd-rom."
511	1	"Starring Tia Carrere"--Container.
521		Ages 13+
530		Also issued for Windows.
650	0	Computer adventure games $v Software.
700	1	Carrere, Tia.
710	2	Virgin Interactive Entertainment, Inc.
710	2	Mechadeus (Firm)

Figure 5.9   The Daedalus encounter.

Discussion for Figure 5.9

- Fixed field, 007: Code g in File indicates computer game. Code e in Audn is used because "ages 13+" covers at least two audience groups listed for the Audn element, and OCLC input standards instruct that the higher group should be used to code this element. Codes in field 007 describe physical characteristics of this item: computer file ("c"), optical disc ("o"), color ("c"), in 4 ¾ in. ("g"), and with sound ("a").

- 245: The relationship between "Mechadeus" and this file is clarified by the information on the rim of the disc, so it is entered in subfield c of field 245.

- 300: Information on the sound and color of the file is entered in subfield b.

- 538: The instruction manual lists the minimal system requirements and the requirements for best performance. This note illustrates how such information is recorded.

- 500: "Mac cd-rom" is on the disc label and indicates that this file is designed for Macintosh machines, so it is presented as a note.

- 511: The featured performer is recorded in field 511 and traced in field 700.

- 530: The instruction manual contains information for PC CD-ROM for Windows and MAC CD-ROM, so this note is provided to indicate the availability of the PC CD-ROM for Windows. If the cataloger feels such a note is not useful to local users, it can be omitted.

- 650: The subject heading describes the nature of the game. Form subdivision --Software is used to indicate a computer program.

- 710: Corporate bodies related to the creation and publication of the file are traced.

Title screens:

SPLENDORS
of
IMPERIAL CHINA

TREASURES from the
NATIONAL PALACE MUSEUM, TAIPEI

---

an electronic catalogue of more than 475 masterworks from the imperial collections of China

COPYRIGHT © 1996 THE METROPOLITAN MUSEUM OF ART, NEW YORK, AND
THE NATIONAL PALACE MUSEUM, TAIPEI

****

Type: m		BLvl: m File: m
007		c $b o $d c $e g $f a
090		N3750.T32
092		709.510747471
110	2	Kuo li ku kung po wu yüan.
245	10	Splendors of imperial China $h [computer file] : $b treasures from the National Palace Museum, Taipei : an electronic catalogue of more than 475 masterworks from the imperial collections of China.
246	30	Treasures from the National Palace Museum, Taipei
256		Computer data and program.
260		New York : $b Metropolitan Museum of Art, New York, $c c1996.
300		1 computer optical disc : $b sd., col. ; $c 4 3/4 in.
538		System requirements for Macintosh: Power PC or 68040 processor; 8 MB RAM (16 MB recommended); System 7 or later; 640 x 480+ color monitor; double-speed CD-ROM.
538		System requirements for Windows: Pentium or 486 processor; 8 MB RAM (16 MB recommended); Windows 95; Windows 3.1 or later; SVGA video card and 640 x 480, 245+ color monitor; Windows-compatible sound card; double-speed CD-ROM.
500		Title from title screens.
500		Produced in conjunction with the exhibition, "Splendors of Imperial China: Treasures from the National Palace Museum, Taipei," organized by the National Palace Museum, Taipei, and The Metropolitan Museum of Art, New York.
500		Based on: Possessing the past : treasures from the National Palace Museum, Taipei.
536		The electronic catalog was funded by a grant from the National Endowment for the Humanities.
520		An electronic catalog of images and details accompanied by essays, glossary entries, artists' biographies, maps, pronunciations of Chinese names and terms and translations.
610	20	Kuo li ku kung po wu yüan $v Exhibitions.
650	0	Art, Chinese $v Exhibitions.
650	0	Art $z Taiwan $z Taipei $v Exhibitions.
710	2	Metropolitan Museum of Art (New York, N.Y.)
730	0	Possessing the past: treasures from the National Palace Museum, Taipei.

Figure 5.10   Splendors of Imperial China.

Discussion for Figure 5.10

- This item contains texts, images, and sound, and links related information for user exploration. But the navigation paths are linear. So this item is cataloged as a computer file.

- File: Code "m" (combination) is used to indicate that the file includes several types of files.

- 090, 092: The LCC number is for this particular museum. The DDC number is built from 709 (art), 51 (China), 074 (museum exhibition), and 7471 (the location of the exhibit, New York).

- 110: This item describes the resources of a corporate body, so the corporate body is designated as the main entry (*AACR2* 21.1B2). The LC Name Authority file lists the authorized form for this body in the romanized form.

- 245: The title screens consist of three screens. The third screen has a more detailed explanation of the file and that information is recorded as the second piece of other title information. An alternative treatment is to present this information in a quotation note.

- 538: The file is designed to run on Macintosh and Windows machines. Since the requirements are platform specific, two 538 fields are provided.

- 500: The exhibition information provides a context for this file.

- 500: This note indicates the source of this file's contents, and the source is presented in a citation format specified by 9.7B7.

- 536: Funding sources are recorded in field 536.

- 700: The name-title entry is added according to Rule 21.30G for related works.

- 710: The Metropolitan Museum of Art is traced for publishing this item. The form is taken from the LC Name Authority file.

Disc label:

FACTS ON FILE
WORLD NEWS
CD-ROM

1998 No. 1   Jan. 1980
                    March 1998

© Facts on File News Services — A PRIMEDIA company.
Software by Electronic Press Services Group — A division of DIGEX, Inc.
Search software by Personal Library Softwrae Inc.

****

Type: a   ELvl: I   Srce: d   GPub: Ctrl: Lang: eng
BLvl: s   Form: Conf: 0   Freq: q   MRec: Ctry: nyu
S/L: 0   Orig: EntW: Regl: r   ISSN: Alph:
Desc: a   SrTp: p   Cont: DtSt: c   Dates: 1998,9999

T006: m   Audn: File: m   GPub:
007   c $b o $d u $e g
090   D839
092   909.0805
245   00   Facts on file world news CD-ROM $h [computer file].
246   30   World news CD-ROM
256   Computer data and program.
260   New York : $b Facts on File News Services, $c 1998-
300   computer optical discs ; $c 4 3/4 in.
310   Quarterly.
362   0   1998, No. 1 (Jan. through March 1998)-
538   System requirements: 486 processor or higher; 16 MB RAM; 7
              MB free hard-disk space (custom install for fastest searching, 25
              MB); Microsoft Windows 3 or Windows95; color monitor, mouse,
              double-speed or faster CD-ROM drive; printer recommended.
500   Title from disc label.
520   Presents the full text of Facts on File since 1980 along with
              primary source documents, photographs, maps, biographies,
              and country profiles. Designed as a universal reference system
              on facts of U.S. and worldside news and history.
650   0   World politics $z 20th century $v Periodicals.
650   0   Foreign news $v Periodicals.
650   0   Geography $v Periodicals.
650   0   History, Modern $y 20th century $v Periodicals.
710   2   Facts on File News Services.

Figure 5.11   Facts on file.

Discussion for Figure 5.11

- Chapters 12 (for serials) and Chapter 9 (for computer files) of *AACR2R* are consulted for the cataloging of electronic serials. Since February 1998 the national standards stipulate that language-based electronic serials be cataloged on **serials format** and that field 006 be used to describe the computer aspect of the file. Field 007 is also used to provide additional details on the characteristics of a computer file.

- Fixed field: Code "s" in BLvs stands for serial; code "p" in SrTp (serial type) stands for periodical; code "q" in Freq refers to quarterly publication; and code "r" in Regl indicates regular publication. For serials two dates are provided, the beginning date and ending date of the publication.

- 006: Code "m" in T006 indicates computer file, and code "m" in File indicates the file contains several file types.

- 007: The codes specify that the file is on an optical disc ("o") with a diameter of 4 ¾ in. ("g").

- 260: The description of a serial should be based on the first issue and the beginning date of publication is recorded in subfield c of field 260.

- 310: This field specifies the frequency of the serial.

- 362: This field records the information about the numerical/chronological designation of a publication when the first issue is available.

- 500: The source of the title proper is always recorded for computer files.

- 650s: Topical headings with subdivision --Periodicals are assigned to indicate the subject coverage of this serial. *LC Subject Cataloging Manual* advises that for electronic serials that are reference-type of works, the subdivision --Database should not be assigned (H1580.5). Both LC and NLM have established "electronic journal" as a subject heading. But "electronic journal" is not a form heading yet.

- 710: The publisher is traced per 21.1B3.

Disc label:

Unclassified
JOINT ELECTRONIC LIBRARY
PEACE OPERATIONS
CD-ROM   JEL-PO-2(U)
December 1995
JOINT WARFIGHTING CENTER
FT. MONROE, VA
ISO
9660
re: Search
Contained copyrighted material
Copyright © 1989, 1992 by MicroRetrieval Corporation

Developed by OC, Incorporated
for the
Joint Warfighting Center

****

Type: a	ELvl: I	Srce: d	GPub:	Ctrl:	Lang: eng
BLvl: s	Form:	Conf: 0	Freq: a	MRec:	Ctry: vau
S/L: 0	Orig:	EntW:	Regl: r	ISSN:	Alph:
Desc: a	SrTp: p	Cont:	DtSt: c	Dates: 19uu,9999	

T006: m	Audn:	File: m	GPub: f

007		c $b o $d u $e g
090		JX1981.P7
092		327.172
245	00	Joint electronic library peace operations CD-ROM $h [computer file] / $c Joint Warfighting Center.
246	30	Peace operations CD-ROM
256		Computer data and program.
260		Ft. Monroe, VA : $b The Center,
300		computer optical discs ; $c 4 3/4 in. + $e 1 instruction booklet (16 p.).
310		Annual
538		System requirements: IBM AT or compatible; minimum 510K RAM; Windows 3.0 or higher; EGA video card; DOS 5.0 or higher; Laserjet printer for printing images.
500		"ISO 9660."
520		An electronic version of documents pertinent to peace operations, including bibliographies; books, articles and papers; doctrine, policy, and JTTP; lessons learned & after action reports; training; and user information. Supports browsing, searching, and printing of documents.
500		Description based on: JEL-PO-2(U) (Dec. 1995); title from disc label.
650	0	International police.
650	0	Peace.
610	20	United Nations $x Armed Forces.
710	2	Joint Warfighting Center (U.S.).

Figure 5.12 Joint electronic library.

Discussion for Figure 5.12

- Fixed field: Since this record is not based on the first issue, the dates element is coded to show the beginning date is not known.

- 006: Code "m" in T006 indicates a computer file, code "m" in File indicates the item contains several file types, code "f" in GPub indicates the file is issued by a federal agency.

- 256: The item contains text files, image files, and a program for searching the texts.

- 260: Since the Joint Warfighting Center is named in the statement of responsibility, the cataloger can refer to it as "The Center" in this area. Subfield c is not included because this record is not based on the first issue.

- 310: This note records the frequency of a serial.

- 500: ISO 9660 is an important technical standard. Since it is on the disc, it is presented as a quotation note.

- 500: When the first issue is not the basis for a record, the issue used should be noted. This note is usually combined with the note on the source of the title proper.

- 650s & 610: This item contains mainly full-text documents. Because LC recommends against assigning subdivision --Databases to files that are mainly textual (H1520). The 610 heading is the authorized form for UN peacekeeping forces.

■NOTES

1. Sheila S. Intner, "Intellectual Access to Patron-Use Software," *Library Trends* 40, no. 1 (summer 1991): 42–62.

2. Ingrid Hsieh-Yee, "Organization of Nonprint Resources in Public and Academic Libraries," unpublished report, May 30, 1999.

3. *Guidelines for Using AACR2 Chapter 9 for Cataloging Microcomputer Software* (Chicago: ALA, 1984).

4. Ray Templeton and Anita Witten, *Study of Cataloguing Computer Software: Applying AACR2 to Microcomputer Programs* (London: British Library, 1984).

5. Nancy B. Olson, "History of Organizing Microcomputer Software," in *The Library Microcomputer Environment: Management Issues*, edited by Sheila S. Intner and Jane Anne Hannigan (Phoenix: Oryx Press, 1988), 22–34.

6. Jean Weihs, "Organizing the Collection: State of the Art," in *The Library Microcomputer Environment: Management Issues*, edited by Sheila S. Intner and Jane Anne Hannigan (Phoenix: Oryx Press, 1988), 35–44.

7. *ISBD (CF): International Standard Bibliographic Description for Computer Files* (London: IFLA Universal Bibliographic Control and International MARC programme, 1990).

8. *Guidelines for Bibliographic Description of Interactive Multimedia* (Chicago: American Library Association, 1994).

9. See, for example, Kyle Banerjee, "Describing Remote Electronic Documents in The Online Catalog: Current Issues," *Cataloging & Classification Quarterly* 25 (Number 1 1997): 5–20.

10. See, for example, Carol A. Mandel, and Robert Wolven, "Intellectual Access to Digital Documents: Joining Proven Principles with New Technologies," *Cataloging & Classification Quarterly* 22, nos. 3/4 (1996): 25–42 and Norman Oder, "Cataloging the Net: Can We Do It?" *Library Journal* 123 (October 1, 1998): 47–51.

11. Nancy B. Olson, ed., *Cataloging Internet Resources: A Manual and Practical Guide*, 2nd ed. (Dublin, Ohio: OCLC, 1997).

12. *ISBD (ER): International Standard Bibliographic Description for Electronic Resources* (Munchen: K. G. Sauer, 1997).

13. Available: http://www.oclc.org/oclc/cataloging/type.htm, accessed June 2000.

14. Ann Sandberg-Fox and John D. Byrum, "From ISBD (CF) to ISBD (ER): Process, Policy, and Provisions," *Library Resources & Technical Services* 42 (April 1998), 89–101.

15. Dru W. Mogge, ed., *Directory of Electronic Journals, Newsletters and Academic Discussion Lists*. 7th ed. (Washington, D.C.: Association of Research Libraries, 1997).

16. *CONSER Cataloging Manual Module 31: Remote Access Computer File Serials*, available: http://lcweb.loc.gov/acq/conser/module31.html, accessed June 2000.

17. Carol Liheng and Winnie S. Chan, *Serial Cataloging Handbook*, 2nd ed. (Chicago: American Library Association, 1998).

18. *Guidelines on Subject Access to Microcomputer Software* (Chicago: American Library Association, 1986).

19. *Library of Congress, Subject Cataloging Manual: Subject Headings*, 5th ed. (Washington, D.C.: Cataloging Distribution Service, Library of Congress, 1996).

20. Ingrid Hsieh-Yee, "Organization of Nonprint Resources in Public and Academic Libraries," unpublished report, May 30, 1999.

21. *Library of Congress, Subject Cataloging Manual: Classification* (Washington, D.C.: Cataloging Distribution Service, Library of Congress, 1992).

22. See, for example, Intner (1991) and Weihs (1988).

23. Jean Weihs, *The Integrated Library: Encouraging Access to Multimedia Materials*, 2nd ed. (Phoenix, Ariz.: Oryx Press, 1991).

24. Denise M. Beaubien, Bruce Emerton, Erich Kesse, Alice Primack, and Colleen Seale, "Patron-Use Software in Academic Library Collections," *College & Research Library News* 49 (November 1988): 661–67.

25. See, for example, Jean Polly, "Circulating Software: Some Sensible Groundrules," *Wilson Library Bulletin* 60 (June 1986): 20–22; and Scott Seaman and Nancy Carter, "Do Not Desensitize: Developing a Policy for Accompanying Electronic Materials," *Information Technology and Libraries* 16 (June 1997): 86–92.

■ SUGGESTED READINGS

Coyle, Karen, ed. *Format Integration and Its Effect on Cataloging, Training, and Systems.* Chicago: American Library Association, 1993.

Intner, Sheila S. "Intellectual Access to Patron-Use Software," *Library Trends* 40, no. 1 (summer 1991): 42–62.

Sandberg-Fox, Ann, and John D. Byrum. "From ISBD (CF) to ISBD (ER): Process, Policy, and Provisions," *Library Resources & Technical Services* 42 (April 1998), 89–101.

Seaman, Scott, and Nancy Carter. "Do Not Desensitize: Developing a Policy for Accompanying Electronic Materials," *Information Technology and Libraries* 16 (June 1997): 86–92.

Weitz, Jay. 1999. *Cataloging Electronic Resources: OCLC-MARC Coding Guidelines.* Available: http://www.oclc.org/oclc/cataloging/type.htm (Accessed June 2000).

SIX ← INTERACTIVE MULTIMEDIA

Cataloging rules for computer files have evolved since the publication of the *Anglo-American Cataloguing Rules* in 1978. While the rules for cataloging of computer files had stabilized in the late 1980s (notably Chapter 9 of *AACR2R*), the inadequacy of these rules in describing interactive multimedia became obvious. After years of deliberation and discussion, American Library Association published *Guidelines for Bibliographic Description of Interactive Multimedia* to assist catalogers in describing interactive multimedia.[1] These *Guidelines* supplement the second edition, 1988 revision of the *Anglo-American Cataloguing Rules*. Catalogers are to consult Chapter 9 of *AACR2R* and the *Guidelines* when cataloging interactive multimedia. Where the two differ catalogers should prefer the 1994 *Guidelines*.

Interactive multimedia resources make use of computer technology, video technology, and sound technology to present a work that combines two or more media formats (text, images, or sound) and support users' nonlinear navigation within the work. The 1994 *Guidelines* provide a definition of interactive multimedia and instructions on how to identify the chief and prescribed sources of information, and information related to areas 1, 2, 4, 5, and 7. They stipulate that an interactive multimedia can reside in one or more physical carriers or be retrievable via computer networks. Two characteristics are essential for determining whether a work is an interactive multimedia. First, it should support "user-controlled, nonlinear navigation" (p. 1) by computer technology. Second, the item should make use of two or more media. Specifically, the guidelines recommend that catalogers consider the following issues:

1. The use of sophisticated computer technology in the work. The cataloger needs to determine if a work requires the use of a microcomputer, a Level III or higher videodisc player, or sophisticated computer technology, because such technology is required in interactive multimedia.

2. The level of interactivity. The cataloger can determine the levels of interactivity built into the work by its designer by reading documentation and using the work.

3. The support for nonlinear navigation. Nonlinear navigation refers to a user's ability to explore the work by hyperlinks or other similar features and to retrieve information "freely or randomly" (p. 3). The cataloger can obtain this information by reading documentation or descriptive materials for the work or testing the work.

4. Hardware requirements. System requirements often reveal the nature of a work. Any requirement for sound boards, video playback programs (such as QuickTime), a videodisc player, or a multimedia computer suggests that a work is an interactive multimedia.

5. Descriptive phrases. Words such as interactive media, multimedia, new media, and hypermedia, may suggest an interactive multimedia work. But the presence of such words should not be taken literally. The cataloger should always consider if a work contains the two defining characteristics mentioned above: user-controlled nonlinear navigation and the use of two or more media.[2]

In addition, the *Guidelines* list several types of material that should not be considered interactive multimedia. They include "textual or graphic applications software programs ... computer-assisted instruction (CAI), database management systems, graphical user interface systems (GUI), children's books which present text, audio and/or graphics in linear fashion, primarily textual databases with some graphics or images, and video games employing predetermined software paths" (p. 4). The *Guidelines* also warn against treating works that were published and cataloged separately earlier as a set and regard them as interactive multimedia. After considering the above issues and reviewing the categories that should not be considered interactive multimedia, if the cataloger has any doubt about the nature of a work, it should not be treated as interactive multimedia.

The major challenge in cataloging interactive multimedia is to determine if a work is indeed interactive multimedia. The *Guidelines* offer helpful instructions, but the application of the rules still requires judgment. It is usually easy to identify the number of media contained in a work, but the interactive aspect requires actual interaction with the work. Another difficulty is that sometimes different parts of a work present the same type of information differently. For instance, "Macintosh" appears at the head of the title on the disc, but it is "Macintosh version" on the container, and "Macintosh edition" on accompanying material. The cataloger will need to determine whether these statements are meant to specify the type of computer required to run the program or to indicate a new edition.

■ MARC FIELDS FOR INTERACTIVE MULTIMEDIA

The MARC fields commonly used to encode interactive multimedia are the same as those for computer files. The Type element is almost always coded "m" for non-serial interactive multimedia because such works contain more than one media and require the use of computer technology. The File element is code i for the interactive aspect. Field 007 is required for all files with code m in Type.

Type:	m	
File:	i (for interactive multimedia)	
007	$a computer file $b SMD $d color $e dimensions $f sound	
245 _ _	Title proper $h [interactive multimedia] : $b other title information / $c statement of responsibility.	
250	Edition statement.	
256	File characteristics (computer data, program, or both)	
260	Place of publication : $b name of publisher, $c date of publication.	
300	Number of special material designation : $b sound, color, etc. ; $c dimension + $e accompanying material.	
4XX _ _	Series statement	
538	System requirements note	
538	Mode of access (for works located remotely)	
500	Source of title proper. (A required note)	
500	Persons involved in the creation of the entire work.	
520	Summary.	
505 _	Contents note listing individually named parts of the work.	
6XX _ _	Subject added entries.	
700 _	Personal name added entry.	
710 _	Corporate body added entry.	
730 _ _	Uniform title.	

■ DESCRIPTION

Rules for Descriptive Cataloging

Chief Source of Information

Unlike other media, the chief source of information for interactive multimedia is **the entire work**, which according to the *Guidelines*, includes internal sources such as title screens or title frames and external sources such as carrier labels, container, and printed or online accompanying textual materials. Catalogers should look for "information that applies to the work as a whole and that includes a collective title" (p. 4). If these sources present information in varying fullness, the source with **the most complete information** is preferred.

If these sources do not present the needed information, catalogers may take information from other published description of the work (this source is preferred) or other sources such as the publisher's brochures.

The source of the title proper for an interactive multimedia should always be recorded in a note (field 500). This practice is consistent with the treatment of computer files in *AACR2R*.

Prescribed Sources of Information

The prescribed sources of the areas are summarized below:

245, 250, 260, 4xx (Areas 1, 2, 4, 6)	Chief source (the entire work)
300, 5xx, 02X (Areas 5, 7, 8)	Any source (chief source, published description, other sources.)

Area 1. Title Proper and Statement of Responsibility (MARC field 245)

The chief source of information should include a title for the entire work. When several forms of the title appear in the chief source, the *Guidelines* recommend that the fullest title be used as the title proper. If this is not possible, the cataloger should select as title proper the title that best represents the work.

Title screen: JULIA CHILD

                   Home Cooking with Master Chefs

Disc label: JULIA CHILD

                   Home Cooking with Master Chefs
                   Interactive Cooking Lessons from 16 All-Star Chefs

User guide: Home Cooking with Master Chefs

                   Interactive Cooking Lessons from 16 All-Star Chefs

Transcribed as:

245 00   Julia Child $h [interactive multimedia] : $b home
                   cooking with master chefs : interactive cooking
                   lessons from 16 all-star chefs.

246 30   Home cooking with master chefs

500   Title from disc label.

General Material Designation (GMD): A new GMD, "interactive multimedia," was formulated for interactive multimedia.

Statement of Responsibility: Individuals responsible for the entire work are recorded in area 1 and persons involved in the creation of parts of the work are recorded in a note if they are considered important.

245 00   Medieval realms $h [interactive multimedia] : $b
                   Britain 1066 to 1500 / $c produced by the British
                   Library.

508   Project managers, Karen Brookfield and Roger
                   Watson ; software development, Sadler Johnson
                   and Mike Peterson.

Area 2. Edition (MARC field 250)

The edition statement that applies to the item as a whole is entered in field 250. If it is not clear whether a statement covers the entire work, it is recorded in a note. Because different parts of a multimedia may carry different information, the *Guidelines* require that the source of the edition statement be recorded in a note. Some catalogers have combined the edition source note with the source note for the title proper.

250	Interactive ed.
500	Ed. statement from disc label.
250	Version 2.0 for Windows.
500	Title from title screen.
500	Ed. statement from container.

Area 3. File Characteristics (MARC field 256)

Currently computer data, computer programs, and computer data and program(s) can be used in this field. Because interactive multimedia by definition must includes two or more types of media, "computer data and program" is frequently used for this area, even though they are clearly not specific enough about the nature of the files. *ISBD (ER)* has listed many more descriptive terms for file characteristics. If adopted in the next version of the standard cataloging rules, terms such as computer games will become available for better description.

Area 4. Publication, Distribution, Etc. (MARC field 260)

The place of publication and the name of the publisher should be recorded according to *AACR2R*. As for the date information, the *Guidelines* recommend the use of the **latest date**. When the dates of parts of the work appear in a work, the cataloger should consider all dates as applying to the entire work and use the latest date in Area 4. The most typical date seen on interactive multimedia is the copyright date.

Area 5. Physical Description (MARC field 300)

300	Number of specific material designation : $b sound, color, etc. ; $c dimension + $e accompanying material.

The specific material designations for interactive multimedia depend on the type of physical carrier used to store the information. Files created with older technology may have "videodisc" as the carrier, whereas more recent interactive files tend to be stored on laser optical disc. Rules 9.5 list several SMDs for computer files. The *Guidelines* recommend that "disc" be used for computer optical disc such as CD-ROM and "disk" be used for disks that are magnetically encoded. If a work is on one physical carrier, the rules for physical description in Part I of *AACR2R* (rules x.5 of the appropriate chapters) should be followed.

300	1 videodisc (90 min.) : $b sd., col. ; $c 12 in. + $e 1 booklet.
300	2 computer optical discs : $b sd., col. ; $c 4 3/4 in. $e 1 user guide.

If a work has multiple physical carriers, methods (a) and (b) of rule 1.10C2 of *AACR2R* should be used. This means the cataloger has two options: (a) to describe the carriers in one 300 field or (b) to provide a separate statement for each carrier (repeating the 300 field as necessary). Method (c) of 1.10C2 should not be used.

245	00	Dead Sea scrolls revealed $h [interactive multimedia]
300		1 computer optical disc : $b sd., col.; $c 4 3/4 in. + $e 1 computer disk (3 1/2 in.) + 1 vial of sand.

The cataloger should keep in mind that interactive multimedia may be retrievable through computer networks. But for any work that is available only remotely, no area 5 should be provided. This practice is consistent with the treatment of remotely accessed computer files in Chapter 9 of *AACR2R*.

245	00	Grandcascade SMF Textures Series MIDI files $h [interactive multimedia]
538		Mode of access: Internet.
856	40	$z For instructional purposes use only at UVA $u http://www.lib.virginia.edu/dmc/midi.html

[Field 538 and field 856 indicate this work is available on the Internet. Field 300 is therefore not provided.]

Area 6. Series (MARC field 4xx)

This area is recorded per Rules x.6 of the appropriate chapters in Part I of *AACR2R*.

440	0	Microsoft Home
440	0	Golden books interactive

Area 7. Notes

While notes are optional for interactive multimedia, they are very important for users to understand the work. The order of the notes is the same as that specified by Rules 9.7. Catalogers should note that *CONSER* participants enter notes in numerical order. Before they make an effort to present the notes in proper order, catalogers should know how notes are processed by their local online system to avoid unnecessary frustration. The notes that are commonly provided for interactive multimedia are discussed below.

System Requirements (MARC field 538): If a work is on one physical carrier, one system requirements note is given. This note is one of the most important ones for interactive multimedia and is often presented first. Following *AACR2R* the *Guidelines* specify the elements and their order as follows:

the make and model of computer(s) or videodisc player to run the files;

the memory required;

the operating system;

the software requirements (and the programming language);

the kind and characteristics of any required or recommended peripherals.

538   System requirements: Macintosh LC II; 4 MB RAM; System 7.0 or above; 13" or larger 256 color monitor; CD-ROM drive.

If a work can be played on several systems, a separate note is provided for the requirements of each system:

538   System requirements for Macintosh: Mac LC III or higher (040 recommended); 8 MB RAM; double-speed CD ROM drive; 13" monitor or larger.

538   System requirements for PC: MPC 386 DX or higher (486 recommended); 8 MB RAM; double-speed CD ROM drive; sound card; SVGA monitor.

If a work is on several physical carriers, the cataloger can record system requirements for the carriers in one note or list the requirements for each carrier individually, repeating field 538 as needed.

538   System requirements: 386 16 Mhz IBM compatible computer; 4 MB RAM or better; 3.5" 1.44 MB floppy drive and hard disk (3 MB) ; MS-DOS 5.0 or higher ; Microsoft windows 3.1 ; MCI Laserdisc drivers for Windows ; printer optional.

Alternative treatment:

538	System requirements: 386 16 Mhz IBM compatible computer; 4 MB RAM or better; 3.5" 1.44 MB floppy drive and hard disk (3 MB); MS-DOS 5.0 or higher; Microsoft windows 3.1; printer optional.
538	System requirements: MCI Laserdisc drivers for Windows.

Mode of Access (MARC field 538): If an interactive multimedia is only available remotely, this note should be given. The old practice to include the address of the site that hosts the file has been discontinued.

538	Mode of access: Internet.

Languages (MARC field 546): If an item involves more than one language, that should be noted in field 546 and coordinated with the "Lang" element in the fixed field and field 041.

Lang: eng

041	engfre
546	Text in English and French.

If special language provision is provided for a particular group, the information is presented in field 546 also.

546	Closed-captioned.

Source of Title Proper (MARC field 500): This is a required note.

500	Title from title screen.
500	Title from disc label.

Variant Titles (MARC field 246): Variations to the title proper, if important, should be recorded in field 246 so that additional access points can be provided. Because interactive multimedia usually appear on several carriers and variant titles can appear in documentation or on container, it is not uncommon for such files to have several 246 fields.

245	00	Critical mass $h [interactive multimedia] : $b America's race to build the atomic bomb.
246	30	America's race to build the atomic bomb

Statements of Responsibility (MARC fields 500, 511, 518): If the statement of individuals responsible for the entire work is lengthy, an optional treatment is to record such a statement in a note. Individuals responsible for only aspects or parts of the work may be given in a note if the cataloger consider them important. Performances in motion pictures, videorecordings, and sound recordings that are part of the interactive multimedia, if judged to be important by the cataloger, may be given in the note area. In these instances, fields 511 (for cast) or 508 (for production credits) should be used.

508   Programmer, Daniel Beer; producer, Paul Benedetti.

Edition and History (MARC field 500): If an interactive multimedia includes materials published before, that information should be given in a note. The source of the edition statement is always noted. Some catalogers have combined this note with the note for the source of the title proper.

245   00   Living cells.

250   Version 1.0

500   Title from container.

500   Ed. statement from disc label.

Physical Description (MARC field 500): Important physical details of the work that are not included in area 5 should be given in a note. Sound characteristics such as stereo can be recorded in a 500 note.

Summary (MARC field 520): A succinct, unbiased summary of the content of an interactive multimedia should be prepared unless the rest of the record provides enough details.

245   00   Multimedia Beethoven $h [interactive multimedia] : $b the Ninth symphony, an illustrated interactive musical exploration.

520   Robert Winter examines Beethoven's Ninth symphony as performed by the Vienna State Opera Chorus and Vienna Philharmonic Orchestra in an illustrated and interactive program.

245   00   The art historian $h [interactive multimedia]

520   Presents a comprehensive collection of images of art works from all periods together with text and audio. Offers multiple options for navigation and allows the user to compile customized presentations.

Contents (MARC field 505): If the parts of an interactive multimedia are individually named, a contents note can be given to present such information. Catalogers can make the titles searchable by tagging the second indicator 0.

> 505　0　　　History -- Great dreadnoughts -- Famous liners -- U.S. Navy -- British Navy -- Freighters -- WWII -- Great sailing ships -- Cruise ships.

Assignment of Access Points

The *Guidelines* recommend that catalogers follow rules in Part II of *AACR2R*. The main entry for interactive multimedia works tend to be the title because there are usually many people or bodies involved in the creation. Persons or bodies responsible for the entire content of the work may be assigned the main entry depending on the number of persons or bodies involved. If there are more than three persons or bodies involved and the principal responsibility is not attributed to any one, then title should be the main entry. Added entries should be assigned according to Rules 21.29 and 21.30 of *AACR2R*. If a person is responsible for only parts of the work, and if that responsibility is considered important, an added entry can be made for that person.

■ SUBJECT ANALYSIS

Interactive multimedia are treated in the same manner as other materials when analyzed for subject. Instructions in *SCM* for the assignment of subject headings (H180) apply to this type of material. For topical multimedia, appropriate topical headings are assigned and form subdivision "--Interactive multimedia" are used. The form subdivision is usually the last element in a subject heading string. If a form subdivision is used, it should be used with all topical headings assigned to a work.

> 245　00　　　History of ships & navies $h [interactive multimedia].
>
> 650　0　　　Ships $x History $v Interactive multimedia.
>
> 650　0　　　Navies $x History $v Interactive multimedia.
>
> 610　10　　　United States. $b Navy $x History $v Interactive multimedia.

Since interactive multimedia are a kind of computer file, the classification and shelf arrangement of interactive multimedia are the same as the organization of computer files. Readers are referred to Chapter Five for a discussion of the classification and arrangement of computer files.

■ CATALOGING EXAMPLES

Disc label:

THE
AMERICAN HERITAGE
TALKING DICTIONARY

WINDOWS 96
COMPATIBLE
WINDOWS 3.1

COMPACT
DISC
DIGITAL DATA   **SoftKey**

© 1998 Learning Company Properties Inc., a subsidiary of The Learning Company, Inc., and its licensors. All rights reserved. ...

AMH744CE-CD

****

Type: m	BLvl: m	File: i
007		c $b o $d c $e g $f a
020		0763022713
090		PE1628
092		423
245	04	The American Heritage talking dictionary $h [interactive multimedia].
246	30	Talking dictionary
256		Computer data and programs.
260		Cambridge, MA : $b SoftKey, $c c1998.
300		1 computer optical disc : $b sd., col., ; $c 4 3/4 in. + $e 1 installation sheet.
538		System requirements for IBM: IBM PC or compatible, 386/25 or higher; 4 MB RAM; 2 MB hard disk (18 MB if dictionary resides on hard disk); Windows 3.1 or higher; CD-ROM drive; 8-bit sound card (MPC-compliant).
538		System requirements for Macintosh: Any Macintosh; 2 MB RAM (System 6.x), 4 MB (System 7), 500K hard disk (15 MB if dictionary resides on hard disk); CD-ROM drive.
500		Title from disc label.
520		Contains The American Heritage dictionary of the English language, The dictionary of cultural literacy, and an English electronic thesaurus. Provides definitions, proper usage, hyphenation, idioms, synonyms, homographs, pronunciations and inflections, abbreviation, and sample sentences. Supports random searches, searches by word fragment and retrieval by definition.
500		"AMH744CE-CD."
650	0	English language $x Dictionaries $v Interactive multimedia.
650	0	English language $x Synonyms and antonyms $v Interactive multimedia.
700	12	Hirsch, E. D. $q (Eric Donald), $d 1928- $t Dictionary of cultural literacy.
710	2	SoftKey International, Inc.
730	02	American Heritage dictionary of the English language.

Figure 6.1   The talking dictionary.

Discussion for Figure 6.1

- This item combines texts, images, and sound, and supports random access to words, phrases, and concepts, so it is cataloged as an interactive multimedia.
- Type, 007: All interactive multimedia files make use of computer technology and are recorded on the computer format (code "m" in Type). Field 007 describes physical characteristics of this item: computer file ("c"), optical disc ("o"), colored ("c"), 4 ¾ in. in diameter ("g"), and with sound ("a").
- 245 & 246: The title proper is transcribed according to Rule 1.1B1. Since "talking dictionary" is more prominent by typography, a variant title is provided for it. Indicator 3 will produce an added entry but not a note for this title, indicator 0 explains this title is part of the title proper.
- 250: Although the copyrights of several parts of this work are found in the "copyrights" page, there is no edition statement that covers the entire work. So no edition statement is provided.
- 256: The item contains data files and programs to search them, so this phrase is used.
- 260: Place of publication is found on the item under "readme" and also on the back of the container. SoftKey is a unit within the Learning Company that produced this file, so it is recorded as the publisher (see Rule 1.4D2 and examples). Several parts of this item have their own copyright date, but only the date that covers the entire work is recorded in subfield c.
- 300: The number of SMD is recorded in subfield a, sound and color characteristics in subfield b, dimensions in subfield c, and accompanying materials in subfield e.
- 538: This file can run on two different platforms, so a 538 field is created for each platform. The requirements are re-arranged to follow the order specified by the *Guidelines*. The original wording, "18 MB of free hard disk space if the dictionary is to reside on the hard disk," is revised for this note.
- 500: The note for the source of the title proper is a required note.
- 520: An objective summary is recorded to indicate the content of the file and its features.
- 500: This number appears on the disc label, so it is presented as a quotation note. If it is verified to be a stock number, it can be entered in field 037 (e.g., 037 AMH744CE-CD $b SoftKey International).
- 650: Subdivision --Interactive multimedia is a form subdivision, and is coded as subfield v, according to the latest practice.
- 700: A name-title added entry is provided per Rule 21.30G1 for related work.
- 710: The corporate body is traced per 21.30E.
- 730: An analytical added entry is provided for the work included in this item. Indicator 2 identifies this entry as an analytic.

Title Screen:

Microsoft
WINE GUIDE

The Essential Multimedia Wine Reference with World Expert Oz Clarke

WINE TASTING WITH OZ   ALL ABOUT WINE
[video introduction by Clarke]
OVERVIEW
WORLD ATLAS OF WINE   WINE ENCYCLOPEDIA

CONTENT   WINE SELECTOR   INDEX   FIND   FIND AGAIN
OPTIONS   HELP ...

© & (p) 1995 Microsoft Corporation. All rights reserved.

****

Type: m		BLvl: m File: i
007		c $b o $d c $e g $f a
090		TP548
092		641.22
245	00	Microsoft wine guide $h [interactive multimedia] : $b the essential multimedia wine reference with world expert Oz Clarke.
246	1	$i Title on disc label: $a Wine guide, your essential multi-media wine reference
246	30	Wine guide
256		Computer data and programs.
260		[Redmond, Wash.] : $b Microsoft Home, $c c1995.
300		1 computer optical disc : $b sd., col. ; $c 4 3/4 in. + $e 1 user's guide.
538		System requirements: Multimedia PC, 386SX or higher; 4 MB RAM; 1 MB hard disk; MS-DOS version 5.0 or later; Micro-soft Windows 3.1 or later; CD-ROM drive; Super VGA with 256-color (or better) display; Microsoft mouse or compatible pointing device; audio board and headphones or speakers.
500		Title from title screen.
505	0	Wine tasting with Oz -- All about wine -- World atlas of wine -- Wine encyclopedia -- Wine selector.
650	0	Wine and wine making $v Interactive multimedia.
700	1	Clarke, Oz.
710	2	Microsoft Home (Firm)

Figure 6.2   Wine guide.

Discussion for Figure 6.2

- This item combines text, images, videos, and sound to present a reference tool on wine. The parts are carefully linked by hypertext and users can explore the file at will and access topics randomly from the search program. So this item is cataloged as an interactive multimedia.

- 007: The codes indicate that this is a computer file ("c") on an optical disc ("o") that is multicolored ("c"), $4\frac{3}{4}$ in. in diameter ("g") and contains sound ("a").

- 245 & 246: Title on the title screen is chosen over the title on the disc label because it has fuller information. To enable users to search by the disc label title, it is presented in field 246. Indicator 1 will produce a note explaining the source of this title and an added entry for this title.

- 260: The place of publication is found outside of the chief source, so it is bracketed. "Microsoft Home" appears on the disc label and the user's guide. LC name authority file identifies this as the imprint, so it is entered in subfield b and traced by field 710.

- 505: Titles of parts of the work are listed to indicate its contents. Since these headings are clear in showing the file's contents, no summary note (field 520) is used.

- 650: Form subdivision --Interactive multimedia is coded in subfield v.

- 700: As the host of this program, Clarke is traced.

- 710: The corporate body is traced per 21.1B3.

Title screen [the first title has an image of two angels as background, the second title has a white background]:

THE BIBLE
A MULTIMEDIA EXPERIENCE

World Library's
THE BIBLE: A MULTIMEDIA EXPERIENCE

Windows Ver. 4.4
Copyright 1991-1995 World Library, Inc.

Disc label:

THE
BIBLE:
A MULTIMEDIA EXPERIENCE

WINDOWS 96
COMPATIBLE
WINDOWS 3.1

COMPACT
DISC
DIGITAL DATA   SoftKey

© 1997 Learning Company Properties Inc., a subsidiary of The Learning Company Inc. © 1995 World Library Inc. All rights reserved.
SoftKey and The Learning Company are registered trademarks of Learning Company Properties Inc. The Bible: A Multimedia Experience is a trademark of World Library Inc.
HYB344FE-CD

```
*******************************************************************
Type: m         BLvl: m       File: i
007                 c $b o $d c $e g $f a
020                 1564349675
090                 BS186
092                 220.5203
130      0          Bible. $l English. $s Authorized. $f 1997.
245     14          The Bible $h [interactive multimedia] : $b a multimedia experience.
250                 Ver. 4.4.
256                 Computer data and programs.
260                 Cambridge, MA : $b SoftKey, $c c1997.
300                 1 computer optical disc : $b sd., col. ; $c 4 3/4 in. + $e 1 insert.
538                 System requirements: PC 386 or higher; 2 MB RAM; Windows 3.1 or
                    higher; VGA monitor; CD-ROM drive; mouse recommended but not required.
500                 Title from disc label.
500                 Ed. statement from title screen.
500                 Originally created by World Library, Inc.
520                 Features the complete text of The King James Bible, full-motion video
                    scenes from the four Gospels, audio of popular verses, and colored Biblical
                    illustrations. Data searchable by word, date, or name and Bible indexed by
                    book, chapter, and verse. Supports bookmark, notepad, print and save functions.
500                 "HYB344FE-CD."
630     00          Bible $v Interactive multimedia.
710     2           SoftKey International, Inc.
710     2           World Library, Inc.
```

Figure 6.3   The Bible.

Discussion for Figure 6.3

- This item includes texts, videos, audio, and images and supports random access to information in the file, so it is cataloged as an interactive multimedia.

- 007: The codes indicate that this is a computer file ("c") on an optical disc ("o") that is multicolored ("c"), 4 ¾ in. in diameter ("g") and contains sound ("a").

- 020: The ISBN is found on the container.

- 130: A uniform title main entry heading is provided to bring different manifestations of the same work together. The uniform title is formulated according to Rules 25.18, and includes language, version, and year of publication.

- 245: The title screen and the disc label essentially present the same title proper except that a title on the title screen includes the original creator of the file. Because this phrase is not an integral part of the title proper, a 246 field is not provided for this alternate form of the title.

- 250: The edition statement is found on the title screen.

- 260: World Library is listed as the earlier copyright owner of this work, while SoftKey has the 1997 copyright, so SoftKey is recorded as the publisher. Information about World Library is included in a 500 note later.

- 500: The disc label was chosen as the source of the title proper because the information there is clearer than that on the title screen.

- 500: A separate note is provided for the source of the edition statement.

- 500: A note is provided to indicate that World Library, Inc. is the original creator of this product. Such information is usually not included but since World Library is prominently presented on the title screen, it is recorded.

- 500: The number appears on the disc label and is recorded because it can be helpful for identifying the item. If it can be verified to be the stock number of the publisher, this information can also be presented in a 037 note.

- 710: World Library, Inc. is traced because it appears on the title screen and contributes to the creation of this work.

Disc label:

VOYAGER
A HARD DAY'S NIGHT

COPYRIGHT 1964
PROSCENIUM FILMS LTD.

CDRM112350
QT8

****

Type: m		BLvl: m File: i
007		c $b o $d c $e g $f a
020		1559402652
090		PN1997
092		791.4372
245	02	A hard day's night $h [interactive multimedia].
246	1	$i Title on the container: $a Beatles in A hard day's night, the complete uncut movie
256		Computer data and programs.
260		New York, NY : $b Voyager, $c c1993.
300		1 computer optical disc : $b sd., col. ; $c r 3/4 in. + $e 1 user guide (7 p.).
538		System requirements: Macintosh; at least 4 MB RAM; System 6.0.7 (or later); 256-color (13" or larger) or 256-grayscale (12" or larger) monitor (Apple 12" RGB color monitors can play the video segments, but without supplemental text); QuickTime-compatible CD-ROM drive (double-speed recommended).
500		Title from disc label.
520		Contains the original movie; the original script; profiles of the Beatles, cast, and crew; clips from the director's early work; a critic's essay; the theatrical trailer; and the 1982 movie re-release prologue. Search feature supports random access to and navigation through the video and text.
500		"CDRM112350."
610	20	Beatles.
630	00	Hard day's night (Motion picture)
650	0	Feature films.
650	0	Musical films.
710	2	Beatles.
710	2	Voyager Company.

Figure 6.4   A hard day's night.

Discussion for Figure 6.4

- This item combines video, sound, text, and images. Users can play video clips, zoom in and out of images, change screen displays, explore the file through hypertext, and search topics by a search engine. As a result, this item is cataloged as an interactive multimedia.

- 246: The title on the container is prominent and users may search for this item by this title. So a 246 field is provided, with subfield i indicating the source of this title and subfield a the variant title. Following OCLC input guidelines, the initial article is not recorded in field 246.

- 260: The copyright date on the disc is for the movie. The copyright for this multimedia is found on the container and recorded.

- 500: This number appears on the disc label and is recorded because it can be helpful for identifying the item.

- 630: This item contains information about the making of the movie and other information related to the movie, so a heading for the movie is assigned. A uniform heading is used to bring related works together.

- 650: Two genre headings are assigned for the film.

- 710: The musical group that is featured in the multimedia is traced.

- 710: The publisher is traced per 21.1B3.

Disc label:

NASA
National Aeronautics and
Space Administration
Planetary Data System
Welcome to the Planets
Educational CD-ROM

Grades 9 and
above

PDS

Dedicated to
Dr. William L. Quaide
Chief (Ret.)
Planetary Science Branch
SOLAR SYSTEM EXPLORATION DIVISION
NASA HEADQUARTERS

ISO
9660
COMPACT **DISC**
CDRM1248210

USA_NASA_PDS_ED_0001
VERSION 1
GTDA

****

Type: m		Audn: e	BLvl: m	File: i	GPub: f
007		c $b o $d c $e g $f a			
086	0	NAS 1.86:P 69			
090		QB601			
092		523.4			
245	00	Welcome to the planets $h [interactive multimedia] / $c NASA, Planetary Data System.			
246	1	$i Title on the container: $a Planetary data system: welcome to the planets			
250		Version 1.			
260		[Washington, D.C.?] : $b NASA, Planetary Data System, $c 1994.			
300		1 computer optical disc : $b sd., col. ; $c 4 3/4 in.			
538		System requirements for Macintosh: 8 MB RAM; System 7.0 or higher; 640 x 480 screen with 8-bit color.			
500		Title and ed. statement from disc label.			
500		"Educational CD-ROM."			
516		Files presented in Macintosh format and NCSA Mosaic format; all images in GIF format.			
500		"Dedicated to Dr. William L. Quaide, Chief (Ret.), Planetary Science Branch, Solar System Exploration Division, NASA Headquarters."			
521		Grades 9 and above.			
520		Contains 190 selected images and associated information from the NASA planetary exploration program. The intent is to give teachers an overview of planetary exploration at about a high school or college level.			
500		"ISO 9660."			
500		"USA_NASA_PDS_ED_0001."			
500		"CDRM1248210."			
650	0	Planets $v Databases.			
710	1	United States. $b National Aeronautics and Space Administration. $b Planetary Data System.			

Figure 6.5   Welcome to the planets.

Discussion for Figure 6.5

- This item contains a database of planet images, text and video to illustrate NASA's effort in planetary exploration. Files in the database are linked and users can interact with the files as they wish. This item is therefore cataloged as an interactive multimedia.

- Fixed field: GPub is coded "f" because this file is produced by a federal agency. The stated audience group includes several age groups listed for the "Audn" element. Following OCLC guidelines, the highest age group, adult ("e"), is used to code this element.

- 245: The layout of the information on the disc label suggests that NASA Planetary Data System is responsible for the creation of this file. This information is confirmed by a voice introduction of the file. So this statement is recorded in subfield c of field 245. The full name of NASA is in smaller font and serves to clarify the name of the agency, so it is not transcribed here.

- 246: This information appears on the back cover of the container, so it is recorded in field 246 in case users search for this item by this title. Subfield i indicates the source and subfield a records the alternative title.

- 250: Version information is on the disc label.

- 260: The file lists the unit for users desiring further information, but provides no information on place of publication. Since the place of publication is uncertain, it is followed by a question mark and bracketed.

- 538: Full information on system requirements is included in the volinfo.txt file which explains the purpose, scope, and coding structure of the file.

- 500: Because the source of the title proper and that of the edition statement are the same, the notes are combined into one.

- 500: "Educational CD-ROM" appears on the disc label and indicates the purpose of this file, so it is quoted as a note.

- 516: Information on file formats is found in the volinfo.txt file. Since this information is not presented elsewhere in the record, it is recorded in field 516, the field for file characteristics.

- 500: The statement of dedication is quoted because it appears prominently on the disc label. Since this item is not a Festschrift, no added entry is provided for Dr. William L. Quaide.

- 521: The audience information is presented in field 521 and used to code the Audn element in the fixed field.

- 500s: A technical specification and two numbers appear on the disc label. Each is presented as a quotation note.

- 650: The volinfo.txt file explains how the data are organized and encoded in the file; this information makes it clear that this file is a database. Subdivision --Databases is therefore assigned to the topical heading, Planets.

- 710: The unit responsible for this file is traced per 21.1B3. The form of the agency's name is established according to Rules 24.18 and 24.19.

Disc label:

The ultimate encyclopedia of military aircraft and aviation

WARPLANES

MODERN FIGHTING AIRCRAFT

© 1994 Maris Multimedia and its licensors

****

Type: m	BLvl: m	File: i
007		c $b o $d c $e g $f a
090		UG1240
092		358.4183
245	0 0	Warplanes $h [interactive multimedia] : $b modern fighting aircraft : the ultimate encyclopedia of military aircraft and aviation.
246	30	Modern fighting aircraft
246	30	Ultimate encyclopedia of military aircraft and aviation
250		Version 1.
256		Computer data and programs.
260		London, England : $b Maris Multimedia ; $a [Orinda, CA : $b Distributed in North America by Maxis], $c c1994.
300		1 computer optical disc : $b sd., col. ; $c 4 3/4 in. + $e 1 user's guide (17 p.) + 1 installation guide.
538		System requirements for IBM: IBM compatible with 386SX processor or better; 4 MB RAM; Windows 3.1, DOS 3.3 or above, MSCDEX 2.0 or later; SVGA graphics card with 512K RAM; Sound Blaster or Adlib compatible sound card; CD-ROM drive; mouse.
538		System requirements for Macintosh: Macintosh LC II; 4 MB RAM; System 7.0 or above; 13" or larger 256 color monitor; CD-ROM drive.
538		System requirements for Power Macintosh: Power Macintosh 6100; 8 MB RAM; System 7.1.2 or above; 13" or larger 256 color monitor; CD-ROM drive.
500		Title from disc label.
500		Ed. statement from user's guide.
520		Contains flight simulators and information on more than 500 military aircraft and 200 weapons systems in service between 1976 and 1994.
650	0	Airplanes, Military $x Encyclopedias $v Interactive multimedia.
650	0	Airplanes, Military $x History $v Interactive multimedia.
650	0	Flight simulators $v Interactive multimedia.
710	2	Maris Multimedia (Firm).

Figure 6.6   Warplanes.

Discussion for Figure 6.6

- This item contains flight simulation programs, photos, descriptions of military aircrafts, and weapon systems and sound information. Navigation paths can be controlled by users. It is therefore cataloged as an interactive multimedia.

- 245 & 246: In Area 1 each piece of other title information is preceded by a colon. Because of the layout and the meaning of these two pieces of other title information, two 246 fields are used to create added entries. Indicator 3 will produce an added entry, and indicator 0 explains the title is a part of the title proper. Following OCLC input guidelines, the initial article is not recorded.

- 250: Edition statement is found in the user's guide.

- 260: Information about the distributor is taken from a promotion sheet, so it is entered in brackets.

- 538s: The file can be played on three types of computers, so three separate 538 fields are used to record the system-specific requirements.

- 500s: Both source notes are required for interactive multimedia.

- 650s: Form subdivision --Interactive multimedia is assigned to each topical heading.

- 710: The corporate body is traced per 21.1B3.

Disc label:

THE WAR IN VIETNAM
A Multimedia Chronicle from
CBS News & The New York Times

Windows and
Macintosh   MACMILLAN
CD-ROM   DIGITAL USA
The New York Times
CBS News

Copyright © 1995 Simon & Schuster Macmillan
Digital USA and its licensors.
Copyright © 1995 CBS Inc. and The New York Times Company.
All rights reserved.
ISBN 1-57595-005-7

****

Type: m	BLvl: m	File: i

Tag	Ind	Field
007		c $b o $d c $e g $f a
020		1575950057
043		n-us---
090		DS558
092		959.7043373
245	04	The war in Vietnam $h [interactive multimedia] : $b a multimedia chronicle / $c from CBS News & the New York Times.
256		Computer data and programs.
260		New York, NY : $b Macmillan Digital USA, $c c1995.
300		1 computer optical disc : $b sd., col. ; $c 4 3/4 in.
538		System requirements for Windows: Multimedia PC, 486/33 MHz or better; 8 MB RAM; Windows 3.1 or higher or Windows 95; double speed CD-ROM drive; multimedia PC compatible audio board; color monitor.
538		System requirements for Macintosh: Performa or better/25 MHz; 8 MB RAM; System 7.0.1 or higher; double speed CD-ROM drive; color monitor.
500		Title from disc label.
500		"Windows and Macintosh CD-ROM"--Disc label.
520		Includes New York Times articles and photos, 40 minutes of CBS News broadcast clips, biographical essays, maps, specifications and photos of weapons and planes of the Vietnam War, and a searchable database of Americans who died in the war and are recorded on the Vietnam Veterans Memorial in Washington, D.C.
650	0	Vietnamese Conflict, 1961-1975 $v Interactive multimedia.
651	0	Untied States $x History $y 1945- $v Interactive multimedia.
710	2	CBS News.
710	2	New York Times.
710	2	Macmillan digital USA.

Figure 6.7   War in Vietnam.

Discussion for Figure 6.7

- This item contains text, images, and video clips. Contents are linked for nonlinear exploration. It is therefore cataloged as an interactive multimedia.

- 043: When a place name is used in the subject headings, field 043 can be used to indicate the geographic area covered. The seven-character code is taken from the OCLC-MARC geographic area codes list.

- 090 & 092: DS558 is for general works about the involvement of foreign country in Vietnam conflict. The *DDC* number is built from the number for the participation of specific country in the Vietnam War (959.70433) and the number for the United States (73).

- 245: *AACR2R* stipulates that statement of responsibility be transcribed in the form it appears, so "from" and "&" are recorded in the statement of responsibility.

- 538: This item can run on two platforms, so two separate 538 fields are used to record the platform-specific requirements.

- 500: "Windows and Macintosh CD-ROM" appears prominently on the disc label and indicates the CD-ROM is designed for both systems, so this note is presented as a quotation note.

- 650: The file is about U.S. involvement in the Vietnam War. Since *LCSH* does not have a heading for this subject, two headings are assigned. Form subdivision --Interactive multimedia is assigned to each heading.

Title screen:

AMERICAN GOVERNMENT
The Political Game
Stephen E. Frantzich
United States Naval Academy

Based on the textbook by
Stephen E. Frantzich and Stephen Percy

Brown &
Benchmark

====================

Disc label:
3M
CD-ROM

AMERICAN GOVERNMENT CD-ROM
MACINTOSH VERSION
Manufactured in USA by 3M

****

Type: m	BLvl: m	File: i
007		c $b o $d c $e g $f a
020		0697234592
043		n-us---
090		JK274
092		320.473
100	1	Frantzich, Stephen E.
245	10	American government $h [interactive multimedia] : $b the political game / $c Stephen E. Frantzich.
246	1	$i Title on disc surface: $a American government CD-ROM
250		Macintosh version.
260		Dubuque, Iowa : $b Brown & Benchmark, $c c1994.
300		1 computer optical disc : $b sd., col. ; $c 4 3/4 in. + $e 1 user's manual (26 p.) + 1 insert.
538		System requirements: LC III or higher Mac with System 7.1 or later; 8 MB RAM; a monitor with 256-color display that can display at least 640 x 480 pixels; QuickTime version 1.6.1 or later; CD-ROM drive.
500		Title from title screen.
500		Ed. statement from disc label.
500		"Based on the textbook by Stephen E. Frantzich and Stephen Percy."
500		"Produced by Lunaria"--Container.
520		Contains the original text of American government, the political game, and an expanded archive of primary sources, including texts, videos, graphics, and photos.
651	0	United States $x Politics and government $v Interactive multimedia.
700	1	Percy, Stephen L. $t American government, the political game.
710	2	Brown & Benchmark Publishers.

Figure 6.8 **American government.**

Discussion for Figure 6.8

- This item is based on Frantzich's textbook and enhances it with images, photos, videos, and games. Users can play political games, test the timelines, and use hypertext links to access information. Because the file can be explored nonlinearly, this item is cataloged as an interactive multimedia.

- 043: When a geographic name is used in the subject heading, field 043 can be added to indicate the geographic focus of the item. The seven-character code is taken from the "USMARC Code List for Geographic Areas."

- 100: Frantzich appears prominently on the title screen and the relationship between this interactive multimedia and a textbook is made clear on the title screen as well. So Frantzich is presented as the main entry heading.

- 245 & 246: The title on the title screen is fuller than that on the disc label, so it is transcribed in field 245. The disc label title is presented in 246, with subfield i indicating the source and subfield a the alternative title. Indicator 1 will produce a note and an added entry.

- 250: The edition statement is taken from the disc label and the source of this statement is noted in field 500 below.

- 260: Place of publication and date of publication are taken from the user's manual. Since the chief source for interactive multimedia is the entire work, no square brackets are needed.

- 500: The basis of this interactive multimedia's content is presented in a quotation note because that is the most efficient way to convey this information.

- 500: Information about Lunaria appears on the container but the role of this company is not further explained, so the quotation note is provided to indicate the involvement of Lunaria, but Lunaria is not traced.

- 700: A name-title added entry is provided for a related work (Rule 21.30G1).

- 710: The corporate body is traced per 21.1B3.

Title screen:

The
ENDURING VISION

A HISTORY OF THE AMERICAN PEOPLE

INTERACTIVE EDITION, 1993 VERSION

BOYER • CLARK • KETT
SALISBURY • SITKOFF • WOLOCH

DEVELOPED BY
BRYTEN, INC.

****

Type: m	BLvl: m	File: i
007		c $b o $d c $e g $f a
020		0669340707 (disc)
020		0669324612 (container)
020		0669340693 (guide)
043		n-us---
090		E173
092		973
245	04	The enduring vision $h [interactive multimedia] : $b a history of the American people / $c Boyer ... [et. al.] ; developed by Bryten, Inc.
250		Interactive ed., 1993 version.
256		Computer data and program.
260		Lexington, MA : $b D.C. Heath, $c 1993.
300		1 computer optical disc : $b sd., col. ; $c 4 3/4 in. + $e 1 user guide (15 p.) + 1 help sheet.
538		System requirements: Macintosh LC or II series computer; 4 MB RAM; 1.5 MB hard disk available; System 6.0.7 or higher; QuickTime 1.5; 13 in. color monitor; CD-ROM drive.
500		Title and ed. statement from title screen.
500		"Macintosh CD-ROM"--Container.
520		An electronic version of the second edition of The enduring vision by Paul Boyer et al. In addition to the original text, this version includes audio, video, maps, charts, graphics and a search engine to support users' exploration of the documents and data on this file.
651	0	United States $x History $v Interactive multimedia.
700	1	Boyer, Paul S. $t The enduring vision.
710	2	Bryten, inc.
710	2	D.C. Heath and Company.

Figure 6.9   The enduring vision.

Discussion for Figure 6.9

- This item contains text of *The Enduring Vision* and enhances it with audio, video, maps, charts, and graphics. Users can randomly access the text and media resources on this file. This item is therefore cataloged as an interactive multimedia.

- 020s: This item has three ISBNs, so field 020 is repeated to record the numbers and the parts that carry these numbers.

- 043: When a geographic name is used in the subject heading, field 043 can be added to indicate the geographic focus of the item. The seven-character code is taken from the "USMARC Code List for Geographic Areas."

- 245: The last names of six authors are on the title screen. Following Rule 1.1F5 of *AACR2R*, only the first author is recorded in subfield c. The company that developed this work is separated from the authors by a semicolon.

- 250: Edition statements are transcribed exactly from the title screen.

- 500: Since the title proper and the edition statement are transcribed from the same source, the information is combined into one note.

- 500: The information about Macintosh appears in different forms. On the disc label "Macintosh" appears below the title proper; on the disc case "Macintosh version" appears at the bottom of the cover; and on the container "Macintosh CD-ROM" appears near the developer's name. It seems that the creators mainly want to convey that this file is intended for Macintosh machines. This quotation note is therefore provided to make that point.

- 520: The basis of this file is incorporated into the summary note to indicate its contents and features.

- 700: A name-title added entry is provided for a related work (Rule 21.30G1).

- 710s: The developer and the publisher are traced per 21.1B3.

Disc label:

STAR TREK

MAC
CD-ROM

OMNIPEDIA

START TREK and ©1995 Paramount Pictures. All Rights reserved. STAR TREK and related properties are trademarks of Paramount Pictures. ©1995 Simon & Schuster Interactive, a division of Simon & Schuster, Inc.

****

Type: m		BLvl: m	File: i
007		c $b o $d c $e g $f a	
020		0671528785	
090		PN1992.8.S73	
092		791.4575	
245	00	Star Trek omnipedia $h [interactive multimedia].	
260		New York, NY : $b Simon & Schuster Interactive, $c c1995.	
300		1 computer optical disc : $b sd., col. ; $c 4 3/4 in. + $e 1 user guide (28 p.) + 1 voice commands card.	
538		System requirements: Macintosh LC-III, Performa or better; 8 MB RAM; System 7.01 or later; 13" color monitor with 256 colors; double-speed CD-ROM drive. Requirements for voice activation: Power Macintosh or Quadra A/V model Macintosh; Plaintalk microphone or microphones of similar quality.	
500		Title from disc label.	
500		"A voice-activated guide to the future"--Container.	
500		"MAC CD-ROM."	
511	0	Special multimedia topic features narrated by Mark Leonard (Sarek); featuring Majel Barrett, the official voice of Star Trek's computer systems.	
500		Based on The Star Trek encyclopedia by Michael Okuda, Denise Okuda and Debbie Mirek and The Star Trek chronology by Michael Okuda and Denise Okuda.	
520		An electronic reference guide to the Star Trek universe, including episodes, events, characters, actors, planets, alien life-forms, history, technology, and resources. Indexed entries from three of the TV series and six feature films are illustrated with photos, videos, graphics, and audio. A search engine supports access to charts, maps, starship diagrams and 3-D realistic renderings. Also features more than 100 QuickTime movies and animations.	
650	0	Star Trek television programs $x Encyclopedias $v Interactive multimedia.	
650	0	Star Trek films $x Encyclopedias $v Interactive multimedia.	
700	1	Leonard, Mark.	
700	1	Barret, Majel.	
700	1	Okuda, Michael. $t Star Trek encyclopedia.	
700	1	Okuda, Michael. $t Star Trek chronology.	
710	2	Simon & Schuster Interactive (Firm)	

Figure 6.10   Star Trek omnipedia.

Discussion for Figure 6.10

- This item includes text, photos, videos, graphics, and audio information. It also supports random access to information in the encyclopedia. So this file is cataloged as an interactive multimedia.

- 090 & 092: 1992.8 is for television programs, special topic A-Z, and the Cutter number is based on the first word of this item, "star." 791.4575 is for multiple television programs.

- 260: Simon & Schuster Interactive is recorded as the publisher because it is the division that published this work (see Rule 1.4D2 of *AACR2R*).

- 300: There is no particular order in recording the accompanying materials, but it is a good practice to record more substantial items first.

- 538: The optical disc and the voice commands card each has its own system requirements. The cataloger can enter the requirements in one 538 field or use a separate 538 field for the requirements for voice activation. Either approach is acceptable.

- 500: "A VOICE-ACTIVATED GUIDE TO THE FUTURE" appears prominently on several sides of the container, so it is recorded as a quotation note.

- 500: "MAC CD-ROM" appears on the disc label and serves to indicate the CD-ROM is intended for Macintosh machines, so it is presented as a quotation note.

- 511: Performers featured in the work are noted here. This note will make it clear to users why these individuals are assigned as added entries.

- 500: The sources of this file's content are recorded in a 500 note. This note will justify the provision of two name-title added entries.

- 700s: The two performers are traced for their contribution to this work.

- 700s: Name-title added entries are provided for related works (Rule 21.30G1).

- 710: The publisher is traced per 21.1B3.

■NOTES

1. *Guidelines for Bibliographic Description of Interactive Multimedia* (Chicago: American Library Association, 1994).

2. *Guidelines*, pp. 2–4.

SEVEN ← INTERNET RESOURCES

The rapid growth of electronic resources, and Internet resources in particular, has contributed to libraries' change of their operating philosophy from ownership to access. Users are relying more and more on the Internet for their information needs. For instance, a study of faculty and students found that 83.2 percent of the respondents have used the Internet for information related to academic studies and 73.8 percent have used it for information not related to academic studies.[1] In response, libraries are offering access to Internet resources and actively collecting resources of value to their communities. An ALA study of academic libraries, for instance, discovered that 87 percent of respondents from doctorate-granting institutions have provided access to Internet resources by their home pages.[2] A recent survey showed that 97 percent of large academic libraries and 59 percent of large public libraries have collected Internet resources.[3] The need to organize Internet resources is a concern to all types of libraries.

Internet resources are different from prints and other nonprint materials in a number of ways. They are dynamic and subject to change. In addition, they can be interactive and can contain multimedia. But the main attraction of Internet resources is the hyperlink capability that links related resources for presentation. One major problem of these resources is that they are unstable due to network traffic or change of file name or location. There are also too many resources of questionable quality. Because cataloging used to be applied to static objects and Internet resources have been growing exponentially, many have questioned the wisdom of cataloging Internet resources[4] and information professionals have continued to search for ways to organize such resources.[5] But after the initial skepticism and much discussion,[6] the consensus is that cataloging is a good way to integrate Internet resources into collections—as long as the resources have been carefully evaluated and judged valuable to users. Cataloging rules have been developed, tested, and revised. Encoding standards have improved to ensure better indexing and retrieval of such resources. Major tools needed for cataloging Internet resources include:

- *AACR2R* (Chapters 9, 12, 21 in particular)

- *Cataloging Internet Resources: A Manual and Practical Guide*, edited by Nancy B. Olson. Dublin, Ohio: OCLC, 1997. Available: http://www.purl.org/oclc/cataloging-internet (Accessed June 2000).

- *CONSER Cataloging Manual Module 31: Remote Access Computer File Serials.* Available: http://lcweb.loc.gov/acq/conser/module31.html (Accessed June 2000).

- *Guidelines for Coding Electronic Resources in Leader/06.* Available: http://lcweb.loc.gov/marc/ldr06guide.html (Accessed June 2000).

- Library of Congress. *Draft Interim Guidelines for Cataloging Electronic Resources.* Available: http://lcweb.loc.gov/catdir/cpso/dcmb19_4.html (Accessed June 2000).

- Library of Congress. *Field 856 Electronic Location and Access.* Available: http://lcweb.loc.gov/marc/856guide.html (Accessed June 2000).

- OCLC. *856 Electronic Location and Access (R): Input Standards.* Available: http://www.oclc.org/oclc/bib/856.htm (Accessed June 2000).

- OCLC. *Cataloging Electronic Resources: OCLC-MARC Coding Guidelines.* By Jay Weitz. Available: http://www.oclc.org/oclc/cataloging/type.htm (Accessed June 2000).

For subject analysis catalogers should consult the latest *Library of Congress Subject Headings*, *Library of Congress Classification*, and *Dewey Decimal Classification*. Library of Congress subject cataloging manuals for subject headings and classification are helpful also.

But before cataloging begins, a few questions need to be answered.

1. Which resources should be selected and cataloged? Who should make the decision? Many libraries catalog resources they subscribe to, such as electronic journals. In addition, libraries also catalog items recommended by users and approved by collection development librarians; and resources recommended by the staff, including bibliographers, subject specialists, collection development librarians, catalogers, and reference librarians. The evaluation criteria are similar to those for print resources, with newer criteria such as network capability and graphic design recommended.[7]

2. What should be the unit or the level of analysis? Should an entire Web site be cataloged or would it be more helpful to catalog individual Web pages on that site? The answer lies in the nature of the Web pages and the site and should be based on users' needs. Sometimes it is appropriate to catalog an entire site as a whole, sometimes it is better to catalog few Web pages on a site.

There are also occasions to use both approaches. Some libraries follow the "two-click" rule to make sure users do not need to go through several levels to get to a page.[8]

3. Is the item a monograph or a serial? *AACR2R* defines a serial as "a publication in any medium issued in successive parts bearing numeric or chronological designations and intended to be continued indefinitely" (p. 622). Many Internet resources are not treated as monographs because they are updated frequently, nor as serials because they do not meet the definition of *AACR2R*. Hirons and Graham explained the complex seriality issue and suggested "ongoing publications" as a better description of Web resources such as home pages and resources that are updated continuously.[9] Hirons completed a report on seriality for the Joint Steering Committee for Revision of *AACR*.[10] The report has important implications for the revision of *AACR* and is sure to generate much discussion. The Library of Congress's *Draft Interim Guidelines* treat ongoing publications as monographs and apply the rules for loose-leaf publications to them.[11] OCLC follows the same practice and cautions that while a print publication is cataloged as a serial, its online version may be treated as a monograph because it is continuously updated. To help catalogers in determining the nature of resources, OCLC has identifies several remotely accessed electronic resources as monographs.[12] Because of the importance of this message, the categories are listed verbatim here:

- Databases (including directories, A&I services, etc.)
- Electronic discussion groups (e.g., SERIALIST)
- Electronic discussion group digests (e.g., AUTOCAT digest)
- Gopher servers (e.g., LC-MARVEL)
- Online public access catalogs (e.g., OCLC, RLIN)
- Online services (e.g., America Online)
- Web sites (e.g., the *CONSER* home page)

4. Should catalogers follow the one record approach or the separate record approach? Some electronic resources have print counterparts, while others are available online only. For the former the cataloger has the options of creating a new record for the electronic version or adding relevant information to the record for the print form. *CONSER* allows the single record approach, but recommends catalogers to create separate records.[13] OCLC also prefers catalogers to follow the separate record approach.[14] Graham and the *CONSER* Working Group recently completed

a report on these two approaches.[15] They explained when the one-record approach is appropriate and discussed the pros and cons of both approaches on the basis of factors such as patron convenience, expense, and maintenance.

The one-record approach enables libraries to catalog resources quickly and make them available to users with less cost, less staff time, and less record maintenance. It may also facilitate access by informing patrons of the existence of several formats of the same item. A major drawback is patrons may be confused by seeing the print and the electronic versions represented by the same record. The advantage of the separate-record approach is that there is less confusion over what a record represents, but the cost of creating a separate record is inevitable. A recent survey found that 72 percent of the responding academic and public libraries have taken the one-record approach,[16] perhaps for economic reasons. Examples of these approaches are discussed in the section on field 530.

5. Another issue to consider is how to catalog aggregators that provide access to many resources. Project Muse, for instance, provides full-text access to journals published by the Johns Hopkins University Press. Should a collection-level record be created? Are item-level records needed? Depending on available resources and the capabilities of local systems, libraries may make their own decision.

■ MARC FIELDS FOR INTERNET RESOURCES

The MARC fields commonly used to encode ongoing monographs or serials accessible via the Internet are listed below. Field 006 is required if the Type element is not coded "m." It is also required of electronic serials. Field 007 records additional physical characteristics and is required for all computer files.

1XX		Main entry (name or uniform title)
245	_ _	Title proper $h [computer file] : $b other title information / $c statement of responsibility.
246	_ _	Variant title
250		Edition statement.
256		File characteristics.
260		Publication place : $b publisher, $c date.
310		Frequency of publication (for serials).
362		Numerical/chronological designation (for serials).
4XX	_ _	Series title.
516		Scope, nature, file type, format, or genre.
538		System requirements.
538		Mode of access.
500		Source of title proper note.
506		Restrictions on use.
521	_	Audience.
520		Summary.
505	_	Contents.
530		Other available formats.
6XX	_ _	Subject headings.
700	_	Personal name added entries.
710	_	Corporate name added entries.
730	_ _	Uniform title added entries.
740	_ _	Related/analytical title added entries.
776	_	Additional physical form entry.
856	_ _	Electronic location and access.

Step 1: In creating MARC records for Internet resources in OCLC, first determine the primary characteristic of an item and use that to select a workform. Except for language materials (coded "a" in "Type"), the "Type" code alone will determine which fixed field will be used for coding.

Step 2: If the "Type" code is "a," the cataloger will need to determine if the item is a monograph or a serial. This will result in the coding of the "Blvd" element. For language materials, the codes in "Type" and "Blvd" will determine which fixed field is used for the record. A Web page that is primarily textual, for instance, will have code "a" in "Type" and code "m" in "Blvd" (for monograph). So the 008 field for book will be used for the record. A model for selecting field 008 is presented in Chapter Two (p. 26).

Step 3: The cataloger then determines if the item has other characteristics that are not covered by the fixed field and should be represented by one or more 006 fields. A common example is an electronic journal. Since the new definition of code "m" in "type of record" is much narrower than before according to Update no. 3 to USMARC, the cataloger will code "Type" as "a" (language material), "Blvd" as "s" (serial), and select the serial fixed field for the record. 006 field is added for the computer aspect.

Step 4: The cataloger determines if the item has other physical characteristics that need to be recorded. If so, field 007, physical characteristics fixed field, is used.

File: This element specifies the type of computer file being cataloged, and the types cover computer data files and program files. Eleven types have been identified and encoded. They include numeric data ("a"), computer program ("b"), graphic data ("c"), text files ("d"), bibliographic data ("e"), font ("f"), game ("g"), sound ("h"), interactive multimedia ("i"), and online system or service ("j"), and a combination of data and programs ("m"). These types are more explicit than the file characteristics presented in field 256 and can be incorporated into field 256 if appropriate. For instance, if "File" is coded "h" for a sound file, "computer sound data" can be used in the 256 field.

Field 006: This field is used when an item has multiple characteristics and when an item is a nontextual serial. As far as Internet resources are concerned, field 006 is mandatory if "Type" is not coded "m" and if the item being cataloged is a serial computer file. This field has 18 character positions for coding special aspects of the item that cannot be coded in field 008. Field 006 has a tree structure by which the form of the material (the first element coded) determines what other data elements are allowed for subsequent character positions. For instance, if the first element is coded "a" for monographs, then the data elements for Books Format 006 are used:

Books Format 006 Information

T006: a	Ills:	Audn:	Form:	Cont:	GPub:
Conf: 0	Fest: 0	Indx: 0	Fict: 0	Biog:	

OCLC provides prompts for data input. Field 006 has no indicator values or subfield codes, and data elements are identified by their position. In the OCLC system brackets are used to present this field. For example, if a Web page is basically textual, the workform for monograph is used to create a record, and the "Type" is coded "a." To represent the computer aspect of this item, the cataloger enters "n006 com" (without the quotation marks) and presses <F11>, then a screen for Computer Files Format 006 input will appear:

Computer Files Format 006 Information

T006: m   Audn: File: u   GPub:

A computer text file will be coded and displayed as: 006   [m   d   ] where "m" represents a computer file and "d" textual data.

    Field 007: Required for all computer file. Five subfields are used in OCLC:

$a = Class of material; code "c" for computer files

$b = Specific material designation, including codes for tape cartridge, magnetic disc, and optical disc. Use "r" for remote access files.

$d = Color

$e = Dimensions

$f = Sound.

If an element applies to the file being cataloged, but the needed information is not available, code "u" (unknown) is used. But if an element does not apply to the file being cataloged, then code "n" (not applicable) is used. For remote access files, for instance, $e will be coded "n".

■ DESCRIPTION

Rules for Descriptive Cataloging

Chief Source of Information

    For Internet resources the chief source of information, according to Olson's guidelines, includes several possibilities—title screen, HTML source code, "about" link, "readme" file (especially for FTP files), TEI header (for texts encoded by Text Encoding Initiative), file printout (if no equipment is available for reading the material), publication about the site, and so on.

Rule 9.0B1 designates the title screen(s) of computer files as the chief source. For electronic serials, the chief source is the title screen of the first issue or the earliest available issue. If the title screen is not available, catalogers may take any formal statements in the publication that provide information on the title, publisher, and/or designation of the serial. *CONSER* also recommends that catalogers consider journal home page, publisher's statement page, volume contents page, etc. while creating a record.[17]

Area 1. Title and Statement of Responsibility (9.1, MARC Field 245)

Title proper should be transcribed exactly as to wording and order, but not necessarily to capitalization or punctuation (see Rule 1.1B1).

Title screen: Welcome to the CATCMB Web-page

Title displayed on the browser title bar: The Center for Advanced Training in Cell and Molecular Biology

Transcribed as:

245	00	CATCMB web-page $h [computer file]
246	1	$i Title in HTML source code: $a Center for Advanced Training in Cell and Molecular Biology
245	00	DoD base reuse implementation manual $h [computer file]
246	30	Base reuse implementation manual

The source of title proper is recorded in field 500. This note is required (9.7B3). Possible sources are home page screen, main menu, the "about" page, title bar display (the TITLE tag in the HTML source code), or any other internal sources. *CONSER* users have been instructed to follow LCRI 12.7B3 and include the date the material being cataloged was viewed.[18] This information is added at the end of this note.

500	Title from title screen (viewed March 20, 1998).
500	Title from HTML header (viewed April 23, 1997).

General Material Designation (GMD): The general material designation (GMD) for Internet resources is "computer file," according to *AACR2R*. *ISBD* (*ER*) recommends "electronic resource" and the cataloging community has been enthusiastic about adopting this phrase.[19] This change may be incorporated into *AACR* in the future.

Statement of Responsibility: This information is not always available on the title screen. It is more likely to appear at the bottom of a home page, then the statement is recorded in a 500 field, instead of field 245.

Title screen: Blake Digital Text Project

At the bottom of the screen: site maintained and comments welcomed by Nelson Hilton

Transcribed as:

100	0	Hilton, Nelson.
245	0 0	Blake Digital Text Project $h [computer file]
270		$m hilton@ug.edu
500		Site maintained and comments welcomed by Nelson Hilton.

[Information at the site indicates that Hilton is the compiler.]

The "About" link is another potential source for a more detailed explanation of the purpose of the Web page and the people and corporation bodies responsible for its creation. In recent years Web page creators have used meta tags to include information on author, description, and keywords to make it easier for search engines to index their pages. In Netscape catalogers can view meta tags by pulling down the "VIEW" menu and selecting "Page Source." In Internet Explorer catalogers pull down the "VIEW" menu and selecting "Source" to see the HTML source code. The author information presented in the HTML source code, however, should be verified at the Web site because it frequently refers to the person responsible for the markup of a page instead of the contents.

For example, a meta tag for the CATCMB site presents the following information: <meta name = "Author" content = "Bernard A. Lynch">

Since this information is not on the title screen and Lynch does not appear to be responsible for the contents of this site, it is recorded in a note instead of the subfield c of field 245. Libraries vary in their decision to provide an added entry for a Webmaster. Some consider Webmasters to be editors and trace them, while others do not because they believe Webmasters do not contribute to the intellectual contents of a work. The resource is transcribed as:

245	1 0	CATCMB Web-page $h [computer file]
246	3	Welcome to the CATCMB Web-page
500		Author information in HTML source code: Bernard A. Lynch.
700	0 0	Lynch, Bernard A. (optional)

Some Web pages have titles that include phrases such as "Welcome to." Treatment of such phrases varies by library. If information on the Web page indicated the title proper is the part following the phrase, it is recorded in field 245. The "Welcome to" title may be given as a variant title. If a Web page clearly identifies an author and a Webmaster who was responsible for the markup of the page, the author information in entered in $c of field 245, and the Webmaster is recorded in a 500 note. Occasionally the Webmaster information will be included in places such as the "about" link or the "Developers" link. So catalogers will want to check out those links. The decision to provide added entry for the Webmaster is a local one.

100	1	Van Helden, Albert.
245	1 4	The Galileo Project $h [computer file] / $c Albert Van Helden, Elizabeth Burr.
500		Webmaster: Krist Bender.
700	1	Bender, Krist.

[Information on the Webmaster is found in the "developers" link which explains the extent of his involvement in this project.]

If no information is available on the parties responsible for a Web page, no information is transcribed for $c of field 245.

245	00	Central and East European legal, political, business and economics WWW resources $h[computer file]

Area 2. Edition (9.2, MARC field 250)

AACR2R is liberal in defining the edition statement of computer files. If a file has any wording indicating the existence of the same information in different form, it can be interpreted as an edition statement. Olson's guide states that in case of doubt, a statement can be treated as an edition statement. Edition statements do not appear very often in Internet resources, however. Catalogers should look for words such as edition, version, and release as an indication of the presence of an edition statement. For example, the electronic version of a historical text is so noted in field 250 because the edition statement appears prominently.

245	00	The end of an era $h [computer file] / $c John Sergeant Wise, 1846-1913.
250		Electronic ed.

["Electronic Edition" appears below the title proper.]

245	00	Proceedings of the Workshop and Conference on Grand Challenge Applications and Software Technology 1993 $h [computer file]
250		Electronic version.

["Electronic version edited by Rick Stevens" appears on the title screen.]

Some resources indicate the version of software needed to read the files. This should not be interpreted as the edition statement for the files.

An update statement indicates when a Web resource was last revised. Libraries vary in their treatment of this information. Some consider it an edition statement and enter it in field 250, while others use a note for the update statement or add it to the note for title proper source. The objective is to indicate which version was used for cataloging purposes. A recent practice, recommended by a rule interpretation to Rule 12.7B3 for electronic serials (CSB 79) and endorsed in the *CONSER Cataloging Manual*, is to include viewing date in the source note for title proper. This serves a similar function and seems to be used by more and more libraries.

Old practice: 250	Updated August 8, 1998.
Old practice: 500	Title from home page; last updated Feb. 6, 1998.
New practice: 500	Title from title screen (viewed March 5, 1998).

The cataloging community has been sensitive to the importance of edition and a practice encouraged by *AACR2R* and OCLC is to create a new bibliographic record for each new edition. This practice, however, cannot be applied to Internet resources because such resources undergo continuous changes. The new practice above is a good compromise.

Area 3. File Characteristics
(9.3, MARC field 256)

This field is required for Internet resources. Currently three phrases are used for this field, including "computer data," "computer program," and "computer data and program." If more specific information is available, it can be used with these phrases. For example, "computer sound data" and "computer text data" can be used for files containing a particular type of data. The inadequacy of the three phrases listed above is obvious and *ISBD (ER)* has proposed an expanded list of terms for file characteristics.

CONSER guidelines indicate that field 256 is not used with electronic journal. *AACR2R* Chapter 12 specifies that for serial Area 3 typically includes numeric or chronological designation and field 362 is used for this purpose.

362 0   1982-

362 0   Issue 1 (June 1997-)

362 1   Began publication in May 1995.

[when the first issue is not available but its publication date is known.]

Area 4. Publication, Distribution, Etc. (9.4, MARC field 260)

All Internet resources are considered published, and the publication information is recorded in Area 4. Unlike print resources, Internet resources are not always published by commercial printing houses. Web pages can reside on the Web server of an organization, a government agency, a company, or an educational organization. The place of publication is often not readily available, and any information supplied by the cataloger will need to be presented in square brackets. If no publisher is clearly named, but there is evidence that the item emanates from a particular organization, that organization can be considered the publisher and the location of the organization the place of publication.[20]

Assigning a date to Internet resources can be a challenge because most of these resources are dynamic in nature and many have multiple copyright dates and update statements. *AACR2R* is usually followed to select the date of publication. For static publications that are not expected to change, a closed entry is used. Many government documents, articles, and conference proceedings have finite dates and are recorded as such.

100 1   Carver, Gary P.

245 14   The metric path to global markets and new jobs $h
              [computer file] : $b a question-and-answer and
              thematic discussion / $c Gary P. Carver.

260   Gaithersburg, MD : $b Dept. of Commerce, Technology
              Administration, National Institute of Standards and
              Technology, Metric Program, Technology Services,
              $c 1994.

[Publication date June 1994 appears on the title screen.]

245 00   Education reforms and students at risk $h [computer
              file] : $b a review of the current state of the art

260           $c 1994.

["January 1994" appears below the title.]

LC *Draft Interim Guidelines* for electronic resources treat single-part ongoing resources as nonserial publication and apply rules for loose-leaf publications to them. OCLC supports this treatment. So for Web sites that are continuously updated, such as home pages and databases, an open entry is used.

245	00	Yahoo $h [computer file]
256		Computer online service
260		[Stanford, Calif.] : $b Yahoo, $c 1994-
245	00	CEESource: Central and East European legal, political, business and economics WWW resources $h [computer file]
260		Spokane, Wash. : $b Gonzaga University School of Law, $c c1997-

[Copyright 1997-1998, because this is an ongoing publication we use an open entry.

For a serial on the Internet, if the first issue is available, an open entry is used.

| 260 | Madison, Wis. : $b Computer Science Dept., University of Wisconsin, $c 1995- |

When the first issue is not available, the date information for the electronic serial is blank and a note is given to specify the basis of the description.

245	PAS-L $h [computer file]
260	Houston : $b University of Houston,
500	Description based on: Vol. 2.

MARC Field 270. Primary address: Field 270 is a new field created to present contact information for Internet resources. Information on the address, phone number, and e-mail address of the contact person can be included. Such information is usually found on Web pages under links for "contact us," "comment," "feedback," and other similar terms.

270	Address $b City $c State $e Postal code $k phone $m e-mail $p contact person $z Public note.
270	$m librarian@vh.org
270	Alzheimer's Association, 919 N. Michigan Ave., Suite 1000 $b Chicago $c IL $e 60611-1676 $k (312) 335-8770 $m webmaster@alz.org

Area 5. Physical Description.
Field 300 is not used for Internet resources.

Area 6. Series (MARC fields 4XX):
Series title information is similar to that for print resources.

Area 7. Notes.

Area 7 is one of the most important areas for Internet resources because catalogers tend to use notes to provide a detailed description of such resources. The notes may include description of the resource or information on a resource's creation, content, location, its relationship with other resources, the system required to access it, and many other characteristics. Field 500 is used for many of these purposes. *AACR2R* stipulates that the notes are to be presented in the order specified under 9.7, but *AACR2R* also allows notes that are most important to users to be entered first. The *AACR2R* order of notes follows the order of the eight areas for bibliographic description. *CONSER*, however, instructs catalogers to enter notes in the order of the tag number. Local systems may rearrange the order of the notes, and catalogers should be aware of how their local system processes their notes.

Notes that are common to Internet resources include:

9.7B1a. Scope and Nature of the File (MARC field 516). Information such as type of file, format, or genre of a remote access computer file is recorded in field 516, if it is not clear from the rest of the record. Information on multiple formats is also recorded in field 516.

516	Text in PDF and images in JPEG format.
516	Numeric (statistics)
516	Electronic journal articles available in HTML format; selected articles available in PDF format.
516	PDF, PostScript, and TIFF formats available for printing.

For serials, serial frequency is recorded (Rule 12.7B1) in filed 310.

310	Updated daily.
310	Quarterly

9.7B1b. System Requirements (MARC field 538): For resources accessed remotely, this note indicates the program(s) and/or other devices needed to access the resources.

| 538 | System requirements: Acrobat Reader; QuickTime. |

| 538 | System requirements: RealPlayer; PostScript printer. |

9.7B1c. Mode of access (MARC field 538): A required note to indicate how the file can be accessed. Field 856 provides the address of the file, so this note in field 538 is usually brief. The old practice to enter host address is discontinued.

| 538 | Mode of access: World Wide Web. |

| 538 | Mode of access: FTP and Gopher via the Internet. |

9.7B2. Language(s) (MARC field 546): This information should be coordinated with the "Lang" element in the fixed field and with the 041 field.

| 546 | Text in English and German. |

9.7B3. Source of Title Proper (MARC field 500): This is a required note. Typically sources of title proper are title screen, main menu, "readme" file, "about" link, HTML header or HTML source code, TEI header, and others. A recent practice is to add the last viewing date to this note to inform users which version of the file was used to create the bibliographic record.

| 500 | Title from title screen. |

| 500 | Title from HTML source code (viewed May 5, 1995). |

| 500 | Description based on: No. 27; title from "about" documentation (viewed July 14, 1996). |

9.7B6. Statement of Responsibility (MARC fields 500 and 536): If the author information is not included in Area 1 because the information is not on the title screen, it is recorded in a 500 field to justify the selection of access points. Information on sponsors is entered in field 536.

| 500 | Authors: Lou Bernard and Richard Light. |

| 536 | Funded by the New York State Library. |

| 536 | Sponsored by the AT&T Fund. |

9.7B7. Edition and History (MARC field 500): *AACR2R* stipulates that if the source of the edition statement is different from that of the title proper, a note should be provided. In addition, Information about the edition and its history, if important, can be presented in a 500 note.

500   File first released in 1990.

9.7B8. File Characteristics (MARC field 500): This note is different from field 516 in that it provides additional information, not available in other areas of the description, about a resource, while field 516 indicates the type, format, or genre of a remote computer file.

516   Text in HTML and SGML.

500   Encoded according to TEI-lite.

9.7B9. Publication, Distribution, etc. (MARC field 500): This note is for any important publication information not included in Area 4. If information on date appears on the file, it is usually presented in a quote note.

500   "June 25, 1997."

Field 500 for serial records created not based on first issue (12.7B23)

500   Description based on: No. 7 (1996).

9.7B10. Physical Description (MARC field 500): This note describes information about sound, color, and other physical characteristics of the item if it is not included elsewhere in the record.

500   Audio content of the conference proceedings available through RealPlayer.

9.7B14. Intended Audience (MARC field 521): If a formal statement of the intended audience is in the item, it is recorded in field 521. A print constant, "Audience:" will display before the note if the first indicator is blank. Rating information is also entered in field 521. If indicator 8 is used, no print constant will be displayed. Catalogers should not impose personal judgment on the intellectual level of an item.

521   Ages: 8–10.

521   Adult users only.

521 8   Rated G.

9.7B16. Other Formats (MARC field 530): If the same information is available in other formats, it should be noted in field 530.

245 10   Access to multimedia technology by people with sensory disabilities.

530   Also available on CD-ROM.

If a record for a print publication exists and an online version becomes available, the cataloger has two choices:

1. Single record approach:

   a. Add a 530 field to the print record to indicate the availability of the online version.

   b. Add a 856 field to indicate the location of the online version.

   c. Add a 740 field if the title of the online version differs from that of the print version.

   d. Optionally, a computer file 007 field may be added for the online version.

245	00	Management of digital resources.
530		Also available in online version.
856	41	$u http://www.mdr.com/

   [Explanation: The second indicator ("1") of 856 indicates the URL is for an electronic version of the item (the print one) represented by the record.]

2. Separate record approach:

   a. Create one record for the online version.

   b. To the online record add a 530 field to indicate the availability of the print version and a 776 field to link to the record of the print version.

   c. To the print record add a 530 field to indicate the availability of the online version, a 776 field to link to the online version, and an 856 field to indicate the location of the online version.

   d. Add a 730 field if the title of the online version differs from that of the print version.

   • Record for the online version:

130	0	Management of digital resources (Online)
245	00	Management of digital resources $h [computer file]
530		Also available in print version.
776	1	Management of digital resources.
856	40	$u http://www.mdr.com/

   [Explanation: Because the online version and the print version have the same title, a uniform title with a qualifier is used for the new title. The second indicator ("0") in 856 indicates the URL is for the item (the online one) represented by the record.]

- Record for the print version:

245	00	Management of digital resources.
530		Also available in online version.
776	1	Management of digital resources (Online).
856	41	$u http://www.mdr.com/

  [Explanation: The title 776 refers to is the online version, and the second indicator ("1") of 856 indicates the URL is an electronic version of the print publication.]

9.7B17. Summary (MARC field 520): This note describes the purpose and/or contents of an item and may serve to provide linkage to related resources. The statement should be concise and objective. To create a formal note, the first indicator is "blank" and a display constant "Summary:" will be displayed. If an informal note is desired, value "8" is used for the first indicator. When an item has a clear statement of its objectives, it is acceptable to create a quote note with it.

245	00	Developmental Biology Cinema $h [computer file]
520		DBC's mission is "to get video sequences of developing embryos (organisms), and experimental techniques, from the developmental biologist's lab to the eyeballs of interested individuals in a user-friendly and inexpensive form."

9.7B18. Contents (MARC field 505): This note complements the summary note. It informs users of the contents of a resource by listing the main headings from a Web page. The first indicator value "0" will produce a display constant "Contents:".

245	00	Yahoo $h [computer file]
505	0	What's new? -- What's cool? -- What's popular? -- A random link -- Art -- Business -- Computers -- Economy -- Education -- Entertainment -- Environment and nature -- Events -- Government -- Health -- Humanities -- Law -- News -- Politics -- Reference -- Regional information -- Science -- Social science -- Society and culture.

If catalogers wish to index parts of an item, they can enter the parts under subfield t and use "0" on the second indicator to produce an "enhanced" contents note.

505	00	$t / $r author -- $t / $r author 2 -- $t / $r author 3.

9.7B20. Restrictions on Access (MARC fields 506 and 590): This note specifies how access to the file is restricted.

506	Restrictions on access: Site subscription required.
506	Some files restricted to CUA users only.

Information on local access is recorded in field 590.

590	Electronic access sponsored by VIVA, the Virtual Library of Virginia.

Electronic Location and Access (MARC field 856): This field was developed to provide the address of a file that is accessed remotely. Many subfields are allowed, and there is **no prescribed order** for entering the subfields. The first indicator specifies the access method (gopher, ftp, telnet, http, etc.), while the second indicator indicates the relationship between the file listed in field 856 and the item represented by the bibliographic record. In 1998 MARBI (Machine-Readable Bibliographic Information) approved changes to field 856 by adding a new value ("4" = http) for the first indicator. OCLC began implementing these changes on March 16, 1998. LC will implement these changes in the future. [21]

If the file listed in field 856 and the item represented by the record are the same, which is usually the case when the item is an electronic resource, the second indicator value "0" is assigned. Subfield u presents the Uniform Resource Locator in a standard syntax and can be repeated if necessary.

245	00	Field 856 guideline $h [computer file]
856	40	$u http://lcweb.loc.gov/marc/856guide.html

But when the file listed in field 856 is a part of the item represented by the record, the second indicator value is blank and a subfield 3 is used to record information about the part. This method is used most often when we have a collection - level record and field 856 is used to list the constituent parts of the collection.

A common situation is mirror sites. Sites that are considered of interest to global audience tend to be mirrored in various countries. Catalogers will need to verify the contents of the mirror sites before recording the URLs of those sites. These URLs are recorded to provide users alternate access to the same information.

245	00	Virtual Hospital $h [computer file]
856	41	$z Mirror site (Australia) $u http://australia.vh.org/ International/australia.html
856	41	$z Mirror site (Taiwan) $u http://taiwan.vh.org/ International/taiwan.html

Internet resources can also be accessed by gopher, FTP, telnet, e-mail, and other methods. These methods can all be recorded in field 856. Details of the subfield codes can be found at the *MARC21* site and the OCLC input standards site. Typical subfields for e-mail, ftp, telnet, and http are included below to illustrate the use of field 856.

E-mail: An e-mail message is sent to a processor at a host site and an instruction is usually included for the host to process the request. To send an e-mail request, users need to know the host site (subfield a), the processor (subfield h), and the instruction for the processor (subfield i).

856   0   host name $h processor of request $i command $z
               public information

856   0 $z send e-mail message to $h listserv $a
               infoserv.nlc-bnc.ca $i subscribe DIGLIB your name

[This note instructs users to subscribe to the DIGLIB discussion group by sending a message "subscribe DIGLIB your name" to listserv@infoserv.nlc-bnc.ca. Subfield z is a public message to be displayed, subfield h lists the part appearing before the @ sign, and subfield a lists the host name, the part appearing after the @ sign. Subfield i contains the command for the processor. There is no prescribed order for entering the subfields.]

FTP: Information at FTP sites is stored in files and in directories. To access such information users need to know the host of an FTP site (subfield a), the directory name (subfield d), and the file name (subfield f). If information about password and logon is needed for access, subfield k is used for password and subfield l for logon instruction.

856   10   host name $d path of file $f filename $k guest $l
               anonymous

856   10   rtfm.mit.edu $d /pub/usenet/news.answers/ $f ftp-list/

Subfield u is designed for the uniform resource locator, which has a standard syntax for locating Internet resources using existing Internet protocols. Catalogers may use subfield u instead of several subfields to represent the address of an item. For instance, the next two 856 fields represent the same FTP file:

856   10   ftp.sunet.se $d /pub/music/pictures/Beatles/ $f
               paul.gif

856   10 $u ftp://ftp.sunet.se/pub/music/pictures/Beatles/
               paul.gif

TELNET: By TELNET users connect to a remote computer, so the address of the remote computer (subfield a), and any information on terminal emulation (subfield t), password (subfield k), or login (subfield l) is recorded in the 856 field for a telnet site.

856	20	host name $t terminal emulation $k password $l logon
856	20	nyplgate.nypl.org $b 149.123.1.2 $l nypl
856	20	database.carl.org $p 192.54.81.76 $t vt100
856	20	library.city.ac.uk $b 138.40.164.101 $l library $k library

If subfield u is used, this note would be

856	20	$u telnet://library.city.ac.uk $l library $k library

HTTP: By http users access resources on the Web, so the address of the remote file is the most important information for the 856 field. Any information for the public is recorded in subfield z.

856	40	$u URL $z public note.
856	40	http://www.arl.org
856	40	http://cgi.pbs.org/weta/twib/
856	40	http://www.lib.virginia.edu/dmc/midi.html/ $z For instructional purposes use only at UVA

Special characters: URLs sometimes include special characters such as the underscore (_) and the tilde (~). Because some local online catalogs cannot recognize these characters, the current practice is to enter the hexadecimal value of these characters preceded by a percent sign. Use %5F for spacing underscore and %7E for spacing tilde. For example: http://www.oneday.com/~travel/ should be entered as http://www.oneday.com/%7Etravel/.

Remote Access Electronic Serials

The *CONSER Cataloging Manual* provides the most authoritative guidance for the cataloging of electronic serials.[25] There are in fact more similarities than differences between the cataloging of print serials and that of electronic serials. Several steps are similar. For example, the chief source is the title screen(s) of the first issue or the earliest available issue. The numerical/chronological designation of the first issue is recorded, and if the first issue is not available, a note "Description based on:" should be entered in field 500. The frequency of the serial is recorded if known.

In addition, following *CONSER* practice, notes in records for regular serials and electronic serials are arranged in numerical order.

Importance differences between print and electronic serial records include:

1. The 006 field is required of all records for electronic serials. For a language-based electronic serial, the serials format is used for the record and a 006 field is added to cover the computer file characteristics. For a non-language-based electronic serial, the primary characteristic (sound or computer file, for example) decides the fixed field format for the record, and a 006 field is added to indicate the serial aspects of the item. (This is the result of a new definition of "type of record" code "m," which was implemented in early 1998 and has a narrower scope for code "m".)

2. The source of the title proper of a remote access electronic serial is always presented in a 500 note, with the last viewing date included in parentheses.

3. A uniform title qualified by the physical medium is used when the electronic version and its counterpart in another format have the same title.

4. A 516 field is used to record the formats in which the file is available (e.g., PDF format and ASCII format).

5. A 530 field is used to indicate the availability of the serial in other forms.

6. A 538 field is used to indicate mode of access.

7. 856 field or fields is used to indicate access method(s).

Two records are included here to illustrate some of these similarities and differences:

Type: a   Elvl: Srce: d   Gpub: Ctrl: Lang: eng

BLvl: s   Form: Conf: 0   Freq: q   MRec: Ctry: cau

S/L: 0   Orig: EntW: Regl: r   ISSN: 1   Alph: a

Desc: a   SrTp: p   Cont: DtSt: c   Dates: 1997,9999

006		[m d]
007		c $b r $d c $e n
022	0	1093-7927
130	0	Advances in environmental research (Online)
245	00	Advances in environmental research $h [computer file].
260		Berkeley, CA : $b [s.n., $c 1997-
310		Quarterly
362	0	Vol. 1, no. 1-
500		Title from title screen (viewed March 15, 2000).
516		Electronic journal in HTML and PDF formats.
530		Also available in print.
538		System requirements: Adobe Acrobat Reader needed to view PDF files.
538		Mode of access: World Wide Web.
776	1	$t Advances in environmental research $x 1093-0191
856	40	$u http://www.sfo.com/~aer/

Explanation

Fixed field, 006, 007

- This record reflects the current practice of using the serials format for electronic serial (coded "s" in BLvl). Several fixed field elements are unique to this format, including S/L (successive/latest entry, code 0 for successive entry), SrTp (serial type, code p for periodical), Freq (frequency, code q for quarterly), Regl (regularity of the serial, code r for regular), DtSt (publication status, code c for current, and ISSN (International Standard Serial Number, code 1 for presence of an ISSN). The Dates element usually includes the beginning date and closing date of a serial. A 006 field is used to indicate the computer file characteristics, with code m representing a computer file, code d textual data. A 007 field is required for computer files, and the codes identify this item as a computer file (code c) that is accessed remotely (code r), multicolored (code c), and no dimensional elements apply (code n).

Variable fields

- 130: The uniform title is the print title qualified by the physical medium. It serves to tell the two titles apart.

- 310 & 362: Frequency note and the note for numerical designation are the same for print and electronic serials.

- 500: The source of title for a remote access electronic serial is always recorded and the last viewing date included.

- 516: This field records the type, file, or format of a title.

- 530: This field indicates the existence of a print version.

- 538s: A system requirement note and a mode of access note are common to remote electronic serials.

- 776: This note links this title to the print title, and the ISSN of the print title is included.

- 856: The note records the location of the item, with the indicator 4 identifying http as the access method, and the indicator 0 indicating that the file at this location is the one represented by the bibliographic record.

Type: a Elvl: Srce: d Gpub: Ctrl: Lang: eng

BLvl: s Form: Conf: 0 Freq: b MRec: Ctry: ilu

S/L: 0 Orig: EntW: Regl: r ISSN: 1   Alph: a

Desc: a SrTp: p Cont: DtSt: c Dates: 1998,9999

006		[m d]
007		c $b r $d c $e n
022	0	1523-018X
037		$b ALCTS, 50 E. Huron St., Chicago, IL 60611
245	00	ALCTS newsletter online $h [computer file]
260		Chicago, IL : $b Association for Library Collections & Technical Services, American Library Association, $c c1998-
310		Six no. a year
362	0	Vol. 10, no. 1 (Dec. 1998)-
500		Title from newsletter homepage (viewed March 15, 2000).
516		Online newsletter in HTML format.
538		Mode of access: World Wide Web.
610	20	Association for Library Collections & Technical Services $v Periodicals.
650	0	Cataloging $v Periodicals.
650	0	Information retrieval $v Periodicals.
650	0	Abstracting and indexing $v Periodicals.
650	0	Library science $v Periodicals.
710	2	Association for Library Collections & Technical Services.
780	00	$t ALCTS newsletter $x 1047-949X $w (DLC)91649699 $w (OCoLC)20820888
856	40	$u http://www.ala.org/alcts/alcts_news/archive.html

Explanation

Fixed field, 006, 007

- This record reflects the current practice of using the serials format for electronic serial (coded "s" in BLvl). Several fixed field elements are unique to this format, including S/L (successive/latest entry, code 0 for successive entry), SrTp (serial type, code p for periodical), Freq (frequency, code b for every two months), Regl (regularity of the serial, code r for regular), DtSt (publication status, code c for current, and ISSN (International Standard Serial Number, code 1 for presence of an ISSN). The Dates element usually includes the beginning date and closing date of a serial. A 006 field is used to indicate the computer file characteristics, with code m representing a computer file, code d textual data. A 007 field is required for computer files, and the codes identify this item as a computer file (code c) that is accessed remotely (code r), multicolored (code c), and no dimensional elements apply (code n).

Variable fields

- 037: Like print serial records, this field replaces field 265 for the recording of subscription address of a publisher.

- 362: The numerical designation of the first online issue is recorded, with the chronological designation in parentheses, and an open entry is used in subfield c of field 260. Because this title continues a print publication, the volume number does not begin with number one.

- 500: The source of title for Internet resources is a required note that is presented in field 500 and the last viewing date is included in parentheses.

- 516: This note records the nature of this publication and its file characteristics.

- 538: A required note for all Internet resources.

- 610 & 650s: Because the serial covers activities of the Association as well as subjects of interest to its members, subject access is provided through the corporate body and the topics. A form heading, "periodicals" (coded subfield v), is assigned to all subject access points.

- 780: The immediate predecessor of this title is recorded to link related titles together. The ISSN, LC Card number, and OCLC number of the predecessor are included in appropriate subfields.

- 856: The note records the location of the item, with indicator 4 identifying http as the access method, and the indicator 0 indicating that the file at this location is the one represented by the bibliographic record.

Assignment of Access Points

Rules for the selection of access points apply to print and electronic resources alike. Personal names, corporate bodies, and titles can serve as main entries if the criteria are met. Web pages created by individuals often have their creators as the main entry, and compilers of subject guides are considered authors. Resources issued or hosted by a corporate body that belongs to one of the six categories enumerated in Rule 21.1B2 will have the corporate body as the main entry. Title becomes the main entry when authorship is diffuse or unknown, when a work is under editorial direction, when a work is the sacred scripture of a religious group, or when a work is issued by a corporate body but the corporate body is not the main entry. Uniform title is selected as the main entry when it is necessary to bring together various manifestations of a work. According to LCRI 25.5B, a computer file serial that is also published in another format is not considered a reproduction, so a uniform title qualified by the medium should be used to describe the item. *CONSER* indicates the term "online" may be sufficient to distinguish the electronic version from the other version.[22]

245	00	Journal of child psychology [the print title]
130	0	Journal of child psychology (Online)
245	00	Journal of child psychology $h [computer file]

Rules 21.29 and 21.30 guide the selection of added entries. Individuals or corporate bodies that are named prominently and contribute to the creation, publication, and access to a remote access serial can be selected as added entries. Webmasters or Web page creators, for example, can be added entries if their contribution is significant. This information is often found in an "about this page" link or similar links. Some Webmasters include their name in the meta tag as "author" (meaning author of the Web page), which should not be interpreted

as the person responsible for the intellectual content of the work. The corporate body that hosts a Web page is often made an added entry. Title is usually an added entry when it is not the main entry. In addition, added entries are made for related works. For instance, if a work is the electronic version of a print publication, besides indicating that in a note, the cataloger will want to provide an added entry for the original work. If a personal author is known, it will be a 700 entry; if the item has a title main entry, a 730 entry will be used. Analytical added entries can also be made.

500		Based on Interactive SGML by Mark Smith.
700	1	Smith, Mark. $t Interactive SGML.
500		Based on the Cambridge companion to Galileo.
730	0	Cambridge companion to Galileo.

■ SUBJECT ANALYSIS

In assigning subject headings catalogers should treat Internet resources the same as other types of material. Principles regarding the specificity and the number of heading to be assigned also apply to Internet resources (see *SCM* H180). Subject information of these resources can often be learned from the title, subtitle, table of contents, "about" link, hyperlinks, and the metadata in the source code. Regardless of how resources are accessed (by gopher or by FTP, for instance), the same headings should be assigned to resources on the same subject. It should be noted that subdivision "--Computer network resources" is not a form subdivision and should not be assigned automatically to indicate that an item is an electronic resource. It is often used under a topical heading for a collection of electronic resources on a topic. Library of Congress does not have a form subdivision such as "electronic resources" to describe Internet resources, but it has "electronic journals" now for remote access computer file serials.

The decision to classify Internet resources was controversial because classification numbers tend to be associated with the location of a work. Since libraries do not physically own Internet resources, some catalogers were reluctant to classify them. But many catalogers and researchers have pointed out the importance of classification for browsing and searching, and the benefit for collection development and management.[23] The DESIRE project analyzed several classification schemes for their retrieval power and concluded that classification could be an efficient way for searching electronic resources.[24]

The classification of Internet resources is the same as that of other resources. After the cataloger determines the main thrust of a work, the most specific number is assigned, including building a number that is not listed in the selected classification schedule. Many libraries add "Internet" to their call numbers to alert users that these resources are not on site, while others list "Internet" in their location field for it to be displayed right next to the call number. Some have used terms such as electronic journal, Web site, and Online U.S. document to sort search results.

Cataloging Examples begin on page 232.

■ CATALOGING EXAMPLES

Title screen:

ACCESS TO MULTIMEDIA TECHNOLOGY BY PEOPLE
WITH SENSORY DISABILITIES

March 13, 1998
National Council on Disability
1331 F Street, NW, Suite 1050
Washington, DC 20004-1107

202-272-2004 Voice
202-272-2074 TTY
202-272-2022 Fax
http://www.ncd.gov

This report is also available in braille and large print and on diskette and audiocassette.

The views contained in this report do not necessarily represent those of the administration, as this document has not been subjected to the A-19 Executive Branch review process.

****

TYPE: a

T006: m		Audn:	File: d	GPub:
007		c $b r $d a $e n		
043		n-us---		
090		HV1569.5		
092		362.4		
110	2	National Council on Disability (U.S.)		
245	10	Access to multimedia technology by people with sensory disabilities $h [computer file] / $c National Council on Disability.		
256		Computer text data.		
260		Washington, DC : $b The Council, $c 1998.		
538		Mode of access: World Wide Web.		
500		Title from title screen (viewed April 2, 1998).		
500		"March 13, 1998."		
530		Also available in braille and large print and on diskette and audiocassette.		
650	0	Computerized self-help devices for the handicapped $z United States.		
650	0	Computers and the handicapped $z United States.		
650	0	Interactive multimedia $z United States.		
650	0	Visually handicapped $x Services for $z United States.		
650	0	Hearing impaired $x Services for $z United States.		
856	40	$u purl.access.gpo.gov/GPO/LPS764		

Figure 7.1   Access to multimedia technology.

Discussion for Figure 7.1

- Type, 006, and 007: Type is coded "a" for language material, and a 006 field is added to represent the computer aspect of this item. This step will make the item retrievable when a search is qualified by format "COM." Code d in File indicates text file. Field 007 describes the physical characteristics of this page: computer file ("c"), remote access ("r"), one color ("a"), and dimensions not applicable ("n").

- 043: When a work has a geographic focus that is reflected by a geographic heading or a subdivision, 043 can be used to code the geographic area. The seven-character code is taken from the OCLC-MARC geographic area codes list.

- 110: The corporate body presents the study and concludes with its recommendations, so it is selected as the main entry.

- 256: This is an electronic document, so "computer text data" is used.

- 260: The Council is recorded in the statement of responsibility, so it is referred to here as "The Council." The publication date is clearly stated on the screen, so a close entry is used. It is acceptable to include the complete date information as a quotation note.

- 538: This note indicates the mode of access. It is always provided for Internet resources.

- 500: The source of title proper must be recorded in a note. LCRI 12.7B3 (CSB 79) recommends adding the date the title was viewed to remote access electronic serials. This practice has been applied by many libraries to Internet resources.

- 530: This field indicates the availability of the file in other formats.

- 856: Indicator "4" identifies HTTP as the access method and indicator "0" indicates the file at this URL is the item represented by the record.

```
Title screen:

[image of the following text information]
Virtual Hospital ® is the Apprentice's Assistant (TM)

Virtual Hospital ® is a registered trademark of The University of Iowa and
is registered in the United States.

Presented by the Electric Differential Multimedia Laboratory, Department of
Radiology, University of Iowa College of Medicine, Iowa City, Iowa.

Supported by University of Iowa Health Care.

  * Welcome to Virtual Hospital
    Look here to learn how to use Virtual Hospital, find out what's new,
    and discover who we are.

  * Departments and Clinical Services
    Look here for information about the University of Iowa Hospitals and
    Clinics Departments and Clinical Services.

  * For Patients
    Look here for the Iowa Health Book of educational materials for
    patients and families in the form of brochures and books.

  * For Healthcare Providers
    Look here for educational materials for healthcare providers in the
    form of multimedia textbooks, teaching files, patient simulations and
    lectures.
  ...
  * INFORMM (requires password & 3270 terminal emulation)
    For authorized University of Iowa students, faculty and affiliates
    only...
----------------------------------------------------------------------
View this page at the Virtual Hospital location nearest you: Australia |
Taiwan | United States

All contents copyright © 1992-1999 the Author(s) and the University of Iowa.
All rights reserved.
**********************************************************************
Type: m      BLvl: m      File: m    DtSt: m    Dates: 1992,9999
007                       c $b r $d c $e n
090                       Z699.5.M39
092                       025.0661
245          00           Virtual hospital $h [computer file] : $b the apprentice's assistant / $c presented by the
                          Electric Differential Multimedia Laboratory, Department of Radiology, University of
                          Iowa College of Medicine.
256                       Computer data and programs.
260                       Iowa City, Iowa : $b The University, $c 1992-
538                       Mode of access:  World Wide Web.
500                       Title from title screen (viewed April 2, 1999).
500                       "Supported by University of Iowa Health Care."
506                       The "Informm" section and the "Healthnet" section are restricted to University of Iowa
                          students, faculty, and affiliates.  Both require password.  The "Informm" section also
                          requires 3270 terminal emulation.
520                       A continuously updated digital health sciences library that provides information for
                          patients, practicing physicians and other healthcare professionals. Includes texts, photos,
                          videos.  The site is international in scope but includes some information specific to Iowa.
505          0            Welcome to Virtual Hospital -- Departments and clinical services -- For patients -- For
                          healthcare providers -- Beyond Virtual Hospital -- Virtual Children's Hospital --
                          Continuing education -- Informm -- HealthNet.
650          0            Health $x Computer network resources.
650          0            Medicine $x Computer network resources.
710          2            University of Iowa. $b College of Medicine. $b Electric Differential Multimedia
                          Laboratory.
710          2            University of Iowa Health Care.
856          40           $u http://www.vh.org/
856          41           $z  Mirror site in Australia $u http://australia.vh.org/
856          41           $z  Mirror site in Taiwan $u http://taiwan.vh.org/
```

Figure 7.2   Virtual Hospital.

Discussion for Figure 7.2

- Type: Type is coded as "m" for a computer file because this site includes several types of computer material and no predominance can be determined (per OCLC Guides by Weitz). Code m in File indicates several types of files are included. Field 007 describes the physical characteristics of this site: computer files, remote site, multicolor, and dimensions not applicable.

- 260: The University appears in Area 1, so it is referred to as "The University" in this area. This is an ongoing publication, so an open entry is used.

- 506: Information about restriction of access is entered in field 506. The emulation information is included here because it is related to the information in this note. An alternative place for the emulation information is field 538.

- 520 & 505: Sometimes it is appropriate to include a summary and a detailed contents note.

- 856s: The first 856 is for the main site, so the second indicator is "0." Indicator "1" refers to a version of the item represented by the bibliographic record and is used to indicate mirror sites.

Faculty of Classics

[image] External Gateway to Humanities Resources
(Click here for information on the image)

The links on this page lead to individual pages of information, listed by subject area. Every subject page is under 36k.

You may either **Search this Site**, or choose a subject from the selection below. (**Links in brackets**) lead directly to the section listing that topic:

Links: More latin links here

- Ancient History
  (Greek, Mediaeval, Numismatics, Oriental, Religion, Roman, Sexuality)
- Archaeology and AncientArt
  (Aegean, Associations, Departments, Egyptian, Etruscan, Museums, Near East, Sites)

...
[Bottom of the home page]

ARGOS Limited Area Search of the Ancient World

The Cambridge Classics External Gateway to Humanities Resources is an Associate Site of the Argos search engine. Please use the form below to search the Argos database.

...
About this site
Helping with using the WWW and links to other search engines

Cambridge Classics Home Page
Computer Office Faculty of Classics. Update 2.5.99

****

TYPE: a
T006: m   Audn: File: d   GPub:
007   c $b r $d a $e n
090   Z699.5.H8
092   001.3
245   00   External gateway to humanities resources $h [computer file] / $c Faculty of Classics.
246   30   Cambridge classics external gateway to humanities resources
256   Computer data and programs.
260   Cambridge : $b Cambridge Classics, $c 1992-
538   Mode of access: World Wide Web.
500   Title from title screen (viewed April 2, 1999).
500   An associate site of the Argos search engine.
520   This page contains links to electronic resources by subject area, each subject page is under 36k. Users can follow the link or use the Argos search engine to search the site.
505   0   Ancient history -- Archaeology and ancient art -- Classics: General resources -- Classical departments and associations -- Classical literature and drama -- Linguistics and literary theory -- Modern literature and humanities resources -- Philosophy and ancient science.
650   0   Archaeology $x Computer networked resources.
650   0   Classics $x Computer networked resources.
650   0   Linguistics $x Computer networked resources.
650   0   Humanities $x Computer networked resources.
650   0   Philosophy $x Computer networked resources.
710   2   Cambridge University. $b Classics Dept.
856   40 $u http://www.classics.cam.ac.uk/Faculty/links.html

Figure 7.3   External gateway.

Discussion for Figure 7.3

- Type, 006, 007: Type is coded "a" for language materials. Field 006 is mandatory because Type is not code "m." Code d in File indicates the site is mainly textual. Field 007 encodes the physical characteristics of this site: computer file, remote access, one color, and dimensions not applicable.

- 245: The author statement is transposed to the proper part in Area 1.

- 246: This title is used at the bottom of the Web page, so a variant title added entry is used.

- 260: This subject page is updated frequently, so an open entry is used.

- 520 & 505: 520 explains the nature of the page, its organization, size, and access methods, while 505 lists the main topics. Since both types of information are important, both fields are included.

- 650s: This page contains collections of resources for several topics, so it is appropriate to use this topical subdivision. It is used under every topical heading.

- 856: The URL is entered in subfield u, indicator 4 identifies HTTP as the access method, and indicator 0 explains the file at the URL location is the one represented by the record.

Title screen:
[image THE GALILEO PROJECT - Rice University]

The Galileo Project is a hypertext source of information on the life and work of Galileo Galilei (1564-1642) and the science of his time. The project is supported by the Office of the Vice President of Computing of Rice University. The initial stages were made possible by a grant from the Council on Library Resources to Fondren Library.

Albert Van Helden
Elizabeth Burr

Introduction
   Developers
   Copyright
   Recent Recognition
   Comments and Questions
   RiceInfo
Galileo's Villa
   Family Quarters
      Text about Galileo's family can be found in this room.
   Laboratory
      Information about Galileo's inquiries in mechanics (physics) is
      available in this room

...

The Galileo Project Development Team
August 5, 1996
Copyright ©1995 Albert Van Helden

****

Type: a				
T006: m		Audn:	File: d	GPub:
007		c $b r $d c $e n		
090		QB36.G2		
092		520.92		
100	1	Van Helden, Albert.		
245	14	The Galileo project $h [computer file] / $c Albert Van Helden, Elizabeth Burr.		
256		Computer data and program.		
260		[Houston, TX] : $b Rice University, $c 1995-		
516		Text and graphics.		
538		Mode of access: World Wide Web.		
500		Title from title screen (viewed April 2, 1999).		
500		Webmaster, Krist Burn.		
536		Initial stages of the project supported by a grant from the Council on Library Resources to Fondren Library.		
520		"A hypertext source of information on the life and work of Galileo Galilei (1564-1642) and the science of his time."		
505	0	Introduction -- Galileo's villa -- Resources -- Maps of Galileo's world -- Timeline of Galileo's life & era -- Student work.		
600	10	Galilei, Galileo, $d 1564-1642 $x Computer network resources.		
700	1	Burr, Elizabeth.		
700	1	Burn, Krist.		
710	2	Rice University.		
710	2	Council on Library Resources.		
856	40	$u http://es.rice.edu/ES/humsoc/Galileo/		

Figure 7.4   Galileo project.

Discussion for Figure 7.4

- Type, 006, 007: This site includes several types of data, but text is the predominant type, so Type is coded "a" for language material. Field 006 is added to represent the computer aspect, and code d in File indicates the site is mainly textual. Field 007 describes the physical characteristics of the file: computer file, remote access, multicolored, and dimensions not applicable.

- 100 & 245: The authors are prominently listed in the chief source, so the first author is selected as the main entry.

- 260: The place of publication is taken outside of the page, so it is entered in square brackets. An open entry is used because this is an ongoing publication.

- 516: This note makes explicit the nature of information on this site.

- 500: Webmaster information is from the "developers" link. The description there indicates his role is important, so an added entry is made for this person.

- 536: Funding information is entered in 536 this note also explains why an added entry is made for this corporate body.

- 505: Contents note lists titles of parts of a work. Only the main headings are included.

- 700s: The co-author and the Webmaster are traced for their contribution to this item.

- 710s: Corporate bodies are traced per Rule 21.30.

Title screen:

The EAD Roundtable of the Society of American Archivists
presents
<EAD> HELP PAGES

- MISSION STATEMENT & BACKGROUND
- EAD SOURCE FILES
- READINGS ON SGML/XML
- EAD SITES BY LOCATION (LC list)
- EAD SITES ANNOTATED (Delivery Methods, Encoding Schemes, Contact Information, RLG Participation)
- TRAINING & FUNDING
- TOOLS & HELPER FILES
- INDEXING AND METADATA
- CONVERSION
- I NEED HELP!!!

Disclaimer

Last updated March 1999. Send comments to timothy.young@yale.edu
URL is http://jefferson.village.virginia.edu/ead/index.html

****

Type: a				
T006: m		Audn:	File: d	GPub:
007		c $b r $d a $e n		
090		Z695.2		
092		025.324		
245	04	The EAD Roundtable of the Society of American Archivists presents EAD help pages $h [computer file]		
246	30	EAD help pages		
246	3	Encoded archival description help pages		
256		Computer text data and programs.		
260		[Chicago] : $b Society of American Archivists, $c 1999-		
270		Send comments to $m timothy.young@yale.edu		
538		Mode of access: World Wide Web.		
500		Title from title screen (viewed April 2, 1999).		
500		"Last updated March 1999."		
505	0	Mission statement & background -- EAD source files -- Readings on SGML/XML -- EAD sites by location (LC list) -- EAD sites annotated (delivery methods, encoding schemes, contact information, RLG participation) -- Training & funding -- Tools & helper files -- Indexing and metadata -- Conversion -- I need help!!!		
650	0	Encoded Archival Description (Document type definition)		
710	2	Society of American Archivists. $b EAD Roundtable.		
856	40	$u http://jefferson.village.virginia.edu/ead/index.html		

Figure 7.5   EAD help page.

Discussion for Figure 7.5

- Type, 006, 007: This site is predominantly textual, so Type is coded "a" for language material. Field 006 is added to represent the computer aspect, and code d in File indicates the site is mainly textual. Field 007 describes the physical characteristics of the file: computer file, remote access, multicolored, and dimensions not applicable.

- 245 & 246: The corporate body is transcribed as part of the title proper, but a variant title is provided for the portion following the corporate body to make it searchable. Indicator 3 specifies that no note will be produced, but an added entry will be made for the variant title. Indicator 0 indicates the variant title is portion of the title proper. For the second 246 field the second indicator is blank because there is no appropriate code to indicate it is the same title with the acronym spelled out.

- 256: The resources at this site include text files and conversion programs, so a statement is presented to specify the characteristics of these files.

- 260: Since this resource is an ongoing publication, an open entry is used.

- 270: Contact information is entered in field 270; subfield m is for email address.

- 500: The note for the last update is optional. Some libraries have treated such information as an edition statement, while others have presented it as a quotation note. The purpose is to indicate which version of the Web page was used to create the bibliographic record. If a library adds the date a page was last viewed to the record, this note may not be as useful or necessary.

Title screen:
July, 1994 Common Sense, by Thomas Paine [comsn10x.xxx] [#147]

Common Sense, by Thomas Paine

PROJECT GUTENBERG ETEXT OF _COMMON SENSE_ BY
THOMAS PAINE

****

Type: a					
006		T006: m	Audn:	File: d	GPub:
007		c $b r $d a $e n			
043		n-us---			
090		E211			
092		320.973			
100	1	Paine, Thomas, $d 1737-1809.			
245	10	Common sense $h [computer file] / $c by Thomas Paine.			
246	3	Project Gutenberg etext of Common sense			
256		Computer text data (1 file : 137,327 bytes).			
260		Champaign, IL : $b Project Gutenberg, $c 1994.			
538		System requirements: Personal computer with modem, or Web browser with support for FTP.			
538		Mode of access: FTP via the Internet from Project Gutenberg (ftp uiarchive.cso.uiuc.edu); login as anonymous; password is e-mail address. Directory: /pub/etext/gutenberg/etext94. File names: comsn10.txt or comsn10.zip.			
500		Title from title screen (viewed April 2, 1999).			
500		"Project Gutenberg etext of Common sense by Thomas Paine."			
500		"July, 1994 . . . #147."			
530		May also be issued as ASCII text on diskette, or in print form.			
651	0	United States $x Politics and government $y 1775-1783.			
650	0	Political science $x History $y 18th century.			
650	0	Monarchy.			
710	2	Project Gutenberg.			
856	1	$u ftp://uiarchive.cso.uiuc.edu/pub/etext/gutenberg/etext94/comsn10.txt			
856	1	$u ftp://uiarchive.cso.uiuc.edu/pub/etext/gutenberg/etext94/comsn10.zip			

Figure 7.6   Common sense.

Discussion for Figure 7.6

- Type, 006, 007: This site is predominant textual, so Type is coded "a" for language material. Field 006 is added to represent the computer aspect, and code d in File indicates the site is mainly textual. Field 007 describes the physical characteristics of the file: computer file, remote access, multicolored, and dimensions not applicable.

- 043: When a subject has a geographic focus, field 043 can be added. The code is taken from the OCLC-MARC geographic area codes list.

- 246: The first indicator ("3") specifies that no note will be produced but an added entry will be made for the variant title. This is necessary because a note with the author's name is presented as a 500 note later. The second indicator is blank because there is no appropriate code to indicate this type of variant title.

- 256: The file number and the bytes information are readily available, so they are recorded in Area 3.

- 538s: The first 538 specifies the machinery needed to access the file, and the second explains how to access file. Detailed instructions are provided in case users prefer to retrieve the files this way. The URLs in the 856 fields provide easier access.

- 530: This note indicates the availability of the file in other formats.

- 856s: The file can be accessed in two ways, so two 856 fields are provided.

Title screen:

University of North Carolina at Chapel Hill Libraries
DOCUMENTING THE AMERICAN SOUTH

THE END OF AN ERA:
ELECTRONIC EDITION.
John Sergeant Wise,
1846-1913.

****

TYPE: a		
T006: m	Audn:	File: d	GPub:
007	c $b r $d c $e n
090	E605
092	973.782
100	1	Wise, John S. $q (John Sergeant), $d 1846-1913.
245	14	The end of an era $h [computer file] / $c John Sergeant Wise, 1846-1913.
250		Electronic ed.
256		Computer text data (1 file : 930K).
260		[Chapel Hill, N.C.] : $b Academic Affairs Library, University of North Carolina at Chapel Hill, $c 1998.
516		Text in HTML and SGML formats.
538		System requirements: Panorama viewer for SGML files.
538		Mode of access: World Wide Web.
500		Title from title screen (viewed April 2, 1999).
500		Text scanned (OCR) by Jessica Mathewson. Images scanned by Carlene Hempel. Text encoded by Carlene Hempel and Natalia Smith.
536		Funding from the Library of Congress/Ameritech National Digital Library Competition supported the electronic publication of this title.
500		Digitized version of: The end of an era / by John S. Wise.
500		Part of the UNC-CH digitization project, Documenting the American South, Beginnings to 1920.
504		Includes bibliographical references and index.
600	10	Wise, John S. $q (John Sergeant), $d 1846-1913.
650	0	Plantation life $z Virginia $x History $y 19th century.
650	0	Slavery $z Virginia.
651	0	Virginia $x History $y Civil War, 1861-1865 $x Personal narratives.
710	2	University of North Carolina at Chapel Hill. $b Documenting the American South (Project)
710	2	University of North Carolina at Chapel Hill. $b Library.
856	40	$u http://metalab.unc.edu/docsouth/wise/wise.sgml
856	40	$u http://metalab.unc.edu/docsouth/wise/wise.html

Figure 7.7   The end of an era.

Discussion for Figure 7.7

- Type, 006, 007: This is an electronic document, so Type is coded "a" (for language material). 006 is added to indicate the computer aspect of this work. Code d in File indicates text file. 007 encodes physical characteristics: computer file, remote access, multicolor, and dimensions not applicable.

- 260: The place of publication is taken outside of the page, so it is entered in square brackets. This is a finished work, so a closed entry is used.

- The notes are presented in the order specified by 9.7B.

- 516: The nature and file characteristics of this item are recorded in field 516.

- 538s: When information on system requirements and access mode is available, the note on system requirements is presented first.

- 500: Persons with technical responsibilities are listed here but not traced.

- 536: Funding information is recorded in field 536.

- 500: The basis for the content of this work is recorded in a 500 note.

- 500: The project information note explains the item's relationship to a project, and serves to justify the provision of that project as an added entry.

- 710s: Both the project and the publisher are traced.

- 856s: The file appears in two formats, so two 856 fields are provided.

```
Title screen
                        A Gateway Between the
                        World-Wide Web and PAT:
                        Exploiting SGML Through the
                                    Web
                             John Price-Wilkin
------------------------------------------------------------------------
To retrieve this file, use the following URL: gopher://info.lib.uh.edu:70/00/
articles/e-journals/uhlibrary/pacsreview/v5/n7/pricewil.5n7. Or, send the
following e-mail message to listserv@uhupvm1.uh.edu: GET PRICEWIL
PRV5N7 F=MAIL.

------------------------------------------------------------------------
************************************************************************

Type: a
T006: m          Audn:      File: d        GPoub:
007                         c $b r $d a $e n
090                         QA76.76
092                         005.72
100      1                  Price-Wilkin, W. John $q (William John), $d 1956-
245      12                 A gateway between the World-Wide Web and PAT $h
                            [computer file] : $b exploiting SGML through the Web / $c
                            John Price-Wilkin.
256                         Computer text data.
260                         Houston, TX : $b University Libraries, University of Houston,
                            $c 1994.
440      0                  Public-access computer systems review ; $v v. 5, no. 7
516                         Electronic document in ASCII text.
538                         Mode of access:  Gopher and electronic mail on the Internet.
500                         Title from printout of online display (viewed March 1, 1999).
520                         A technical paper on how to link the Web and the PAT system,
                            Open Text's search engine for SGML-encoded documents, by
                            using the Web's Common Gateway Interface capability and
                            SGML-to-HTML filter programs.
530                         Also available in print form.
650      0                  SGML (Document markup language)
650      0                  Text processing (Computer science).
650      0                  PAT (search engine)
856      0                  $u gopher://info.lib.uh.edu:70/00/articles/e-journals/uhlibrary/
                            pacsreview/v5/n7/pricewil.5n7
856      00                 listserv@uhupvm1.uh.edu $z Send e-mail message to $f
                            PACSReview $h listserv $i GET PRICEWIL PRV5N7
                            F=MAIL $u mailto: listserv@uhupvm1.uh.edu
```

Figure 7.8   A gateway.

Discussion for Figure 7.8

- Type, 006, 007: Code a in Type indicates language material. 006 is added to encode computer aspect of this item. Code d in file reflects text file. 007 describes physical characteristics of the file: computer file, remote access, one color, and dimensions not applicable.

- 090 & 092: QA76.76 is for "Computer Special topics" and 005.72 is for data encoding.

- 516: This note indicates the nature of this item.

- 538: Two modes of access are entered in one 538 field.

- 530: The availability of other format is entered in field 530.

- 856s: Two 856 fields are used to record the two access methods. The gopher one is simpler, with the first indicator blank because there is no specific indicator value assigned for gopher access. The second indicator shows the file represented by this 856 field is the one represented by the bibliographic record. The URL of the file is presented in subfield u. Information for e-mail access is more complex. The first indicator "0" names e-mail as the access method, $z presents the information for public display, $f is the file name, $h is the processor for the request and usually precedes the at sign in the host address, and $i is the instruction for the remote host to process a request. There is no prescribed order for entering subfields in field 856.

Title screen:
[image *SAILOR*: Maryland's Online Public Information Network]

What is *Sailor*?

Sailor is a statewide public network, connecting <u>libraries</u>, <u>schools</u> and <u>government</u> agencies to the <u>global Internet</u>. The *Sailor* Web site focuses on <u>Maryland information</u>, with links to other resources around the world, creating a virtual online library.

(<u>More Information about *Sailor*</u>)

* What's New, Hon?
* Maryland Libraries

* Project Gutenberg (on-line books)
* Cruise the Internet (subject index & Internet search engines)
*E-mail

* Maryland Information
* Infotrac SearchBank (on-line magazines & newspapers)
* GPO Access (on-line government documents)
* Search *Sailor* & Maryland Databases

* Help

Sponsored by your local Maryland Public Library

Sailor Operations Center
Voice: (410) 396-5551 - fax: (410) 396-3722
E-mail: askus@sailor.lib.md.us
http://www.sailor.lib.md.us
page updated 1 May 1999
site updated 1 May 1999

****

Type: m		BLvl: m	File: j
007		c $b r $d c $e n	
090		Z674.82.S3	
092		021.65	
245	00	*Sailor* $h [computer file] : $b Maryland's online public information network.	
246	30	Maryland's online public information network	
256		Computer data and programs.	
260		[Baltimore, MD] : $b *Sailor* Operations Center, $c [1994-	
270		E-mail inquiry to $m askus@sailor.lib.md.us	
516		Computer online service.	
538		Mode of access: World Wide Web.	
500		Title from title screen (viewed May 2, 1999)	
520		"*Sailor* is a statewide public network, connecting libraries, schools and government agencies to the global Internet. The *Sailor* Web site focuses on Maryland information, with links to other resources around the world, creating a virtual online library."	
505	0	What's New, Hon? -- Maryland information -- Maryland libraries -- Infotrac SearchBank -- Project Gutenberg -- GPO Access -- Cruise the Internet -- Search *Sailor* & Maryland databases -- E-mail -- Help.	
610	20	*Sailor* (Computer network)	
650	0	Computer networked resources $z Maryland.	
710	2	Maryland. $b State Dept. of Education.	
856	40	$u http://www.sailor.lib.md.us	

Figure 7.9   *SAILOR.*

Discussion for Figure 7.9

- Type, File, 007: Type is coded "m" for computer online service, File is coded "j" for online service. Field 007 describes physical characteristics of the file: computer file, remote access, one color, and dimensions not applicable.

- 090: 674.8 is for information networks in the United States and 674.82.S42 is the Seymour system, so the Cutter number is adjusted to create .S35 for *Sailor*.

- 246: The other title information is more explicit than the title proper, so it is traced as a variant title. Indicator 3 will produce an added entry but not a note for this title, indicator 0 explains this title is a part of the title proper.

- 256: The site contains data and databases, so this phrase is used.

- 260: The place of publication information is taken from "more information about *Sailor*" and the date is taken from description of the project, so both are entered in square brackets.

- 270: The e-mail address for contact is entered in subfield m of field 270.

- 516: This note explains the nature of this site.

- 520 & 550: It is acceptable to use statements from the site as the summary note. This note complements the information in 505, so both are included.

Title screen:

LITA-L

    Lita-L is an on-line discussion group which allows LITA members (and others interested in library technology) to exchange information, ask questions, and post employment opportunities and other announcements. Lita-L is monitored to prevent "spamming". Thank you Ben Ide!
        To subscribe, send an e-mail message to:
            listproc@ala.org.
            Leave the subject line blank. (Put a space if required by your mailer.)
            In message portion put: subscribe lita-l Yourfirstname Yourlastname
            Your email address will be picked up automatically.

        To post a message to Lita-L:
            Send e-mail to: lita-l@ala.org.

****

Type: m	BLvl: m	File: j
007		c $b r $d a $e n
090		Z678.93.L5
092		025.0285
245	00	Lita-l $h [computer file].
246	3	Library and Information Technology Association discussion group
260		Chicago : $b American Library Association, $c 1996-
516		Computer online service.
538		Mode of access: E-mail via the Internet.
500		Title from LITA Web page (viewed April 2, 1999).
520		A monitored listserv for LITA members and others interested in library technology to exchange information and post job opportunities and other announcements.
650	0	Libraries $x Automation.
710	2	Library and Information Technology Association (U.S.).
856	00	$z e-mail subscription to $h listproc $a ala.org $i subscribe lita-l your firstname your lastname

Figure 7.10   Lita-L.

Discussion for Figure 7.10

- Type, File, 007: Listservs are considered "computer online services," so Type should be coded "m" and File "j." Field 007 describes the physical characteristics of the file: computer file, remote access, one color, and dimensions not applicable.

- 092: The number is built from 025 (library operations) and standard subdivision -0285 for data processing or computer application.

- 246: The name of the group is spelled out to make it clear that this is an electronic discussion group. Indicator 3 will generate an added entry but not a note.

- 260: Because this is an ongoing publication (not considered serials, according to the latest guidelines), an open entry is used.

- 516: This note specifies the nature of the site.

- 856: $z represents a display text, $h lists the processor, $a lists the host name, and $i is the instruction for the remote host to process a request.

■NOTES

1. Xue-Ming Bao, "Challenges and Opportunities: A Report of the 1998 Library Survey of Internet Users at Seton Hall University," *College & Research Libraries* 59 (Nov. 1998), 535–43.

2. Mary J. Lynch, *Electronic Services in Academic Libraries: ALA Survey Report* (Chicago: ALA, 1996).

3. Ingrid Hsieh-Yee, "Organization of Nonprint Resources in Public and Academic Libraries," unpublished report, May 30, 1999.

4. See, for instance, Kyle Banerjee, "Describing Remote Electronic Documents in the Online Catalog: Current Issues," *Cataloging & Classification Quarterly* 25 (1997): 5–20.

5. See, for instance, Gerry McKiernan, *Project Aristotle (sm)*, available: http://www.public.iastate.edu/~CYBERSTACKS/Aristotle.htm, accessed June 2000.

6. See, for instance, Priscilla Caplan, "Cataloging Internet Resources," *Public-Access Computer Systems Review* 4 (1993): 61–66; and Sherry L. Vellucci, "Herding Cats: Options for Organizing Electronic Resources," *Internet Reference Services Quarterly* 1, no. 4 (1996): 9–30.

7. See, for example, *Criteria for Evaluation of Internet Information Resources*, available: http://www.vuw.ac.nz/~agsmith/evaln/index.htm, accessed June 2000.

8. James R. Veatch, "Insourcing the Web," *American Libraries* 30 (Jan. 1999): 64–67.

9. Jean Hirons and Crystal Graham, "Issues Related to Seriality," in *The Principles and Future of AACR: Proceedings of the International Conference on the Principles and Future Development of AACR, Toronto, Ontario, Canada, October 23-25, 1997, 1–16*, edited by Jean Weihs (Ottawa: Canadian Library Association, 1998), 180–212. Also available: http://www.nlc-bnc.ca/jsc/r-serial.pdf, accessed June 2000.

10. *Revising AACR2 to Accommodate Seriality: Report to the Joint Steering Committee on the Revision of AACR*, available: http://www.nlc-bnc.ca/jsc/ser-rep0.html, accessed June 2000.

11. Library of Congress, Cataloging Policy and Support Office, *Draft Interim Guidelines for Cataloging Electronic Resources*, Dec. 1997, available: http://lcweb.loc.gov/catdir/cpso/dcmb19-_4.html, accessed June 2000.

12. Jay Weitz, *Cataloging Electronic Resources: OCLC-MARC Coding Guidelines*, October 25, 1999, available: http://www.oclc.org/oclc/cataloging/type.htm, accessed June 2000.

13. *CONSER Cataloging Manual Module 31: Remote Access Computer File Serials*, available: http://lcweb.loc.gov/acq/conser/module31.html, accessed June 2000.

14. Weitz, 1999.

15. Crystal Graham and the *CONSER* Working Group, *CONSER WG: Single v. Separate Records, Draft Report*, available: http://wwwtest.library.ucla.edu/libraries/cataloging/sercat/conserwg/conserwg.draft.htm, accessed June 2000.

16. Hsieh-Yee, 1999.

17. *CONSER Cataloging Manual.*

18. LCRI 12.7B3 (CSB 79) recommends adding the last viewing date to the source of title note, and *CONSER* supports this move.

19. Messages at InterCat and CORC listserv reflected enthusiasm for "electronic resources."

20. Carol Liheng and Winnie S. Chan, *Serial Cataloging Handbook*, 2nd ed. (Chicago: American Library Association, 1998).

21. Jean Hirons's message to InterCat listserv on March 24, 1998 indicated that while OCLC implemented changes to field 856, LC will implement the changes at a time to be determined.

22. *CONSER Cataloging Manual.*

23. Robert C. Richard, *Adding Classification Numbers to Bibliographic Records for Internet Resources: Summary of Listserv Responses and Annotated Bibliography*, available: http://alexia.lis.uiuc.edu/~rrichard/classnet.htm, accessed June 2000.

24. DESIRE (Development of a European Service for Information on Research and Education), Part 3, *The Role of Classification Schemes in Internet Resource Description and Discovery*, available: http://www.ukoln.ac.uk/metadata/DESIRE/classification, accessed June 2000.

25. *CONSER Cataloging Manual.*

■ SUGGESTED READINGS

Gerhard, Kristin H. "Cataloging Internet Resources: Practical Issues and Concern." *Serials Librarian* 32 (1/2) 1997, pp. 123–37.

Graham, Crystal, and the *CONSER* Working Group. 1999. *CONSER WG: Single v. Separate Records, Draft Report*. Available: http://wwwtest.library.ucla.edu/libraries/cataloging/sercat/conserwg/conserwg.draft.htm (Accessed June 2000).

Mandel, Carol A., and Robert Wolven. "Intellectual Access to Digital Documents: Joining Proven Principles with New Technologies." *Cataloging & Classification Quarterly* 22, nos. 3/4 (1996): 25–42.

Oder, Norman. "Cataloging the Net: Can We Do It?" *Library Journal* 123 (Oct. 1,1998): 47–51.

Webb, John. "Managing Licensed Networked Electronic Resources in a University Library." *Information Technology and Libraries* 17 (Dec. 1998): 198–206.

EIGHT ← CATALOGING AND THE CHANGING INFORMATION ENVIRONMENT

Advances in information technology have affected creators, publishers, and users of information in many ways in the 1990s. In response to such changes, information professionals have explored several options for organizing electronic resources. These topics are presented in this chapter to provide a context for a discussion of the future of cataloging and that of catalogers.

■ CHANGES IN THE INFORMATION ENVIRONMENT

Scholarly Communication

A large part of the information transfer cycle described in Chapter Two continues to apply in the current information environment, but advanced technology has shortened the distance between the stages. For instance, creators of information previously had to go through an elaborate review and quality control process to publish their works. Now the time between creation and publication is shorter because electronic submission is commonplace, the review cycle is shorter (again due to electronic communication), and electronic editing and production are faster than before. In addition, peer-reviewed e-journals grew from seven titles in 1991 to 1,049 in 1997[1] and researchers now have more channels for publications.

Moreover, Web technology affects the information creation stage because it enables people to communicate through new formal and informal channels. Creators can receive and exchange ideas through e-mail, chat rooms, newsgroups, and listservs, and thus benefit from online discussions as well as completed reports. They can also publish as much as they wish informally because anyone with a Web address is a potential author. Such a free flow of information and the new ease of publishing created the rapid growth of information on the Web, but exacts a toll on receivers' time and energy. The quantity and the quality of Web information are such that information users find it difficult to

255

search for relevant quality resources or to digest or manage received information. That's why David Shenk calls for ways to ensure the quality of information[2] and Paul Waddington reports an urgent need for better information organization and management in the business world.[3]

Furthermore, technology has empowered creators by making it easier for them to communicate by means other than text. Books accompanied by CD-ROMs, sound recordings with "Enhanced CD," and Web sites enriched with sound, video, and images illustrate how creators and publishers have combined formats into new forms of intellectual expression. The emergence of multimedia-embedded electronic journals on the Internet suggests that scholarly communication has entered a new phase. Humanities scholars have recognized that information technology presents new opportunities for research in their fields and many have actively experimented with integrating sound, image, text, and other media into their work.[4] And the growth of electronic information centers and digital libraries is also likely to stimulate scholars' interest in combining multiple formats for research presentation.[5]

The implications of these changes for catalogers are twofold. First, the increasing volume of Web resources highlights the importance of the selection and evaluation of information. Assessing the accuracy, authority, objectivity, and currency of electronic resources, especially those on the Web, will continue to be challenging and time-consuming. But this filtering effort by information organizers will save users from fruitless searching on the Web and elsewhere, especially when the filtering is performed with a solid understanding of the needs of a user community. Evaluation criteria for print resources have been expanded to cover electronic resources,[6] and new techniques such as collaborative filtering can alert users of resources used by other users with similar interest.[7]

Second, the amount of information available and the multiple formats in publications will challenge catalogers to describe file formats adequately and efficiently. Catalogers will need some knowledge of file formats to determine if additional equipment or software is required to run a work that consists of several media. In addition, new ways to organize electronic resources need to be explored. *Project Aristotle*[sm], for instance, lists Web sites that experiment with automated categorization or organization of Web resources.[8] It is also necessary to examine the information creation stage and information organization stage. The University of Virginia, for instance, has established a procedure to generate bibliographic records from information submitted by thesis authors.[9]

Information Users

The large amount of information available challenges information seekers and heightens the need for information organization. Recent studies found that not one single search engine can perform a complete search of the Internet and that search engines retrieve many overlapped items and some unique items.[10] A 1998 university survey found that more than 86 percent of students and faculty spent 11 minutes to more than 30 minutes on searching in order to find satisfactory results on the Internet.[11] Although users learn to live with the limitations of existing engines, the need for a powerful search tool is apparent. The catalog adds value to collected resources by saving users' time and effort in searching and evaluating resources. Such value-adding processes can certainly be extended to electronic resources.

Web technology also enables any users with an Internet connection to access a library's catalog. So the diverse background of users, their location, their purposes, and their information-seeking behavior all need to be taken into account when catalogers decide which data elements to include in bibliographic records. For instance, to serve remote users of the catalog well, catalogers would include technical information or requirements specific to a resource so that off-site users would know if they have the necessary setup to use the resource. In addition, more and more users expect information tools to provide not only bibliographic access but also physical access through virtual display of the actual contents. So the catalog needs to support that need as well.

The implications for catalogers are that they must have an efficient way to produce resource descriptions that can assist users in searching, identifying, selecting, and accessing resources.[12] In addition to traditional cataloging elements, field 856, the field for electronic location and access, has supported access by linking bibliographic records to Web resources. Efficient resource description, however, remains a challenge. MARCit, a commercial software, offers a cataloging template for quick description of Web resources,[13] but still requires much human effort. The OCLC CORC Project tests the extent to which a cooperative catalog for Web resources can be created through machine harvesting and analysis of resources.[14]

A related issue is that many tools have been available in the networked environment for users to find and manage information—search engines, databases, online catalogs, e-mail services, and database management systems, to name a few. As libraries make the online catalog the hub for information discovery, it is important that the catalog be compatible with other tools so that it can provide maximum support for users. Many online catalogs can display in several formats (MARC, ASCII, HTML, etc.), offer users several options for saving and processing their search results, and link users to resources accessible on the World Wide Web. These are all steps in the right direction.

Publishing

Advanced technology has prompted publishers to move more and more print resources into electronic format. The latest international periodical directory reports that 10,332 serial titles are available exclusively online or in addition to a paper version.[15] A recent library marketing survey found that many libraries anticipate a substantial part of their budget increase to be spent on electronic media, and publishers also expect libraries to focus more on electronic media.[16] While publishers are concerned about authentication and rights management[17] and new technological standards for electronic resources and audio-visual materials are in development, the implication for catalogers is that more nonprint resources produced according to new standards and in varying packages will need to be organized. In addition to describing rights restrictions and system requirements of electronic resources, catalogers must decide how to catalog an aggregator such as IDEAL (International Digital Electronic Access Library) from the Academic Press that includes the full-text of 175 journals. Would collection-level records for such items be sufficient? Would item-level records be necessary? How many item-level records should be provided? And how should the item-to-item relationship and the item-to-collection relationships be represented?

Similarly, more and more libraries and institutions are developing their own digital collections. Besides the same decisions about record level and relationship, the issue of encoding local collections for display and retrieval must be addressed. Catalogers will need to decide if they will assume the responsibility for encoding objects or to form an alliance with staff specialized in encoding to streamline the cataloging of digitized materials.

■ RESPONSES FROM THE LIBRARY COMMUNITY

Practical Solutions

The library community has responded to such changes in a number of ways. Individually many libraries have mounted subject guides, most of them well organized and with annotations, to present resources they have selected for their users. This process adds value to the resources by reducing users' searching time. To compensate for the fixed order, linear structure of most subject guides, librarians have combined database design and Web technology. Cornell University's gateway (http://campusgw.library.cornell.edu/gateway.html), for instance, allows users to search keywords against resource types to generate a list of information tools for further exploration. Similar services are provided by Virginia Military Institute's *SourceFinder* (http://www.vmi.edu/sourcefinder/) and at Dickinson College (http://library.dickinson.edu/db_index.html). This approach simplifies the maintenance of links to electronic resources and allows users to customize subject guides as needed. Another method to keep subject guides current and dynamic is to embed search statements in them and run the search statements against a database whenever subject guides are viewed. The Pathfinder module of OCLC's CORC Project (Cooperative Online Resource Catalog) offers this feature. The CORC Project also provides links between the CORC database and the Pathfinder module and enables subject guide creators to identify relevant Web resources and import them into a pathfinder.

Another solution is that more and more libraries have cataloged electronic resources, especially Web resources. This practice reflects an evolving view of the catalog, which used to refer to the collection of one library. In 1995 and 1996 AutoCat, a listserv for catalogers, had lively discussions on how to control Web resources—cataloging or indexing.[18] Most participants preferred that the online catalog represent resources selected for the users, regardless of the location of such resources. And this approach has been found feasible. After a thorough analysis of the characteristics of resources on the Internet OCLC launched the InterCat project to assess if the Anglo-American Cataloging Rules and the MARC format would be adequate for cataloging Web resources.[19] The results include an experimental catalog that has continued to grow and a set of guidelines for cataloging Internet resources.[20]

In addition, librarians have also experimented with other metadata standards in their efforts to control digital collections. Libraries such as the University of Virginia Library have extracted information from TEI headers and EAD headers to generate bibliographic records for their online catalogs. Several libraries have begun using Dublin Core to organize media, and the University of Michigan has developed a search engine that supports searching by Dublin Core elements (http://www.images.umdl.umich.edu). University of Washington has mapped metadata from various sources to Dublin Core and created an integrated service that can search 14 media collections individually or simultaneously (see http://content.library.washington.edu).

Theoretical Analysis

In addition to these practical solutions, the library community has also examined the theoretical aspects of cataloging in the hope that the underpinning of cataloging can be strengthened and a solid theory of cataloging will enable catalogers to organize information of any formats. Heaney applied the object-oriented model to the MARC record and proposed the development of an object-oriented cataloging code.[21] Green proposed applying the entity-relationship model to create large bibliographic databases.[22] Tillet offered a taxonomy of bibliographic relationships.[23] In 1997 the International Conference on the Principles and Future Development of *AACR* was held in Toronto to examine the principles and structures of the Anglo-American Cataloging Rules.[24] Topics such as the logical structure of *AACR*, the definition of "work," the principles of *AACR*, access points, and beyond MARC are presented. The Joint Steering Committee (JSC) for Revision of Anglo-American Cataloging Rules has taken the recommendations from the Conference to develop an action plan and has put forward the final report on the logical structure of the *Anglo-American Cataloging Rules* and a report on seriality for review and comment.[25] In 1998 the International Federation of Library

Associations issued a final report on the functional requirements for bibliographic records.[26] When feedback from the cataloging community is received, the JSC will decide which recommendations will be incorporated into the next version of the *Anglo-American Cataloging Rules*.

Another major rule revision that will have far-reaching impact, if adopted, is the *International Standard for Bibliographic Description (ISBD) for Electronic Resources (ER)*.[27] Sanberg-Fox and Byrum described how the ISBD for Computer Files was revised into the ISBD for Electronic Resources (ER) and highlighted significant differences from *AACR2R* in describing electronic resources.[28] *ISBD (ER)* covers the treatment of interactive multimedia and Internet resources, expands the list of internal sources, makes explicit the prescribed sources for each area, replaces the GMD "computer file" with "electronic resources," expands the list of file designations for Area 3, and offers many other changes useful for describing electronic resources. The Committee on Cataloging: Description and Access (CC:DA) of the Association for Library Collections and Technical Services (ALCTS) has analyzed the implications of *ISBD (ER)* and identified *AACR2R* rules that have been affected by *ISBD (ER)*.[29] If Chapter 9 of *AACR2R* incorporates changes proposed by *ISBD (ER)*, the cataloging of electronic resources is likely to be easier in the future.

Metadata

In addition to the above efforts, people outside of the cataloging community have developed standards, sometimes with the help of librarians, to organize electronic resources important to their user communities. Such standards are considered "metadata" because they refer to data about data (i.e., information-bearing entities). The objectives of metadata are for users to identify, describe, and locate the referenced entities and for managers to control the entities' authenticity, use patterns, access rights, contents, and so on.[30] Although the cataloging community may have been alarmed at first when the discussion of metadata became widespread, it soon became clear that cataloging records is one type of metadata. The question is whether cataloging can represent complex resources sufficiently and meet the objectives of metadata. As catalogers refine cataloging rules and the methods of record creation, it has become clear that some awareness of other metadata is important because the display and indexing of digital collections require encoding details that are not covered by the MARC format. The Text Encoding Initiative (TEI), for instance, was developed in 1987 by humanities scholars, publishers, archivists, and librarians to mark up literary texts.[31] TEI encoding enables full-texts to be displayed. Users can browse a text, jump to any section of it, search it, or search across several texts. As an SGML

DTD (Document Type Definition), TEI makes display and searching of electronic texts a reality and facilitates the sharing of electronic texts. While catalogers may not need to know how to tag a poem or a chapter, they do need to have some understanding of the metadata embedded in the TEI Header because this area contains useful information for cataloging purposes. The TEI Header includes information on the file, encoding practice, source, and revision history of a text. It can be displayed with an electronic text, and has been used as the basis for cataloging by many libraries. The University of Virginia, for instance, has established a procedure for cataloging records to be derived from the TEI header.[32] To explore the relationship of TEI to XML and to MARC a "TEI and XML in Digital Libraries Workshop" was held in June of 1998. As a result, a *"Best Practices TEI"* page was published to show how TEI elements correspond to MARC fields and how catalogers can extract such elements to create MARC records.[33] In late 1998 the CC:DA Task Force on TEI issued a final report to aid the cataloging community in understanding the implications of TEI.[34]

Dublin Core (DC) is probably the metadata standard that has received the most attention from the library community. This is because it is easy to understand, extensible to Web resources in any formats, and interoperable with other standards.[35] The standard originated from a meeting at OCLC in Dublin, Ohio, and many countries around the world have participated in its development. In September 1998 the standard was issued as an Internet Engineering Task Force Information RFC (Request for Comments)[36] and may gain broad acceptance in the future.

DC includes 15 core elements that are similar to MARC record elements but require no cataloging expertise to create. Each of the elements is optional and repeatable. The original intent of DC was for authors of Web resources to provide the elements so that machine indexing and searching can be easily performed. Search engines such as AltaVista and Infoseek have supported searching by DC elements but it is not clear to what extent DC has been accepted by Web authors.

The library community, in fact, has experimented more than regular Web authors in creating DC. Several tools are available to facilitate the creation of DC elements, among them the *DC Generator* and the *Dublin Core Metadata Template* are well-known.[37] These elements can be edited and embedded in the HTML head area of Web resources to make them searchable. A *Nordic Web Index* was also set up to illustrate how DC can be used for retrieval purposes.[38] Many libraries around the world have implemented DC-based projects and data conversion information is available at the *NORDIC* site and the DC home page. The following table illustrates the relationship of DC elements to MARC structure:

Dublin Core	MARC
Creator	100, 110, 111; 245 $c
Title	130; 245 $a
Type	245 $h GMD
Title	246 $a
Source, relation	250
Format	256 (file characteristics)
Publisher	260 $b
Date	260 $c
Coverage	500
Description	505 (contents)
Rights	506 (use restrictions)
Format	516 (type of computer file)
Description	520 (summary)
Source, relation	530 (other formats available)
Format	538 (system requirements; mode of access)
Language	546
Subject	6XX (subject headings)
Contributor	700, 710, 711
Title	730, 740
Source, relation	760–787 (linking entry fields)
Identifier	856 (electronic location and access)

Note that the mapping between DC and MARC is not necessarily one-to-one. And if DC is extended, through qualifiers, to support more complex descriptions, the conversion will involve more MARC fields. The Nordic Metadata Project's DC to MARC converter (http://www.bibsys.no/meta/d2m/) illustrates the process and the USMARC office has issued a report on the conversion of Dublin Core to MARC, and to GILS.[39]

The latest major research effort in Dublin Core is the OCLC CORC Project, which aims to create a catalog of Web resources through cooperation and machine assistance.[40] Using *Mantis* (http://purl.oclc.org/mantis) to generate and extract metadata, CORC supports automatic creation of DC records, quick conversion between DC and MARC, online editing in DC and MARC with source page displayed in a frame or a separate window, automatic assignment of Library of Congress subject headings and Dewey Decimal Classification numbers, assignment of subject keywords by WordSmith, authority control, and output in MARC, HTML, and XML formats. It also supports pathfinder generation and management. Plans to support other metadata such as TEI and to extend DC to locally digitized materials are in the works. The enthusiasm for CORC shows that the library community has realized the importance of cooperative efforts in information organization and access. Since DC is international in scope, applicable to all subjects, and mappable to other metadata standards, it is likely to be the metadata that will affect how electronic resources are organized in the changing information environment.

Other metadata standards are narrower in scope but valuable for the discovery and management of selected types of material. Encoded Archival Description (EAD), for instance, has been developed to encode archival finding aids;[41] and Government Information Locator Service (GILS) is for access to information resources produced by federal government agencies.[42] Media-specific metadata standards have also been developed. A well-known example is the Instructional Management Systems (IMS) metadata that describe learning resources such as multimedia courseware and PowerPoint presentations.[43]

The rapid development of standards is overwhelming to anyone interested in information organization. As the leader of the cataloging community, the CC:DA of ALCTS has made serious efforts to help catalogers to understand metadata and its implications. A Task Force Report on TEI was issued in the fall of 1998;[44] a CC:DA Task Force on Metadata has been appointed; and a listserv, *Metamarda-L*, has been created to facilitate the work of the Task Force. The four working groups respectively examined the resource description needs of library, built a conceptual map of the resource description landscape, defined "metadata," "interoperability," and "metadata schema," and identified prototypes that made use of metadata.[45] MARBI (Machine-Readable Bibliographic Information), an interdivisional committee of the American Library Association, is another group that has actively addressed the needs to describe and control electronic resources. For example, at its 1999 midwinter meeting the group discussed the merit of making field 856 repeatable, the value of URN, and the merit of having URL information in fields other than field 856. Attending MARBI meetings or reading their minutes is a good way to keep current with changes in the cataloging field.[46]

Tension Between Metadata and Cataloging Practice

While many libraries catalog Web resources and even draw on portions of metadata to create bibliographic records, tension between metadata, especially Dublin Core, and cataloging exists. Many catalogers are concerned whether Dublin Core will replace cataloging and what other implications Dublin Core may have for the future of information organization. On more than one occasion Dublin Core advocates have mentioned the liberation from cataloging rules as a major benefit of having metadata (see, for example, the *Nordic Metadata Project report* at http://linnea.helsinki.fi/meta/nmfinal.htm). But opponents such as Michael Gorman have pointed out that simplicity is accomplished at the expense of details and specificity.[47]

Furthermore, as expressed by some CORC participants, guidelines are needed for the implementation of the Dublin Core standard. To ensure consistent implementation and sharing of metadata, issues such as the levels of description, the definition of chief source of information and prescribed sources of information, the choice of access points, the semantics of the elements (such as how to record a name or a publication date), and many other issues must be addressed. The University of Chicago's guidelines for using Dublin Core (http://www.lib.uchicago.edu/Annex/TechSvcs/dcguidelines.html) could serve as the basis for developing inputting standards for Dublin Core. Gorman proposes to control electronic resources by creating records of varying details depending on the importance of resources.[48] His four levels of treatment—full cataloging records, enriched Dublin Core records, minimal Dublin Core records, and keywords—provide a helpful example for specifying the levels of cataloging for electronic resources. As these two examples illustrate, the cataloging community can and should contribute to the development of metadata guidelines. That is the best approach to ensure appropriate organization of electronic resources.

Catalogers will also want to keep an open mind about metadata's potential. The effort at the University of Washington to map data elements from various image collections to Dublin Core demonstrates how catalogers can apply their knowledge of cataloging to the creation of a metadata dictionary. The project also makes explicit how services can be enhanced by combining cataloging knowledge with sophisticated tools such as the CONTENT software suite. Electronic resources present opportunities for catalogers to reexamine how they organize information. The efforts by librarians so far suggest many librarians have affirmed the value of systematic human analysis of electronic resource and recognized the benefits in drawing on sophisticated technology and "agents" to enhance services.

■ THE FUTURE OF CATALOGING AND CATALOGERS

The future of cataloging and catalogers is closely tied to the future of libraries. Many believe the libraries of the future will be "integrated" libraries that integrate new forms of intellectual and artistic expression into existing collections and provide strong bibliographic structures that guide users to resources in any formats, whether they are locally owned or not, and support users' interaction with recorded knowledge and information.[49] As libraries evolve, catalogers will need to expand the current bibliographic structures to accommodate resources that combine different media. To prepare for such tasks, catalogers will need to become familiar with cataloging rules for such resources first. Then they should draw on their experience in organizing such resources and their knowledge of the creation, transfer, and use of information to propose ways to improve the cataloging of these resources.[50] By sharing ideas and experience in professional organizations such as ALCTS and IFLA, catalogers will help bring about rule revisions and changes in cataloging practices. When a strong bibliographic structure is in place to support international cooperation in organizing and sharing information resources, the future of cataloging will be further secured.[51]

In addition, catalogers need to work with other professionals to develop or identify appropriate standards and methods for information organization. Digital technology has made it possible for archivists, special collections directors, museum specialists, scientists, and others to present their collections electronically, whether on the Internet or on CD-ROM or DVD. If catalogers are not involved in the planning and implementation of a digital collection, the task of organizing digital objects will become more difficult later. Catalogers have much to offer to other professionals. The principles of cataloging are applicable to digital materials, and cataloging concepts such as collocation, access points, authority control, controlled vocabulary, and subject analysis are highly relevant to the organization of digital materials.[52] Sharing their cataloging expertise with other professionals, catalogers will help others understand critical issues related to resource description and access. Likewise, understanding the purpose and perspectives of other professionals, catalogers will be able to help others in improving standards and accomplishing their objectives through cataloging, metadata, or other methods of information organization.

As more and more digital libraries are taking shape, an inevitable question is: Will cataloging and catalogers be needed in digital libraries? Technology enthusiasts may prefer heavy reliance on technology to create and manage a digital library, but it is humans who make decisions on what technology will do and how technology will carry out instructions. As Levy observed, order is critical for the stability and usability of digital collections, and cataloging efforts, enhanced and facilitated by technology, are critical to bring about order.[53] The organization of digital resources requires that one considers which resources will be cataloged and how much detail should be included in records so that information resources can be identified, discovered, evaluated, and accessed. These goals of cataloging remain the same in the digital environment, but the procedures will evolve. For instance, if future resources have metadata embedded in them, the cataloging process may become simplified. Catalogers will have many areas to apply their expertise. They can, for example, help define how electronic resources, commercially and locally produced, will be described for access; how resources created by different standards and embedded with different metadata will be integrated into the collection; how the collection will be maintained for access; and how to provide interactivity in the system for users to take full advantage of the library's resources.

■ CONCLUSION

Cataloging involves technology, yet technology continues to cause concerns over the future of cataloging. When bibliographic utilities became available in the 1960s, the fear that machines would replace catalogers loomed large but was never realized. In the 1980s paraprofessionals performed most of copy cataloging, while catalogers were busy preparing data for online catalogs, thus technology seemed less threatening than before. But the economic situation in the first half of 1990s led to reduced support for cataloging and large-scale outsourcing was implemented in some institutions. The growth of the Internet caused further concerns that cataloging might be inadequate for describing dynamic Web resources and that search engines would render cataloging unnecessary. But catalogers reaffirmed their belief in the principles of cataloging and the objectives of the catalog, and addressed the challenges directly by developing guidelines for interactive multimedia and Internet resources. Now new forms of intellectual expression, growth of digital collections, proliferation of standards, and users' expectation and demand for virtual displays have posed new challenges to libraries. As librarians seek to redefine their roles in the changing information environment, the need to organize electronic resources for access becomes more urgent. Catalogers have proven that they can successfully integrate new formats such as sound recordings, videorecordings, and computer files into the bibliographic structure. Recent efforts in the cataloging community suggest that catalogers are meeting the new challenges directly. Catalogers' knowledge of information organization and commitment to produce helpful tools for users will help librarians secure their future in the next century.

■ NOTES

1. Dru W. Mogge, ed., *Directory of Electronic Journals, Newsletters and Academic Discussion Lists*. 7th ed. (Washington, D.C.: Association of Research Libraries, 1997).

2. David Shenk, *Data Smog: Surviving the Information Glut*. Rev. and updated ed. (New York: HarperEdge, 1998).

3. Paul Waddington, *Dying for Information? A Report on the Effects of Information Overload in the UK and WorldWide*, available: http://www.cni.org/regconfs/1997/ukoln-content/repor~13.html, accessed June 2000.

4. Pamela Pavliscak, Seamus Ross, and Charles Henry, *Information Technology in Humanities Scholarship: Achievements, Prospects, and Challenges—The United States Focus* (New York: American Council of Learned Societies, 1997). Also available: http://www.acls.org/op37.htm, accessed June 2000.

5. See, for example, David Seaman, "The User Community as Responsibility and Resource: Building a Sustainable Digital Library," *D-Lib Magazine* (July/August 1997): 1–6. Also available: http://www.dlib.org/dlib/july97/07seaman.html, accessed June 2000. Diane Y. Goldenberg-Hart, "Library Technology Centers and Community Building: Yale University Library Electronic Text Center," *Library Hi Tech* 16 (1998): 21–26.

6. See, for example, *Criteria for Evaluation of Internet Information Resources*, available: http://www.vuw.ac.nz/~agsmith/evaln/index.htm, accessed June 2000.

7. *Collaborative Filtering*, available: http://info.berkeley.edu/resources/collab/index.html, accessed June 2000.

8. Gerry McKiernan, *Project Aristotle*ˢᵐ, available: http://www.public.iastate.edu/~CYBERSTACKS/Aristotle.htm, accessed June 2000.

9. Conversation with Jackie Shieh, electronic resources cataloger at UVA. See the UVA Electronic Theses & Dissertations project at http://viva.lib.virginia.edu/etd/, accessed June 2000.

10. Steve Lawrence and C. Lee Giles, "Searching the World Wide Web," *Science* 280 (April 3 1998): 98–100.

11. Xue-Ming Bao, "Challenges and Opportunities: A Report of the 1998 Library Survey of Internet Users at Seton Hall University," *College & Research Libraries* 59 (Nov. 1998): 535–43.

12. These are the functional requirements identified in IFLA's *Functional Requirements for Bibliographic Records: Final Report*, http://www.ifla.org/VII/s13/frbr/frbr.pdf, accessed June 2000. [Adobe Acrobat Reader required to view this document]

13. *MARCit Cataloging the Internet*, available: http://www.marcit.com/, accessed June 2000.

14. *CORC Home Page*, available: http://www.oclc.org/oclc/corc/index.htm, accessed June 2000.

15. *Ulrich's International Periodicals Directory*. 37th ed. (New York: R. R. Bowker, 1999).

16. Preliminary findings announced in *ALCTS Network News*, Volume 17, Number 19, May 27, 1999.

17. See, for example, *A White Paper on Authentication and Access Management Issues in Cross-Organizational Use of Networked Information Resources*, Clifford Lynch, editor. (Revised Discussion Draft of April 14, 1998), available: http://www.cni.org/projects/authentication/authentication-wp.html, accessed June 2000.

18. See *AUTOCAT Archives* at: http://listserv.acsu.buffalo.edu/archives/autocat.html, accessed June 2000.

19. Martin Dillon and Erik Jul, "Cataloging Internet Resources: The Convergence of Libraries and Internet Resources," *Cataloging & Classification Quarterly* 22, nos. 3/4 (1996): 197–238.

20. Nancy B. Olson, ed., *Cataloging Internet Resources: A Manual and Practical Guide*, 2nd ed. (Dublin, Ohio: OCLC, 1997). Also available: http://www.purl.org/oclc/cataloging-internet, accessed June 2000.

21.   Michael Heaney, "Object-Oriented Cataloging," *Information Technology and Libraries* 14 (Sept. 1995): 135–53.

22.   Rebecca Green, "The Design of a Relational Database for Large-Scale Bibliographic Retrieval," *Information Technology and Libraries* 15 (Dec. 1996): 207–21.

23.   Barbara B. Tillet, "A Taxonomy of Bibliographic Relationships," *Library Resources & Technical Services* 35 (April 1991): 150–58.

24.   *The Principles and Future of AACR: Proceedings of the International Conference on the Principles and Future Development of AACR, Toronto, Ontario, Canada, October 23-25, 1997, 1–16*, edited by Jean Weihs (Ottawa: Canadian Library Association, 1998).

25.   *The Logical Structure of the Anglo-American Cataloguing Rules, Part I and Part II*, available: http://www.nlc-bnc.ca/jsc/aacrdel.htm and http://www.nlc-bnc.ca/jsc/aacrdel2.htm; and *Revising AACR2 to Accommodate Seriality: Report to the Joint Steering Committee on the Revision of AACR*, available: http://www.nlc-bnc.ca/jsc/ser-rep0.html, accessed June 2000.

26.   *Functional Requirements for Bibliographic Records.*

27.   *ISBD (ER): International Standard Bibliographic Description for Electronic Resources* (Munich: K. G. Sauer, 1997). Also available: http//www.ifla.org/VII/s13/pubs/isbd.htm, accessed June 2000.

28.   Ann Sandberg-Fox and John D. Byrum, "From ISBD (CF) to ISBD (ER): Process, Policy, and Provisions," *Library Resources & Technical Services* 42 (April 1998): 89–101.

29.   Sandberg-Fox and Byrum, p. 100.

30.   Jean Hudgins, Grace Agnew, and Elizabeth Brown, *Getting Mileage out of Metadata: Applications for the Library* (Chicago: American Library Association, 1999).

31.   *TEI Home Page*, available: http://www.uic.edu/orgs/tei/ and the official TEI guidelines are available: http://www-tei.uic.edu/orgs/tei/p3, accessed June 2000.

32.   See *Description of Text Encoding Initiatives (TEI), Header Elements and Corresponding USMARC Fields*, available: http://etext.virginia.edu/~ejs7y/tei-usmarc.html, accessed June 2000.

33.   *TEI/MARC Best Practices*, available: http://www.lib.umich.edu/libhome/ocu/teiguide.html, accessed June 2000.

34.   *CC:DA Task Force on Metadata and the Cataloging Rules: Final Report*, available: http://www.ala.org/alcts/organization/ccs/ccda/tf-tei2.html, accessed June 2000.

35.   See *Dublin Core Metadata Initiative*, available: http://purl.oclc.org/dc and *Dublin Core Metadata Element Set Version 1.1*, available: http://purl.org/DC/documents/rec-dces-19990702.htm, accessed June 2000.

36.   *Dublin Core Metadata for Resource Discovery*, available: ftp://ftp.isi.edu/in-notes/rfc2413.txt, accessed June 2000.

37.   *DC Dot - Dublin Core Generator*, available: http://www.ukoln.ac.uk/metadata/dcdot/ and *Dublin Core Metadata Template*, available: http://www.lub.lu.se/cgi-bin/nmdc.pl, accessed June 2000.

38. *Nordic Web Index*, available: http://nwi.lub.lu.se/?lang=en, accessed March 2000; no longer available since June 2000.

39. *Dublin Core/MARC/GILS Crosswalk*, available: http://lcweb.loc.gov/marc/dccross.html, accessed June 2000.

40. *CORC Home page*, available: http://www.oclc.org/corc/index.htm, accessed June 2000.

41. *EAD Home Page*, available: http://lcweb.loc.gov/ead, accessed June 2000.

42. *GILS Home Page*, available: http://www.gils.net/, accessed June 2000.

43. *IMS Home Page*, available: http://www.imsproject.org/metadata/, accessed June 2000.

44. *CC:DA Task Force on Metadata and the Cataloging Rules: Final Report*, available: http://www.ala.org/alcts/organization/ccs/ccda/tf-tei2.html, accessed June 2000.

45. Metamarda-l Listserv Archives are located at http://orc.dev.oclc.org:5103/metamarda-l/ and the *CC:DA Task Force on Metadata Summary Report* is available: http://www.ala.org/alcts/organization/ccs/ccda/tf-meta3.html, accessed June 2000.

46. The 1999 midwinter meeting minutes are at http://lcweb.loc.gov/marc/marbi/minutes/mw-99.html, accessed June 2000.

47. Michael Gorman, "Metadata or Cataloguing? A False Choice," *Journal of Internet Cataloging* 2, no. 1 (1999): 5–12.

48. Gorman, 1999.

49. See, for example, Philip Barker, "Electronic Libraries of the Future," *Encyclopedia of Library and Information Science* 59 (1996): 119–53; Walt Crawford, "Paper Persists: Why Physical Library Collections Still Matter," *Online* 22 (January/February 1998): 42–48; and Michael Gorman, "What Is the Future of Cataloguing and Cataloguers?" in the 63rd *IFLA General Conference–Conference Programme and Proceedings*, August 31-September 5, 1997, available: http://ifla.inist.fr/IV/ifla63/63gorm.htm, accessed June 2000.

50. Intner identifies eight topic areas one needs to know about in order to reject standards. See Sheila S. Intner, "Rejecting Standard Cataloging Copy: Implications for the Education of Catalogers," in *Cataloging Heresy: Challenging the Standard Bibliographic Product*, edited by Bella Hass Weinberg (Medford, N.J.: Learned Information, 1992), 119–30.

51. Gorman, 1997.

52. Carol A. Mandel and Robert Wolven, "Intellectual Access to Digital Documents: Joining Proven Principles with New Technologies," *Cataloging & Classification Quarterly* 22, nos. 3/4 (1996): 25–42.

53. David M. Levy, *Cataloging in the Digital Order*, available: http://www.csdl.tamu.edu/DL95/papers/levy/levy.html, accessed June 2000.

■ SUGGESTED READINGS

Forsythe, Kathleen, and Diana Brooking. 1998. *Metadata: Why Should We Care?* Available: http://content.lib.washington.edu/METADATA (Accessed June 2000).

Gaynor, Edward. 1996. *From MARC to Markup: SGML and Online Library Systems.* Available: http://www.lib.virginia.edu/speccol/scdc/articles/alcts_brief.html (Accessed June 2000).

Gorman, Michael. 1997. *What Is the Future of Cataloguing and Cataloguers?* in the 63rd IFLA General Conference–Conference Programme and Proceedings, August 31–September 5, 1997. Available: http://ifla.inist.fr/IV/ifla63/63gorm.htm (Accessed June 2000).

———. "Metadata or Cataloging? A False Choice." *Journal of Internet Cataloging*, 2, no. 1 (1999): 5–22.

International Federation of Library Associations. 1998. *Study on the Functional Requirements for Bibliographic Records.* Available: http://www.ifla.org/VII/S13/frbr/frbr.pdf (Accessed June 2000).

Levy, David M. *Cataloging in the Digital Order.* Available: http://www.csdl.tamu.edu/DL95/papers/levy/levy.html (Accessed June 2000).

Milstead, Jessica, and Susan Feldman. "Metadata Projects and Standards." *Online* 23 (January/February 1999): 32–38, 40. Also available: http://www.onlineinc.com/onlinemag/OL1999/milstead1.html (Accessed June 2000).

Oder, Norman. "Cataloging the Net: Can We Do It?" *Library Journal* 123 (October 1, 1998): 47–51.

The Principles and Future of AACR: Proceedings of the International Conference on the Principles and Future Development of AACR, Toronto, Ontario, Canada, October 23-25, 1997. Ottawa: Canadian Library Association; Chicago: American Library Association, 1998. Also available: http://www.nlc-bnc.ca/jsc/confpap.htm (Accessed June 2000).

Sandberg-Fox, Ann, and John D. Byrum. "From ISBD (CF) to ISBD (ER): Process, Policy, and Provisions." *Library Resources & Technical Services* 42 (April 1998): 89–101.

Seaman, David. "The User Community As Responsibility and Resource: Building a Sustainable Digital Library." *D-Lib Magazine* [electronic journal] (July/August 1997): 1–6. Available: http://www.dlib.org/dlib/july97/07seaman.html (Accessed June 2000).

Webb, John. "Managing Licensed Networked Electronic Resources in a University Library." *Information Technology and Libraries* 17 (December 1998): 198–206.

BIBLIOGRAPHY

■ CATALOGING STANDARDS (PRINT)

Anglo-American Cataloguing Rules. 2nd ed. 1998 revision. Ed. by Michael Gorman and Paul W. Winkler. Chicago: American Library Association, 1998.

Dewey Decimal Classification and Relative Index. 21st ed. Albany, N.Y.: Forest Press, 1996.

Interactive Multimedia Guidelines Review Task Force. *Guidelines for Bibliographic Description of Interactive Multimedia.* Chicago: American Library Association, 1994.

ISBD (ER): International Standard Bibliographic Description for Electronic Resources. Munchen: K. G. Sauer, 1997.

Library of Congress. Subject Cataloging Division. *Library of Congress Classification Schedules.* Washington, D.C.: Cataloging Distribution Service, Library of Congress, 1901- .

Library of Congress Rule Interpretations. 2nd ed. Washington, D.C.: Cataloging Distribution Service, Library of Congress, 1990- .

Library of Congress. Network Development and MARC Standards Office. *USMARC Format for Bibliographic Data: Including Guidelines for Content Designation.* 1994 ed. Washington, D.C.: Library of Congress, Cataloging Distribution Service, 1994- .

Library of Congress. Office for Subject Cataloging Policy. *Library of Congress Subject Headings.* 21st ed. Washington, D.C.: Cataloging Distribution Service, Library of Congress, 1998.

———. *Free-Floating Subdivisions: An Alphabetical Index.* 10th ed. Washington, D.C.: Cataloging Distribution Service, Library of Congress, 1998.

———. *Subject Cataloging Manual: Classification.* 1st ed. Washington, D.C.: Cataloging Distribution Service, Library of Congress, 1992.

Library of Congress. Cataloging Policy & Support Office. *Subject Cataloging Manual: Subject Headings.* 5th ed. Washington, D.C.: Cataloging Distribution Service, Library of Congress, 1996.

271

OCLC. *Bibliographic Formats and Standards.* 2nd ed. Dublin, Ohio: OCLC, 1996.

OCLC Technical Bulletin 212. Format Integration Phase 2. Dublin, Ohio: OCLC, 1996.

Olson, Nancy B., ed. *Cataloging Internet Resources: A Manual and Practical Guide.* 2nd ed. Dublin, Ohio: OCLC, 1997.

■ CATALOGING STANDARDS (ONLINE)

ALCTS/CCS/SAC Subcommittee on Form Headings/Subdivisions Implementation. 1996- . Available: http://www.pitt.edu/~agtaylor/ala/implem.htm (Accessed June 2000).

Brief Guide to LC Policy and Practice for Format Integration. Available: gopher:// marvel.loc.gov:70/00/services/cataloging/policy/brief.guide (Accessed June 2000).

Free-Floating Subject Subdivisions. Available: http://infoshare1.princeton.edu/katmandu/ subj/subd.html (Accessed June 2000).

Guide to the Usage of LCSH Free-Floating Form Subdivisions. Available: http://www. itcompany.com/inforetriever/form_subdivisions_list. htm (Accessed June 2000).

ISBD (ER): International Standard Bibliographic Description for Electronic Resources. Available: http://www.ifla.org/VII/s13/pubs/isbd.htm (Accessed June 2000).

Library Corporation. *Library of Congress Rule Interpretations.* Available: http:// www. tlcdelivers.com/tlc/crs/lcri0000.htm (Accessed June 2000).

——. *Library of Congress Subject Headings—Principles of Structure and Policies for Applications.* Available: http://www.tlcdelivers.com/tlc/crs/shed0014.htm (Accessed June 2000).

——. *USMARC Format for Bibliographic Data.* Available: http://www.tlcdelivers.com/ tlc/crs/bib0001.htm (Accessed June 2000).

Library of Congress. *CONSER Manual Module 31: Remote Access Computer File Serials Contents Page.* Available: http://lcweb.loc.gov/acq/conser/module31.html (Accessed June 2000).

——. *Draft Interim Guidelines for Cataloging Electronic Resources.* Available: http:// lcweb.loc.gov/catdir/cpso/dcmb19_4.html (Accessed June 2000).

——. *Guidelines for Coding Electronic Resources in Leader/06.* Available: http:// lcweb.loc.gov/marc/ldr06guide.html (Accessed June 2000).

——. *Guidelines for the Use of Field 856.* Available: http://lcweb.loc.gov/marc/856guide.html (Accessed June 2000).

——. *MARC Standards.* Available: http://www.loc.gov/marc/marc.html (Accessed June 2000).

——. *MARC21 Concise Format for Bibliographic Data.* Available: http://lcweb.loc.gov/ marc/bibliographic/ (Accessed June 2000).

——. *Subject Headings Weekly Lists.* Available: http://lcweb.loc.gov/catdir/cpso/wls.html (Accessed June 2000).

———. *USMARC Format for Bibliographic Data*, update No. 1, March 1995, Appendix F: Format Change List. Available: gopher://marvel.loc.gov/00/.listarch/usmarc/ ufbdfi95.cha (Accessed June 2000).

OCLC. *Bibliographic Formats and Standards: About This Manual*. Available: http:// www.oclc.org/oclc/bib/about.htm (Accessed June 2000).

———. *Cataloging Electronic Resources: OCLC-MARC Coding Guidelines*. Available: http://www.oclc.org/oclc/cataloging/type.htm (Accessed June 2000).

———. *Input Standards for 856 Electronic Location and Access*. Available: http://www. oclc.org/oclc/bib/856.htm (Accessed June 2000).

Olson, Nancy B., ed. *Cataloging Internet Resources*. Available: http://www.oclc.org/ oclc/man/9256cat/toc.htm (Accessed June 2000).

■ WEB RESOURCES ON CATALOGING AND METADATA

AACR2 and Seriality. Available: http://lcweb.loc.gov/acq/conser/serialty.html (Accessed June 2000).

AUTOCAT: List of Files. Available: http://ublib.buffalo.edu/libraries/units/cts/autocat/ (Accessed June 2000).

AUTOCAT@LISTSERV.ACSU.BUFFALO.EDU-Archives. Available: http://listserv.acsu.buffalo. edu/archives/autocat.html (Accessed June 2000).

Beyond Bookmarks: Schemes for Organizing the Web. Available: http://www.pub- lic.iastate.edu/~CYBERSTACKS/CTW.htm (Accessed June 2000).

Cataloger's Toolbox. Available: http://www.mun.ca/library/cat/cattools.htm (Accessed June 2000).

Cataloging Contacts at the Library of Congress. Available: http://lcweb.loc.gov/catdir/ contacts.html (Accessed June 2000).

Cataloging Policy and Support Office (Library of Congress). Available: http://lcweb.loc.gov/ catdir/cpso/ (Accessed June 2000).

CC:DA TF on Metadata and the Cataloging Rules: Final Report. Available: http://www.ala.org/ alcts/organization/ccs/ccda/tf-tei2.html (Accessed June 2000).

CC:DA Task Force on Metadata: Summary Report. Available: http://www.ala.org/alcts/ organization/ccs/ccda/tf-meta3.html (Accessed June 2000).

Dewey Decimal Classification. New and changed entries. Available: http://www.oclc.org/ oclc/fp/ddc/new_changed_entries.htm (Accessed June 2000).

Dublin Core Metadata Initiative. Available: http://purl.oclc.org/dc/ (Accessed June 2000).

Dublin Core Metadata Template. Available: http://www.lub.lu.se/cgi-bin/nmdc.pl (Accessed June 2000).

Forsythe, Kathleen, and Diana Brooking. 1998. *Metadata: Why Should We Care?* Available: http://content.lib.washington.edu/METADATA (Accessed June 2000).

Gaynor, Edward. 1996. *From MARC to Markup: SGML and Online Library Systems.* Available: http://www.lib.virginia.edu/speccol/scdc/articles/alcts_brief.html (Accessed June 2000).

Graham, Crystal, and the CONSER Working Group. 1999. *CONSER WG: Single v. Separate Records, Draft Report.* Available: http://wwwtest.library.ucla.edu/libraries/cataloging/sercat/conserwg/conserwg.draft.htm (Accessed June 2000).

InterCat. Available: http://purl.org/net/intercat (Accessed June 2000).

International Conference on the Principles and Future Development of AACR. Available: http://www.nlc-bnc.ca/jsc/confpap.htm (Accessed June 2000).

International Federation of Library Associations and Institutions. *Functional Requirements for Bibliographic Record: Final Report.* Available: http://www.ifla.org/VII/s13/frbr/frbr.pdf (Accessed June 2000).

Internet Library for Librarians. Cataloging. Available: http://www.itcompany.com/inforetriever/cat.htm (Accessed June 2000).

LC Cataloging Newsline. Available: http://lcweb.loc.gov/catdir/lccn/ (Accessed June 2000).

Links to Metadata Web Pages. Available: http://www.cic.uiuc.edu/cli/metadatalinks.htm (Accessed June 2000).

Metamarda-l Listserv Archives (by Date). Available: http://orc.dev.oclc.org:5103/metamarda-l/ (Accessed June 2000).

Milstead, Jessica, and Susan Feldman. "Metadata Projects and Standards." *Online* 23 (January/February 1999): 32–38, 40. Also available: http://www.onlineinc.com/onlinemag/OL1999/milstead1.html (Accessed June 2000).

OCLC Technical Bulletins. Available: http://www.oclc.org/oclc/menu/t-tb.htm (Accessed June 2000).

OLAC: Online Audiovisual Catalogers, Inc. Home Page. Available: http://ublib.buffalo.edu/libraries/units/cts/olac (Accessed June 2000).

Persistent URL Home Page. Available: http://purl.oclc.org/ (Accessed June 2000).

Seaman, David. "The User Community as Responsibility and Resource: Building a Sustainable Digital Library." *D-Lib Magazine* [electronic journal] (July/August 1997): 1–6. Available: http://www.dlib.org/dlib/july97/07seaman.html (Accessed June 2000).

UKOLN: DC-Dot, A Dublin Core Generator. Available: http://www.ukoln.ac.uk/metadata/dcdot/ (Accessed June 2000).

User Guidelines for Dublin Core Creation (Nordic Metadata Project). Available: http://www.sics.se/~preben/DC/DC_guide.html (Accessed June 2000).

USMARC Discussion Group Archives Gopher Index. Available: gopher://marvel.loc.gov:70/ 7waissrc%3a/.waissrc/usmarc-m (Accessed June 2000).

Web4Lib Electronic Discussion. Available: http://sunsite.berkeley.edu/Web4Lib/ (Accessed June 2000).

■ HANDBOOKS, GUIDES, TEXTBOOKS, ETC.

Chan, Lois Mai. *Cataloging and Classification: An Introduction.* 2nd ed. New York: McGraw-Hill, 1994.

———. *Dewey Decimal Classification: A Practical Guide.* 2nd ed., rev. for DDC 21. Albany, N.Y.: Forest Press, 1996.

———. *Immroth's Guide to the Library of Congress Classification.* 4th ed. Englewood, Colo.: Libraries Unlimited, 1990.

———. *Library of Congress Subject Headings: Principles and Application.* 3rd ed. Englewood, Colo.: Libraries Unlimited, 1995.

Downing, Mildred Harlow, and David H. Downing. 6th ed. *Introduction to Cataloging and Classification.* Jefferson, N.C.: McFarland, 1992.

Fecko, Mary Beth. *Cataloging Nonbook Resources: A How-to-Do-It Manual for Librarians.* New York: Neal-Schuman, 1993.

Fritz, Deborah A. *Cataloging with AACR2R and USMARC for Books, Computer Files, Serials, Sound Recordings, Video.* Chicago: American Library Association, 1998.

Frost, Carolyn O. *Media Access and Organization: A Cataloging and Reference Sources Guide for Nonbook Materials.* Englewood, Colo.: Libraries Unlimited, 1989.

Furrie, Betty. *Understanding MARC Bibliographic: Machine-Readable Cataloging.* 5th ed. Washington, D.C.: Cataloging Distribution Service, Library of Congress, 1998.

Liheng, Carol, and Winnie S. Chan. *Serials Cataloging Handbook: An Illustrative Guide to the Use of AACR2 and LC Rules Interpretations.* 2nd ed. Chicago: American Library Association, 1998.

Maxwell, Robert L., with Margaret F. Maxwell. *Maxwell's Handbook for AACR2R: Explaining and Illustrating the Anglo-American Cataloguing Rules and the 1993 Amendments.* Chicago: American Library Association, 1997.

Millsap, Larry, and Terry Ellen Ferl. *Descriptive Cataloging for the AACR2R and the Integrated MARC Format: A How-to-Do-It Workbook.* Rev. ed. New York: Neal-Schuman, 1997.

Olson, Nancy B. *Cataloging of Audiovisual Materials and Other Special Materials: A Manual Based on AACR 2.* 4th ed., edited by Sheila S. Intner and Edward Swanson. DeKalb, Ill.: Minnesota Scholarly Press, 1998.

———. *Cataloging Motion Pictures and Videorecordings.* Edited by Edward Swanson. Lake Crystal, Minn.: Soldier Creek Press, 1991.

———. *Cataloging Computer Files.* Edited by Edward Swanson. Lake Crystal, Minn.: Soldier Creek Press, 1992 (with a 1996 update).

Rogers, JoAnn V., with Jerry D. Saye. *Nonprint Cataloging for Multimedia Collections: A Guide Based on AACR2.* 2nd ed. Littleton, Colo.: Libraries Unlimited, 1987.

Saye, Jerry D. *Manheimer's Cataloging and Classification.* 4th ed., rev. and expanded. New York: Marcel Dekker, 2000.

Scott, Mona L. *Dewey Decimal Classification, 21st Edition: A Study Manual and Number Building.* Englewood, Colo.: Libraries Unlimited, 1998.

■ RECOMMENDED READINGS

Avram, Henriette D. *MARC: Its History and Implications.* Washington, D.C.: Library of Congress, 1975.

Coyle, Karen, ed. *Format Integration and Its Effect on Cataloging, Training, and Systems.* Chicago: American Library Association, 1993.

Gorman, Michael. "Metadata or Cataloguing? A False Choice." *Journal of Internet Cataloging,* 2, no. 1 (1999): 5–22.

Gorman, Michael, ed. *Technical Services Today and Tomorrow.* 2nd ed. Englewood, Colo.: Libraries Unlimited, 1998.

Intner, Sheila S., and Richard P. Smiraglia, eds. *Policy and Practice in Bibliographic Control of Nonbook Media.* Chicago: American Library Association, 1987.

Lange, Holley R., and B. Jean Winkler. "Taming the Internet: Metadata, a Work in Progress." *Advances in Librarianship* 21 (1997): 47–72.

Levy, David M. *Cataloging in the Digital Order.* Available: http://www.csdl.tamu.edu/DL95/papers/leve/levy.htm (Accessed June 2000).

Mandel, Carol A., and Robert Wolven. "Intellectual Access to Digital Documents: Joining Proven Principles with New Technologies." *Cataloging & Classification Quarterly* 22, nos. 3/4 (1996): 25–42.

Sandberg-Fox, Ann, and John D. Byrum. "From ISBD (CF) to ISBD (ER): Process, Policy, and Provisions." *Library Resources & Technical Services* 42 (April 1998): 89–101.

Schottlaender, Brian E. C., ed. *The Future of the Descriptive Cataloging Rules: Papers from the ALCTS Preconference, AACR2000, American Library Association Annual Conference, Chicago, June 22, 1995.* Chicago: American Library Association, 1998.

Svenonius, Elaine, ed. *The Conceptual Foundations of Descriptive Cataloging.* San Diego, Calif: Academic Press, 1989.

Taylor, Arlene G. *The Organization of Information.* Englewood, Colo.: Libraries Unlimited, 1999.

Weihs, Jean Riddle. *The Integrated Library: Encouraging Access to Multimedia Materials.* 2nd ed. Phoenix, Ariz.: Oryx Press, 1991.

AUTHOR/TITLE INDEX

SUBJECT INDEX